San Francisco For Dummies
1st Edition

San Francisco's Important Bus Lines

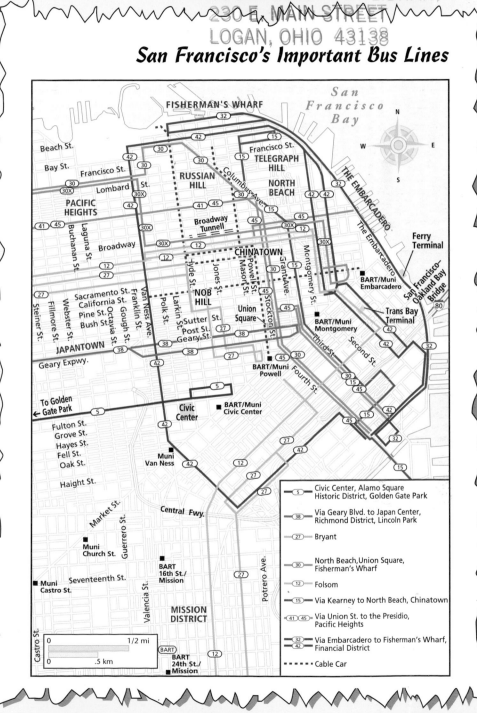

San Francisco Bay

FISHERMAN'S WHARF

TELEGRAPH HILL

RUSSIAN HILL

NORTH BEACH

PACIFIC HEIGHTS

CHINATOWN

NOB HILL

Union Square

JAPANTOWN

Civic Center

Muni Van Ness

To Golden Gate Park

MISSION DISTRICT

THE EMBARCADERO

Ferry Terminal

BART/Muni Embarcadero

Trans Bay Terminal

BART/Muni Montgomery

San Francisco-Oakland Bay Bridge

BART/Muni Powell

BART/Muni Civic Center

Beach St., Bay St., Francisco St., Lombard St., Broadway, Sacramento St., California St., Pine St., Bush St., Sutter St., Post St., Geary St., Geary Expwy., Fulton St., Grove St., Hayes St., Fell St., Oak St., Haight St.

Steiner St., Fillmore St., Webster St., Buchanan St., Laguna St., Octavia St., Gough St., Franklin St., Van Ness Ave., Polk St., Larkin St., Hyde St., Jones St., Mason St., Powell St., Stockton St., Grant Ave., Montgomery St., Columbus Ave., Francisco St.

Market St., Guerrero St., Valencia St., Central Fwy., Potrero Ave.

Muni Church St., Muni Castro St., Seventeenth St., Castro St.

BART 16th St./Mission, BART 24th St./Mission

5	Civic Center, Alamo Square Historic District, Golden Gate Park
38	Via Geary Blvd. to Japan Center, Richmond District, Lincoln Park
27	Bryant
30	North Beach, Union Square, Fisherman's Wharf
12	Folsom
15	Via Kearney to North Beach, Chinatown
41 45	Via Union St. to the Presidio, Pacific Heights
32 42	Via Embarcadero to Fisherman's Wharf, Financial District
- - - -	Cable Car

0 — 1/2 mi
0 — .5 km

For Dummies™: Bestselling Book Series for Beginners

San Francisco For Dummies, 1st Edition

Cheat Sheet

The Napa Valley

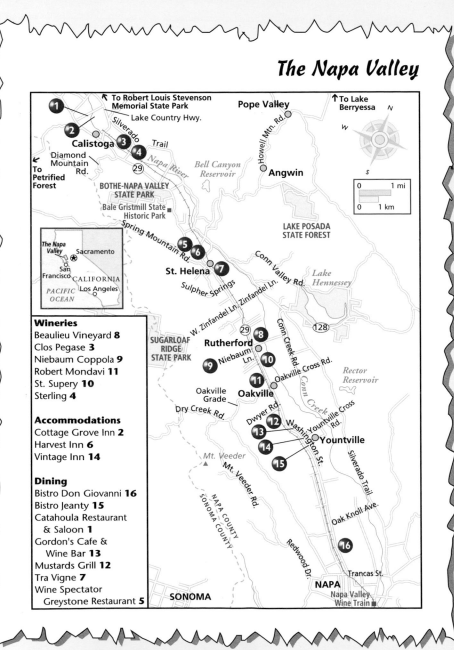

To Robert Louis Stevenson Memorial State Park
Lake Country Hwy.
Pope Valley
To Lake Berryessa

Silverado
Trail
Calistoga
Diamond Mountain Rd.
To Petrified Forest
29
Napa River
Bell Canyon Reservoir
Angwin
Howell Mtn. Rd.

N
W
S

BOTHE-NAPA VALLEY STATE PARK
Bale Gristmill State Historic Park
Spring Mountain Rd.
St. Helena
Sulpher Springs
Conn Valley Rd.
Lake Hennessey
LAKE POSADA STATE FOREST

0   1 mi
0   1 km

The Napa Valley
Sacramento
San Francisco
CALIFORNIA
Los Angeles
PACIFIC OCEAN

W. Zinfandel Ln. Zinfandel Ln.
SUGARLOAF RIDGE STATE PARK
29
Rutherford
Niebaum Ln.
128
Conn Creek Rd.
Oakville Cross Rd.
Rector Reservoir
Conn Creek

Oakville Grade
Dry Creek Rd.
Oakville
Dwyer Rd.
Washington St.
Yountville Cross Rd.
Yountville
Silverado Trail

Mt. Veeder
Mt. Veeder Rd.
NAPA COUNTY
SONOMA COUNTY

Oak Knoll Ave.

Redwood Dr.
SONOMA
NAPA
Napa Valley Wine Train
Trancas St.

Wineries
Beaulieu Vineyard **8**
Clos Pegase **3**
Niebaum Coppola **9**
Robert Mondavi **11**
St. Supery **10**
Sterling **4**

Accommodations
Cottage Grove Inn **2**
Harvest Inn **6**
Vintage Inn **14**

Dining
Bistro Don Giovanni **16**
Bistro Jeanty **15**
Catahoula Restaurant & Saloon **1**
Gordon's Cafe & Wine Bar **13**
Mustards Grill **12**
Tra Vigne **7**
Wine Spectator Greystone Restaurant **5**

IDG BOOKS WORLDWIDE

For Dummies™: Bestselling Book Series for Beginners

 ™

References for the Rest of Us!™

San Francisco

FOR

DUMMIES®

1ST EDITION

San Francisco
FOR
DUMMIES®
1ST EDITION

by Paula Tevis

IDG
BOOKS
WORLDWIDE

IDG Books Worldwide, Inc.
An International Data Group Company

Foster City, CA ✦ Chicago, IL ✦ Indianapolis, IN ✦ New York, NY

San Francisco For Dummies®, 1st Edition

Published by
IDG Books Worldwide, Inc.
An International Data Group Company
919 E. Hillsdale Blvd.
Suite 400
Foster City, CA 94404
www.idgbooks.com (IDG Books Worldwide Web Site)
www.dummies.com (Dummies Press Web Site)

Library of Congress Control Number: 00-103381

ISBN: 0-7645-6161-8

ISSN: 1528-2120

Printed in the United States of America

10 9 8 7 6 5 4 3 2 1

1B/QX/QZ/QQ/IN

Distributed in the United States by IDG Books Worldwide, Inc.

Distributed by CDG Books Canada Inc. for Canada; by Transworld Publishers Limited in the United Kingdom; by IDG Norge Books for Norway; by IDG Sweden Books for Sweden; by IDG Books Australia Publishing Corporation Pty. Ltd. for Australia and New Zealand; by TransQuest Publishers Pte Ltd. for Singapore, Malaysia, Thailand, Indonesia, and Hong Kong; by Gotop Information Inc. for Taiwan; by ICG Muse, Inc. for Japan; by Intersoft for South Africa; by Eyrolles for France; by International Thomson Publishing for Germany, Austria and Switzerland; by Distribuidora Cuspide for Argentina; by LR International for Brazil; by Galileo Libros for Chile; by Ediciones ZETA S.C.R. Ltda. for Peru; by WS Computer Publishing Corporation, Inc., for the Philippines; by Contemporanea de Ediciones for Venezuela; by Express Computer Distributors for the Caribbean and West Indies; by Micronesia Media Distributor, Inc. for Micronesia; by Chips Computadoras S.A. de C.V. for Mexico; by Editorial Norma de Panama S.A. for Panama; by American Bookshops for Finland.

For general information on IDG Books Worldwide's books in the U.S., please call our Consumer Customer Service department at 800-762-2974. For reseller information, including discounts and premium sales, please call our Reseller Customer Service department at 800-434-3422.

For information on where to purchase IDG Books Worldwide's books outside the U.S., please contact our International Sales department at 317-572-3993 or fax 317-572-4002.

For consumer information on foreign language translations, please contact our Customer Service department at 1-800-434-3422, fax 317-572-4002, or e-mail rights@idgbooks.com.

For information on licensing foreign or domestic rights, please phone +1-650-653-7098.

For sales inquiries and special prices for bulk quantities, please contact our Order Services department at 800-434-4322 or write to the address above.

For information on using IDG Books Worldwide's books in the classroom or for ordering examination copies, please contact our Educational Sales department at 800-434-2086 or fax 317-572-4005.

For press review copies, author interviews, or other publicity information, please contact our Public Relations department at 650-653-7000 or fax 650-653-7500.

For authorization to photocopy items for corporate, personal, or educational use, please contact Copyright Clearance Center, 222 Rosewood Drive, Danvers, MA 01923, or fax 978-750-4470.

is a registered trademark under exclusive license to IDG Books Worldwide, Inc., from International Data Group, Inc.

About the Author

A California native, **Paula Tevis** made many treks to San Francisco as a young girl before moving to her favorite city in 1983. After an eclectic, but blessedly brief career that included stints in the computer and nonprofit sectors, she and her husband produced a couple of kids, and Paula happily relinquished the 9-to-5 world for the 24/7 one that parenting brings. Once she regained consciousness, Paula decided to follow her bliss and become a writer. From her humble beginnings word-processing cookbook manuscripts for a local publisher, Paula metamorphosed into a freelance copy editor, and soon received her first break as a professional writer crafting a column on kids who cook for *Parenting* magazine. She has since contributed articles and essays to *Family Fun* magazine, the *San Francisco Chronicle, Citysearch.com, Frommer's Las Vegas, Frommer's New Orleans,* and *California For Dummies,* and is the author of the *Berlitz Vancouver Pocketguide.* She lives with her husband, the girls, and the dog in a somewhat seismically safe neighborhood at the end of the J-Church line.

ABOUT IDG BOOKS WORLDWIDE

Welcome to the world of IDG Books Worldwide.

IDG Books Worldwide, Inc., is a subsidiary of International Data Group, the world's largest publisher of computer-related information and the leading global provider of information services on information technology. IDG was founded more than 30 years ago by Patrick J. McGovern and now employs more than 9,000 people worldwide. IDG publishes more than 290 computer publications in over 75 countries. More than 90 million people read one or more IDG publications each month.

Launched in 1990, IDG Books Worldwide is today the #1 publisher of best-selling computer books in the United States. We are proud to have received eight awards from the Computer Press Association in recognition of editorial excellence and three from Computer Currents' First Annual Readers' Choice Awards. Our best-selling ...For Dummies® series has more than 50 million copies in print with translations in 31 languages. IDG Books Worldwide, through a joint venture with IDG's Hi-Tech Beijing, became the first U.S. publisher to publish a computer book in the People's Republic of China. In record time, IDG Books Worldwide has become the first choice for millions of readers around the world who want to learn how to better manage their businesses.

Our mission is simple: Every one of our books is designed to bring extra value and skill-building instructions to the reader. Our books are written by experts who understand and care about our readers. The knowledge base of our editorial staff comes from years of experience in publishing, education, and journalism — experience we use to produce books to carry us into the new millennium. In short, we care about books, so we attract the best people. We devote special attention to details such as audience, interior design, use of icons, and illustrations. And because we use an efficient process of authoring, editing, and desktop publishing our books electronically, we can spend more time ensuring superior content and less time on the technicalities of making books.

You can count on our commitment to deliver high-quality books at competitive prices on topics you want to read about. At IDG Books Worldwide, we continue in the IDG tradition of delivering quality for more than 30 years. You'll find no better book on a subject than one from IDG Books Worldwide.

John Kilcullen
Chairman and CEO
IDG Books Worldwide, Inc.

Eighth Annual
Computer Press
Awards ≥1992

Ninth Annual
Computer Press
Awards ≥1993

Tenth Annual
Computer Press
Awards ≥1994

Eleventh Annual
Computer Press
Awards ≥1995

IDG is the world's leading IT media, research and exposition company. Founded in 1964, IDG had 1997 revenues of $2.05 billion and has more than 9,000 employees worldwide. IDG offers the widest range of media options that reach IT buyers in 75 countries representing 95% of worldwide IT spending. IDG's diverse product and services portfolio spans six key areas including print publishing, online publishing, expositions and conferences, market research, education and training, and global marketing services. More than 90 million people read one or more of IDG's 290 magazines and newspapers, including IDG's leading global brands — Computerworld, PC World, Network World, Macworld and the Channel World family of publications. IDG Books Worldwide is one of the fastest-growing computer book publishers in the world, with more than 700 titles in 36 languages. The "...For Dummies®" series alone has more than 50 million copies in print. IDG offers online users the largest network of technology-specific Web sites around the world through IDG.net (http://www.idg.net), which comprises more than 225 targeted Web sites in 55 countries worldwide. International Data Corporation (IDC) is the world's largest provider of information technology data, analysis and consulting, with research centers in over 41 countries and more than 400 research analysts worldwide. IDG World Expo is a leading producer of more than 168 globally branded conferences and expositions in 35 countries including E3 (Electronic Entertainment Expo), Macworld Expo, ComNet, Windows World Expo, ICE (Internet Commerce Expo), Agenda, DEMO, and Spotlight. IDG's training subsidiary, ExecuTrain, is the world's largest computer training company, with more than 230 locations worldwide and 785 training courses. IDG Marketing Services helps industry-leading IT companies build international brand recognition by developing global integrated marketing programs via IDG's print, online and exposition products worldwide. Further information about the company can be found at www.idg.com.   1/26/00

Dedication

To my cousins, Irene Levin Dietz and Ina Levin Gyemant, who add so much to my life in San Francisco; and to my mother, Gladys Tevis, who first drove me there.

Author's Acknowledgments

Many thanks to Mary Herczog, who started me on this particular path, and to my dear friend Steve Hochman, who had the good sense to wed her. Thanks also to my editors, Claudia Kirschhold and Jeff Soloway, to Kelly Edmonton of the San Francisco Convention and Visitors Bureau, to Vicki Pate and Cathleen O'Brien, to Grace-Ann Walden, Shirley Fong-Torres, and to my sister, Patience Tevis, who always asks if I'm going to mention her in my next book.

Publisher's Acknowledgments

We're proud of this book; please register your comments through our IDG Books Worldwide Online Registration Form located at http://my2cents.dummies.com.

Some of the people who helped bring this book to market include the following:

Editorial

Editors: Linda Brandon, Jeff Soloway

Copy Editor: Rowena Rappaport

Cartographer: Roberta Stockwell

Editorial Manager: Christine Beck

Editorial Assistants: Melissa Bluhm, Alison Jefferson, Jennifer Young

Production

Project Coordinator: Regina Snyder

Layout and Graphics: Barry Offringa, Heather Pope, Erin Zeltner

Proofreaders: Laura Albert, Vickie Broyles, David Faust, John Greenough, Linda Quigley, Sossity R. Smith

Indexer: Steve Rath

Special Help

Michelle Hacker, Esmeralda St. Clair

General and Administrative

IDG Books Worldwide, Inc.: John Kilcullen, CEO; Bill Barry, President and COO

IDG Books Consumer Reference Group

Business: Kathleen A. Welton, Vice President and Publisher; Kevin Thornton, Acquisitions Manager

Cooking/Gardening: Jennifer Feldman, Associate Vice President and Publisher

Education/Reference: Diane Graves Steele, Vice President and Publisher; Greg Tubach, Publishing Director

Lifestyles: Kathleen Nebenhaus, Vice President and Publisher; Tracy Boggier, Managing Editor

Pets: Dominique De Vito, Associate Vice President and Publisher; Tracy Boggier, Managing Editor

Travel: Michael Spring, Vice President and Publisher; Suzanne Jannetta, Editorial Director; Brice Gosnell, Managing Editor

IDG Books Consumer Editorial Services: Kathleen Nebenhaus, Vice President and Publisher; Kristin A. Cocks, Editorial Director; Cindy Kitchel, Editorial Director

IDG Books Consumer Production: Debbie Stailey, Production Director

IDG Books Packaging: Marc J. Mikulich, Vice President, Brand Strategy and Research

◆

The publisher would like to give special thanks to Patrick J. McGovern, without whom this book would not have been possible.

◆

Contents at a Glance

Cartoons at a Glance

By Rich Tennant

"Yeah, I can tell you how to get there. First, you go down here to Lombard Street, then you take a right, then you take a left, then you take a right, then you take a left, then you take a right..."

page 7

"OK Cookie—your venison in lingonberry sauce is good, as are your eggplant soufflé and the risotto with foie gras. But whoever taught you how to make a croquembouche should be shot."

page 113

Well this is just a whole lot more than I expected from a tour of the Golden Gate Bridge.

page 151

SAN FRANCISCO'S AMAZING CABLE CARS
Travelers can ride from Market Street to the Financial District, through the Rocky Mountains and on to Denver all for the price of one Muni Passport.

page 87

"The problem with wine tastings is you're not supposed to swallow, and Clifford refuses to spit. Fortunately, he studied trumpet with Dizzy Gillespie."

page 229

"For tonight's modern reinterpretation of Carmen, those in the front row are kindly requested to wear raincoats."

page 207

Welcome to the new Haight-Ashbury, Susanne - peace, love, and cell phones.

page 31

"I want a lens that's heavy enough to counterbalance the weight on my back."

page 261

Fax: 978-546-7747
E-mail: richtennant@the5thwave.com
World Wide Web: www.the5thwave.com

Maps at a Glance

Table of Contents

Introduction

● ●

*M*any years ago, way before mandatory seatbelt laws, my mother would occasionally squeeze my sister Patience and me into her little red sports car and literally zoom up Highway 101 for a weekend in San Francisco. We lived 350 miles south in Santa Barbara, but due to my mom's lead foot, we'd be cruising along the bay in no time, past a hill filled with rows of boxy pastel-colored houses, then onto the boulevard that led to our cousin Mildred's beautiful home. My desire to live in a big city (and drive really fast) no doubt developed during these trips, and many subsequent ones in my teens, but my ties to San Francisco actually extend back farther. My grandmother, Sarah, and her sister, Lottie, grew up here. At 18 and 20 years of age they camped in Golden Gate Park after the 1906 earthquake, and in later years lived in a series of houses in the outer Richmond District.

When I had the chance to move to San Francisco nearly 20 years ago, I didn't think twice. My future husband and I rented an apartment a few minutes from Haight Street, and I commuted by Muni to my job on Geary Boulevard in the Richmond District. We then moved to a small neighborhood near the Mission District and Bernal Heights, and eventually I found myself working at one time or another around Civic Center, Potrero Hill, and South of Market. I loved getting well-acquainted with different areas of the city, and in hindsight I realize my early, admittedly dilettantish, professional life helped prepare me for the greatest (and perhaps longest) job I've ever had — writing about San Francisco.

The San Francisco of my grandmother's day was elegant enough to attract the most famous people of its time, yet still wild enough to be exciting. The multicultural, expansive, and liberal city of today continues in that tradition, and even improves upon it. On a daily basis I still continue to marvel at everything San Francisco has to offer, and I'll bet that after a day or two here, you'll do the same.

About This Book

San Francisco For Dummies, 1st Edition, is foremost a reference guide for people who intend to vacation in San Francisco and need basic, clear-cut information on how to plan and execute the best possible trip. If you like, you can begin reading from Chapter 1 and head straight through to the appendixes. But if you turn directly to the restaurant section or to the chapter on wine country, because that's the piece you need at the moment, the book will work just as well. I haven't included absolutely everything San Francisco has to offer in the way of attractions, hotels, restaurants, or diversions — a book that size would be too heavy to pack and probably too bothersome to read. What I have done is pick and choose what I believe to be worth your time and your money. And there is enough variety to please a range of tastes, budgets, and family configurations.

Please be advised that travel information is subject to change at any time — and this is especially true of prices. I therefore suggest that you write or call ahead for confirmation when making your travel plans. The authors, editors, and publisher cannot be held responsible for the experiences of readers while traveling. Your safety is important to us, however, so we encourage you to stay alert and be aware of your surroundings. Keep a close eye on cameras, purses, and wallets, all favorite targets of thieves and pickpockets.

Conventions Used in This Book

So, San Francisco, here you come! You've picked a great destination with a wide variety of wonderful sites to see, fabulous food to try, and interesting places to visit. But, don't be overwhelmed. You've made a smart decision in buying *San Francisco For Dummies,* 1st Edition. This book will walk you through all the nitty-gritty details to make sure that planning your trip goes smoothly, and that the trip itself is divine.

In this book I've included lists of hotels, restaurants, and attractions. As I describe each, I often include abbreviations for commonly accepted credit cards. Take a look at the following list for an explanation of each:

AE – American Express

CB – Carte Blanche

DC – Diners Club

DISC – Discover

JCB – Japan Credit Bank

MC – MasterCard

V – Visa

I've divided the hotels into two categories — my personal favorites and those that don't quite make my preferred list but still get my hearty seal of approval. Don't be shy about considering these "runners-up" hotels if you're unable to get a room at one of my favorites or if your preferences differ from mine — the amenities that the runners-up offer and the services that each provides make all these accommodations good choices to consider as you determine where to rest your head at night.

I also include some general pricing information to help you as you decide where to unpack your bags or dine on the local cuisine. I've used a system of dollar signs to show a range of costs for one night in a hotel or a meal at a restaurant (including appetizer, main course, dessert, one drink, tax, and tip). Check out the following table to decipher the dollar signs:

Cost	SF Hotels	Wine Country Hotels	SF and Wine Country Restaurants
$	75 – 125	100 or less	25 or less
$$	125 – 175	100 – 150	25 – 40
$$$	175 – 250	150 – 200	40 – 50
$$$$	250 or more	200 or more	50 or more

Foolish Assumptions

As I wrote this book, I made some assumptions about you and what your needs might be as a traveler. Here's what I assumed about you:

✔ You may be an inexperienced traveler looking for guidance when determining whether to take a trip to San Francisco and how to plan for it.

✔ You may be an experienced traveler, but you don't have a lot of time to devote to trip planning or you don't have a lot of time to spend in San Francisco once you get there. You want expert advice on how to maximize your time and enjoy a hassle-free trip.

✔ You're not looking for a book that provides all the information available about San Francisco or that lists every hotel, restaurant, or attraction available to you. Instead, you're looking for a book that focuses on the places that will give you the best or most unique experience in San Francisco.

If you fit any of this criteria, then *San Francisco For Dummies,* 1st Edition, gives you the information you're looking for!

How This Book Is Organized

As in all *...For Dummies* guides, this book is organized in parts that contain anywhere from two to five chapters of related information. It isn't necessary to start at the very beginning (though it's a very good place to start); feel free to turn directly to the chapter that intrigues you the most.

Part I: Getting Started

This part gives readers an overview of San Francisco and discusses the details that travel planners need to think about, such as when to come, what the trip may cost, and how to budget. The calendar of events in Chapter 2 may influence your decision on when to arrive, and the text on San Francisco seasons may even dissuade you from showing up in August. Since this book is intended for a varied audience, I include specific advice for family travelers, the disabled, seniors, and gay/lesbian visitors.

Part II: Ironing Out the Details

Because you're reading this, I guess you aren't the type to just show up without an appointment, meaning you intend to do a good bit of pre-planning before your arrival. That's a good idea, and this part covers what you need to know about getting here, particularly if you plan to fly. When it comes to figuring out where to sleep, I include a rundown of the major neighborhoods where visitors stay. That's followed by tips on getting the most room for your money and a brief, but informative, description of my favorite hotels. Of course, we aren't finished yet, because you'll need to decide on whether or not to rent a car and then we pin you down about reserving your tickets for Alcatraz or the American Conservatory Theater (see Chapter 9).

Part III: Settling into San Francisco

In a strange city, it can take days to figure out where you are, but Part III saves time by helping navigate you out of the airport and around the most important neighborhoods. A thorough chapter on local transportation options follows, including everything I know about parking, although exercising luck and patience usually plays a more important role than mere words. And since money is an integral part of any trip, there are a few choice paragraphs on where to get it and what to do if it disappears.

Part IV: Dining in San Francisco

An entire section devoted to food? You betcha. If not in a book devoted to the culinary center of the universe, or at least a good three-quarters of the U.S., then where? Read these chapters and you'll soon be able to discuss the intricacies of the local food scene as if you spend all your weekends dining in these parts. And if you prefer to eat and run, you'll get a head start with a chapter on food to go, and I don't mean fast food.

Part V: Exploring San Francisco

You likely have an idea of what you want to see, and this part provides the information you need to conquer the most popular sites. Along with the big stuff, I've categorized other fun and interesting options under lots of different interests. My three- and five-day itineraries at the end of Part V will help you focus and plan your days with all the precision you care to muster up.

Part VI: Living It Up After the Sun Goes Down: San Francisco Nightlife

As my husband says prior to his annual pilgrimage to JazzFest in New Orleans, "You can sleep when you're dead." But first, you need to figure out where to go after dinner and that's what you'll discover in Part VI. From opera to swing dancing to barhopping, there's always something stimulating around town.

Part VII: Exploring beyond San Francisco: Great Day and Overnight Trips

Leaving already? Don't stay away long, but have a wonderful time investigating a few of the beautiful areas an hour or less from the city. In this part, you take a day trip to Berkley, an overnighter to the coast, and a getaway to wine country, including a winery tour.

Part VIII: The Part of Tens

This is where I get to lurch from the sublime (the best views) to the practical (what to do if it's raining) to the goofy (how not to look like a tourist). But there's plenty of useful info to be gleaned.

You can also find two other elements near the back of this book. I've included an *appendix* — your Quick Concierge — containing lots of handy information you may need when traveling in San Francisco, like phone numbers and addresses, emergency personnel or area hospitals and pharmacies, contact information for babysitters, lists of local newspapers and mazagines, protocol for sending mail or finding taxis, and more. Check out this appendix when searching for answers to lots of little questions that may come up as you travel.

I've also included a bunch of worksheets to make your travel planning easier — among other things, you can determine your travel budget, create specific itineraries, and keep a log of your favorite restaurants so you can hit them again next time you're in town. You can find these worksheets easily because they're printed on yellow paper.

Icons Used in This Book

Find out useful advice on things to do and ways to schedule your time when you see the Tip icon.

Watch for the Heads Up icon to identify annoying or potentially danger-ous situations such as tourist traps, unsafe neighborhoods, budgetary rip-offs, and other things to beware of.

Look to the Kid Friendly icon for attractions, hotels, restaurants, and activities that are particulary hospitable to children or people traveling with kids.

Keep an eye out for the Bargain Alert icon as you seek out money-saving tips and/or great deals.

While it may seem obvious that everything in this book is only to be found in San Francisco, this icon is used for those places that by their very nature can only be found in San Francisco.

Where to Go from Here

Grab some sticky notes to mark the pages that you may want to refer back to later, clear your calendar, check the condition of your suitcase, and let's hit the road.

Part I
Getting Started

"Yeah, I can tell you how to get there. First, you go down here to Lombard Street, then you take a right, then you take a left, then you take a right, then you take a left, then you take a right..."

In this part . . .

San Francisco may appear a formidable place to visit, at least the first time, but let me assure you that it's not. The city is small and friendly, so it won't take long for you to figure out which way is which. Of course, the more you learn about any destination, the more comfortable you'll feel when you arrive. This part of the book is designed to "raise your comfort level," as we like to say in Northern California.

Chapter 1

Discovering the Best of San Francisco

- -

- -

*W*ith a wink and a nod to the past, San Francisco is reinventing itself once again. In its new role as the heartbeat of the Internet economy, the city is sashaying into the twenty-first century with an energy and style that even causes the old-timers to gasp in admiration. Of course, transformation hasn't touched everything: The beautiful scenery continues to dazzle, the top-flight dining continues to garner raves, and the entertainment possibilities continue to grow in sophistication.

San Francisco is consistently rated one of the top tourist destinations in the world, and it's no secret why. The city's treasured cable cars provide both thrills and great views as they whiz down and around the hills; a majestically golden bridge suspends walkers over the deep blue of the bay; and hidden staircases lead to lovely gardens and eye-catching homes. Where else can you savor freshly-made miniature chocolate truffles, meander down the crookedest street in the world, and escape from Alcatraz, all in one action-packed day!

Summarizing San Francisco is not easy. When it comes to culture, it delivers everything from grand opera to leather-clad, fire-dancing performance artists. As for dining, we can down a burrito for lunch and polish off a multi-course designer meal for dinner, but critique both with equal passion. Our neighborhoods can more accurately be called villages, each with its own shopping blocks, parks, and highly distinct personalities. For in the face of rampant cultural homogeneity — the malling of America, so to speak — San Francisco is holding on tight to its individualism and enthusiastically applauds, or quietly salutes, those who do the same. What is consistent about the city, from the top of **Telegraph Hill** to the newly paved sidewalks of **South Park,** is constant surprise. As you round a bend in the road, a lovely vista unexpectedly pops into your line of sight. As you savor a glass of chardonnay, a Chinese funeral cortege may suddenly glide past your cafe table, the band playing a pop classic. Or the smell of roasting coffee beans will waft down the street and completely erase any thought but where to find an espresso.

If You Cook It, They Will Come

San Francisco's reputation as a food lover's paradise is both well-deserved and tested on a daily basis. You can find thousands of restaurants around town, from dives to divas, all with their loyal followings and all under constant scrutiny by critics and self-proclaimed gourmands. Between the competition and the narrowed eyes of the food patrol, a restaurateur has to stay sharp, or at least hire a crackerjack public relations firm, to make it through the first year in business. The constant buzz and change in the food scene can be a little nerve-wracking to track, but it serves to make dining an event for locals and tourists alike. In the end, fortunately, it all comes down to ingredients. And where else but here do you find the freshest, and most beautiful and politically correct fruits, veggies, fish, and organically raised meats? Well, Berkeley, maybe, but certainly nowhere else.

The Hills (and the Views) Are Alive

The clatter and hum of cable cars, the huffing and puffing of out-of-shape joggers, the wooden stairways leading to hidden gardens — San Francisco's famous hills are most certainly alive and well. They serve as the main attraction, as well as the backdrop, for sightseers in the city, and they've worked their way into our collective imagination through the myriad books and films that have immortalized them.

But these hills, gathered between the orange-hued **Golden Gate** and silvery **Bay bridges,** the hypnotic Pacific Ocean and the icy waters of the bay, are just one part of the scenery. For equally breathtaking, if less lofty, views seek out the **Palace of Fine Arts,** the **Museum of Modern Art,** or **Golden Gate Park.** Ride the streetcar down **Market Street** to **Fisherman's Wharf** or in the opposite direction to the **Giants'** fabulous new, **Pac Bell Park.** Revel in the urban gardens at **Yerba Buena Center** and in the crowded sidewalks of **Chinatown.** In these places you can catch a glimpse of what San Francisco was like during its formative years and where the city is headed in the twenty-first century.

The Lowdown on the After Hours

San Francisco has matured greatly from its rough and tumble years during the gold rush. There's no chance you'll get shanghaied on a boat to China any longer, nor are you apt to witness any vigilante groups patrolling the streets as they did during the Barbary Coast heydays. But if you're looking for excitement, the city still delivers. The music and club scene, especially around **North Beach** and **South of Market,** is thriving, for those who want to shimmy as well as those who prefer to groove silently with the horn section. There's no lack of places to relax and make a toast to your vacation, and theater, dance, and classical music lovers can find a great many venues in which to laugh, cry, or clap wildly. We're not exactly an all-nighter town, but we have plenty of activities to keep you occupied.

Day Trading

From the hallowed picture windows of **Union Square** to the curio-packed sidewalks of **Chinatown,** from the boutiques along **Fillmore, Sacramento,** and **Union streets** to the discounters of **SoMa,** if shopping is your bag, San Francisco can fill 'er up. Do you fancy fine wines? Do handmade chocolate truffles have you making promises you have no intention of keeping? Would a unique object d'art be just the right pick-me-up for your old coffee table? This is the town for you!

Urban Renewal

San Francisco, the city in the thick of the new economy, is bursting with growth and ideas these days. New neighborhoods are developing in areas that at best were ignored prior to the dot.com revolution. Traffic, which will forever be a problem, hasn't lightened up, but public transportation is improving and expanding. With more and more people and companies determined to call San Francisco home, gentrification is reaching every nook and cranny with both fortunate and unfortunate consequences. Skid row as a definable geographic location is disappearing slowly, but homelessness seems entrenched. Nary a downtown street nor a median strip is empty of some poor soul holding a sign asking for handouts. While comparing San Francisco to Calcutta, as one travel writer recently did, is a stretch (and a nasty dig), be prepared psychologically and/or financially — whatever suits you. Yet underneath it all, San Francisco stays remarkably the same — youthful, vibrant, beautiful, and a lot of fun.

The Bay Area

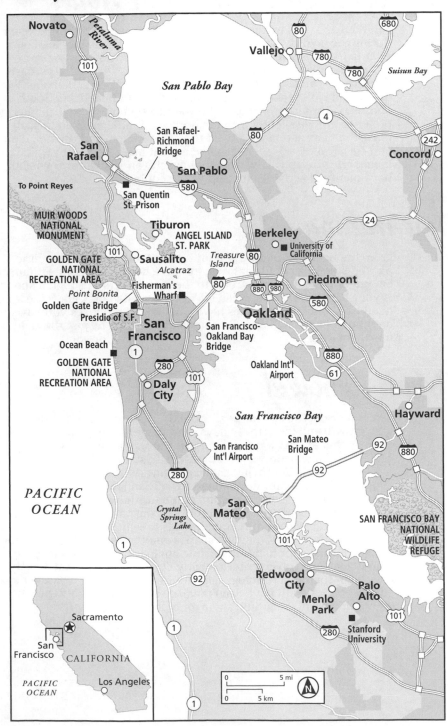

Chapter 2

Deciding When to Go

• •

In This Chapter

▶ Choosing the best season to visit

▶ Finding events that suit your interests

• •

*Y*ou may not have much choice when it comes to scheduling your trip, especially if you have to plan around school vacations and work obligations. But for those who do have some leeway, I've outlined what's going on in San Francisco at different times of the year in terms of weather, crowds, and celebrations. The kind of weather we locals long for is usually balmy temperatures and clear skies. I can only hope you find the same, but just in case, bring a warm jacket and a hat whatever season you plan to visit. Anyway, a little fog never hurt anybody.

The Secret of the Seasons: When to Go and What to Do

Because of its temperate California address, San Francisco hosts tourists and business travelers year-round. However, San Francisco is the most crowded between June and October.

It pays to plan

Push spontaneity aside and plan ahead if you visit during this time of year. In other words, make hotel and car reservations at least six weeks in advance, reserve a table at the more well-known restaurants three to four weeks in advance, and purchase your tickets to **Alcatraz** (see Chapter 16) well in advance of your visit there. Don't think you can arrive in the city with just a suitcase and a camera around your neck. You don't want to waste your time and energy making phone calls or driving around in the car searching for accommodations, or waiting for a table at **Foreign Cinema** (see Chapter 14) for hours and hours.

Something to remember about the San Francisco "summer" is that it might not be the summer you're used to. Temperatures rarely top 70°F and are often quite cool. Bring a jacket and a hat and be prepared for fog — at any time of year.

But the city is at its warmest and most glorious in September and October. These are also the very busiest months. It's when Fisherman's Wharf is packed to the gills, every cable car is overflowing, and there's not a hotel room available in sight. Don't even think about trying to get a discount on accommodations during these months.

School vacation schedules will probably dictate your travel time if you're traveling with children. The days start out heavy with fog in July and August, but eventually clear up enough for you to lose the jacket or sweatshirt. Prepare for big crowds, especially at the most popular tourist destinations. Fortunately, a little imaginative planning can help you entertain your kids and avoid some (though not all) of the crowds. (See Chapter 17 for some offbeat sightseeing ideas.)

During the winter, the crowds do thin out and are most likely in warmer climates such as Florida and even Southern California. (Those seeking tanning locations during winter need to make arrangements in those southern states.) November through March, when the weather can be damp and chilly, are considered slow tourist months in San Francisco. But these are months when you can get a great deal at a nice hotel, or a room upgrade, after you arrive, if you don't mind sightseeing with an umbrella or bundled up in sweaters and a hat. You may even be pleasantly surprised by blue skies and low 60s temperatures in the middle of February. In general, room rates are lowered between November and mid-April, unless a big convention is in town (check with the **Convention and Visitors Bureau** at ☎ **415-391-2000**). A few attractions even reduce their entrance fees at this time.

Wintertime can be a great time to visit San Francisco, in spite of the weather. A good number of the larger hotels offer packages, and some have special events for kids. The Ritz-Carlton hosts a Teddy Bear Tea throughout December, a popular affair that sells out early in the season. Along with sightseeing, you can admire the Christmas windows decorating Union Square, skate around the Embarcadero Center's outdoor ice rink, and take in one of many Nutcracker ballet or music performances.

Travel reasons for each season

Here's the good and the bad of each season. Take a look at Table 2-1 for information on average temperatures and rainfall.

Winter

▪ ✔ The skies may be gray and the air damp

But . . .

> ✔ Hotel prices will be lower, especially on weekends
>
> ✔ Cable cars still have room
>
> ✔ Store windows are decorated for the holidays
>
> ✔ Restaurants won't be as busy

Spring

▌ ✔ Convention season starts, bringing hotel costs up

But . . .

▐ ✔ Flowers are in bloom in the parks
▐ ✔ The weather can be glorious
▐ ✔ Kids are still in school

Summer

▐ ✔ Pier 39 and Fisherman's Wharf are madhouses
▐ ✔ Hotels are packed
▐ ✔ Foggy mornings are downers

But . . .

▐ ✔ Mimes are out in full force
▐ ✔ Kids are out of school and it's the best time to plan a family vacation

Autumn

▐ ✔ Napa Valley is booked
▐ ✔ Heavy events calendar lures additional crowds

But . . .

▐ ✔ Finest weather available all year on average
▐ ✔ Cultural season begins

**Table 2-1   San Francisco's Average Temperatures (°F)
& Rainfall (in.)**

	Jan	Feb	Mar	Apr	May	June	July	Aug	Sept	Oct	Nov	Dec
High	56	59	60	61	63	64	64	65	69	68	63	57
Low	46	48	49	49	51	53	53	54	56	55	52	47
Rain	4.5	2.8	2.6	1.5	0.4	0.2	0.1	0.1	0.2	1.1	2.5	3.5

Mark Your Calendars

You can get a quick glance of San Francisco's most popular special events and festivals throughout the year using the following list. However, many more festivals and events are scheduled during the year than I can list here. For more events and festivals, check out the *Bay Guardian* Web site (www.sfbg.com), the San Francisco Chronicle site (www.sfgate.com), or the Citysearch Web site (www. bayareacitysearch.com), or send $3 to the Convention and Visitors Bureau for their Festivals and Special Events calendar (see the Appendix). Call the phone numbers noted with each event for exact dates and ticket prices.

You pay no charge for street fairs and holiday festivals, but bring along some cash for the crafts booths and food. How do you keep a festival festive? Because parking will inevitably be impossible, don't drive. Take public transportation, or take a cab if you can't walk — it's well worth the expense.

January/February

Chinese New Year, Chinatown. This is an important, well-attended two-week event in San Francisco, with lots of free entertainment, a parade, and colorful sights. Dates vary. ☎ 415-982-3000.

March

St. Patrick's Day Parade, Downtown. St. Patrick's Day is a big holiday around here, and the parade is one of San Francisco's largest. ☎ 415-731-0924.

April

San Francisco International Film Festival, centered at the AMC Kabuki 8 Cinemas at Fillmore and Post Streets and around town. One of the oldest film festivals in the country, it features more than 100 films and videos from over 30 countries. April through early May. Call ☎ 415-929-5000 for a schedule.

Cherry Blossom Festival, Japantown. Celebrate Japanese culture with flower arranging, sumo wrestling, traditional drumming, and a parade. Mid- to late April. ☎ 415-563-2313.

May

Cinco de Mayo Celebration, Mission District. Festivities and a parade are held around the Mission District on the first Sunday of May. ☎ 415-826-1401.

Carnival, Mission District. If you like crowds and scantily dressed samba dancers, this spectacle is a must-see. More than a half-million revelers turn out for this two-day celebration. Memorial Day weekend. ☎ 415-826-1401.

June

Ethnic Dance Festival, Palace of Fine Arts Theater, next to the Exploratorium. Three weekends of world dance and music performances. ☎ 415-474-3914.

Union Street Fair, on Union from Fillmore to Gough Streets. Music and entertainment, food and drink, arts and crafts, and yuppies — this fair has it all. First weekend in June. ☎ 415-441-7055.

North Beach Festival, Grant Street in North Beach. Come for the music, arts and crafts, and the people-watching. This festival is the oldest urban street fair in the country, claim festival organizers. ☎ 415-989-6426.

July

San Francisco Chronicle Fourth of July Waterfront Festival, Fisherman's Wharf. A day-long party culminating in fireworks. ☎ 415-705-5500.

August

Comedy Celebration Day, Golden Gate Park. Four hours of free chuckles and guffaws. ☎ 415-386-5035.

A La Carte, A La Park, Sharon Meadow, in Golden Gate Park. Check this festival out for samplings from the city's best wineries, microbreweries, and restaurants, and for some great music, too. Labor Day weekend. ☎ 415-383-9378.

September

Autumn Moon Festival, Chinatown. Grant Street between California and Pacific Streets. This Chinese festival features moon cakes (which are round pastries with eggs inside), children's activities, and traditional dances. Dates vary. ☎ 415-982-6306.

Latino Summer Festival, 24th Street between Mission and York Streets in the Mission. A celebration of Central and South American independence, with international food, arts and crafts, and four stages with live music. Sunday date varies. ☎ 415-826-1401.

San Francisco Blues Festival, Fort Mason. The biggest outdoor blues event on the West Coast, both national and local musicians perform at this festival. Late September. ☎ 415-979-5588.

Folsom Street Fair, Folsom Street between 7th and 12th Streets. This arts-and-crafts street fair attracts the black leather and dog collar crowd. Usually the last Sunday in September. ☎ 415-861-3247.

San Francisco Fringe Festival, Exit Theater and various venues downtown. A 10-day marathon of experimental theater and performance art. ☎ 415-931-1094.

October

Castro Street Fair. A few hundred thousand people are entertained by community organizations and local merchants at this street fair, which takes place in the Castro from Market to 19th Streets between Noe and Collingwood Streets. The first Sunday in October. ☎ 415-467-3354.

San Francisco Jazz Festival. Held in various venues around the city, this eclectic two-week jazz fest sells out fast. End of October, beginning of November. Call ☎ 415-788-7353 for tickets.

November

San Francisco International Automobile Show, Moscone Center. Cars, and lots of 'em. ☎ 415-331-4406.

December

Teddy Bear Tea, Ritz-Carlton. Starting after Thanksgiving and going through Christmas, this event reserves fast. Reservations start in August, and are recommended, especially for weekends. Call ☎ 415-773-6198.

Chapter 3

Planning Your Budget

● ●

In This Chapter

▶ Figuring out the cost of things

▶ Knowing where to go for money

▶ Cutting your expenses down to size

● ●

*M*oney may or may not make the world go 'round, but nothing spoils a vacation faster than running out of it. This chapter covers everything from figuring the cost of your trip to the nitty-gritty of how to obtain your cash.

Keeping a Lid on Hidden Expenses

My credit card bill never ceases to amaze me. I often wonder where half those charges came from, although digging through the statement often lends itself to fond reminiscing about the recent past. You may not want to be reminded of your vacation in such a potentially harsh manner — better to stick with pictures — but that means paying attention to expenses that are less obvious than shelter and food. For example, remember that the cost of your hotel is more than the stated room rate. A steep hotel tax of 14 percent is added on, and don't forget any minibar, telephone, bar, or room service charges. Parking in San Francisco can bankrupt you. Remember, too, minor things such as film and developing; bridge tolls; warm sweatshirts times the number of people in your family who forgot to pack a jacket; and tips for the bellmen, parking garage attendants, waiters, tour bus drivers . . . they add up quickly. Do you have to kennel your dog? May as well include that on the list.

Adding Up the Elements

Creating a budget is easy; sticking to one can be difficult, especially if the budget is unrealistic. A worksheet at the end of this book can help you get an idea of what your trip will cost. Expenses to consider include transportation to and around the city, hotels, food and beverages, attractions, shopping, entertainment, and incidentals such as telephone calls. After you figure your budget, follow my rule of thumb and add an extra 15 percent. (Unless you are unusually disciplined, you won't come in under budget.)

The Cost of Things to Come

A lemonade	$1.95
A latté in North Beach	$2.50
A 12 oz. microbeer at Thirsty Bear	$3
Lunch for one at the Hayes Street Grill (moderate)	$14
Lunch for one at Pancho Villa (inexpensive)	$8
Dinner for one at Grand Cafe (moderate)	$30
Dinner for one at Chow (inexpensive)	$18
Shuttle from airport to any hotel (excluding tip)	$10–$12
Taxi from airport to city center (excluding tip)	$35
One-way Muni/bus fare to any destination within the city (adult)	$1
One-way Muni/bus fare to any destination within the city (senior/child)	35¢
Movie ticket	$8.50
Theater ticket	$8–$50

Finding the Payment Method That's Best for You

From traveler's checks to cash to credit cards, it's difficult to know what to bring on a trip and what to leave at home. You want security, but you also want flexibility. Read on for a rundown of what each money method entails.

A check of all trades

Traveler's checks were really a great invention for the days before ATMs when people used to write personal checks all the time for their cash. In those days, you couldn't be sure that you would find a place where you could cash a check for cash while on vacation. Traveler's checks were a sound alternative to filling your wallet with cash at the beginning of a trip because they could be replaced if lost or stolen. If you prefer the security of traveler's checks and don't mind the hassle of showing identification every time you want to cash one, you can get them at almost any bank. Here's a listing of companies to contact:

- ✔ **American Express** offers checks in denominations of $10, $20, $50, $100, $500, and $1,000. You have to pay a service charge ranging from 1 percent to 4 percent, though AAA members can obtain checks without a fee at most AAA offices. You can also get American Express traveler's checks over the phone by calling ☎ 800-221-7282; Amex gold and platinum cardholders who call this number are exempt from the 1 percent fee.

- ✔ **Visa** also offers traveler's checks, available at Citibank locations across the country and at several other banks. The service charge ranges from 1.5 percent to 2 percent; checks come in denominations of $20, $50, $100, $500, and $1,000.

- ✔ **MasterCard** also offers traveler's checks. Call ☎ 800-223-9920 for a location near you.

The ABCs of ATMs

Traveler's checks are less necessary these days because most cities have 24-hour ATM machines linked to a national network that most likely includes your bank at home. **Cirrus** (☎ 800-424-7787 or 800/4CIRRUS) and **Plus** (☎ 800-843-7587) are the two most popular networks. You can look on the back of your ATM card to see which network your bank belongs to. The 800 numbers give you specific locations of ATMs where you can withdraw money while on vacation. If you like using cash, using an ATM while in San Francisco may be the route for you. However, it may be in your best interest to make several withdrawals while you're in town, so you don't have a lot of money on you at one time. It's worth it to pay the $1.50 ATM fee than to walk through Fisherman's Wharf with a bulging wallet in the seat of your pants and an ATM receipt sticking out of your pocket.

Charge it!

Credit cards are invaluable while traveling and are a safe way to carry money and provide a convenient record of all your travel expenses when you arrive home. If you are in a pinch, you can also get cash off your credit card with a cash advance transaction at any bank (though you'll start paying high-interest charges on the advance the moment you receive the cash, and you won't receive frequent-flyer miles on an airline credit card). At most banks, you can bypass the teller and go straight to the ATM for a cash advance — if you know your PIN number. If you don't know your PIN number, call the phone number on the back of your credit card and ask the bank to send it to you. It usually takes five to seven business days, though some banks will give you your PIN over the phone provided you give them certain information to ensure your identity.

Here are a few credit-card emergency toll-free numbers in case a problem comes up:

- ✔ **American Express**   ☎ 800-221-7282
- ✔ **Citicorp Visa**   ☎ 800-645-6556
- ✔ **MasterCard**   ☎ 800-307-7309

Cutting Costs: 12 Surefire Money-Saving Strategies

If you're still worried about how you can go on vacation without going into debt, here are some tried-and-true strategies for reducing sticker shock:

1. **Change your date of travel.** Travel on the off-season! You can save big time on airfare and hotel costs if you travel during the winter or early spring. Yes, it may be cold and/or wet, but you might also luck out. Remember, we're talking California — if El Niño doesn't alter the weather patterns, maybe we'll have a drought.

2. **Travel on off days of the week.** Airfares vary depending on the day of the week. If you can travel on a Tuesday, Wednesday, or Thursday, you may find a cheaper flight. When you inquire about airfares, ask if you can obtain a cheaper rate by flying on a different day. Staying over a Saturday night can reduce airfares by more than half.

3. **Always ask for corporate, weekend, senior citizen, or other discount rates.** Membership in AAA, frequent-flyer plans, trade unions, AARP, or other groups may qualify you for discounted rates on car rentals, plane tickets, hotel rooms, and even meals. Ask about a possible discount every time you open your wallet; you may be pleasantly surprised.

4. **Try a package tour.** For many destinations, including San Francisco, you can book airfare, hotel, ground transportation, and even some sightseeing just by making one call to a travel agent or packager, for a lot less than if you tried to put the trip together yourself. (See the section on package tours in Chapter 5 for specific suggestions of companies to call.)

5. **Reserve a hotel room with a kitchenette and do your own cooking.** It may not feel as much like a vacation if you still have to do your own cooking, but you can save a lot of money by not eating out three times a day. Even if you only make breakfast and

an occasional lunch in your room, you'll still save. And you won't have to worry about any unexpected room service bills.

6. **Ask whether kids stay free.** A room with two double beds usually doesn't cost any more than a room with a queen-size bed. And many hotels won't charge you the additional person rate if the additional person is pint-sized and related to you. Even if you have to pay $10 or $15 for a rollaway bed, you can save hundreds of dollars by taking one rather than two rooms.

7. **Research what days your sites of choice have free admission.** Take advantage of free museum entry days and other free admission days.

8. **Skip the souvenirs.** Your photographs and memories should be the best mementos of your trip. You can skip the T-shirts, key chains, salt-and-pepper shakers, and other trinkets, and save a bundle.

9. **Don't rent a car.** The city is easily navigable on foot or by public transportation. You save a bundle on parking by not having a car, too.

10. **Ride public transportation, such as Muni or BART.** Purchase a Muni passport and use it often (see Chapter 11).

11. **Dine out at expensive restaurants for lunch instead of dinner.** Lunch tabs are usually a fraction of what a dinner costs at most top-notch restaurants, and the menu often boasts many of the same specialties.

12. **Don't drink a lot of alcohol at meals.** A restaurant's wine and spirits list is a tidy profit center.

Chapter 4

Planning Ahead for Special Travel Needs

In This Chapter

▶ Getting ready for a trip with the kids, San Francisco-style

▶ Going for high adventure for the disabled or senior traveler

▶ Checking out the coolest places for gay and lesbian travelers

*A*h, for the good old days when you could grab a backpack, throw in a pair of jeans, and venture out into the world. Now there's the family to consider, with junior needing to run around and let off steam every few hours, your teenage daughter needing to check out just one more store, and your spouse needing a break or maybe a beer. Or perhaps you have a physical limitation that makes traveling a challenge. Or maybe you want to take advantage of your status as an elder. Read on, friend. I like nothing better than to dispense advice.

In addition, San Francisco is already well known as a haven for gay and lesbian visitors. If you're gay or lesbian, you want to check out the resources I've listed that can help you find areas of the city and entertainment venues that will be of interest.

Gaining Family Focus

Babies in backpacks and strollers are a common sight on the streets of San Francisco, so you can be assured that kids are welcome here. But taking a vacation with your kids can sometimes mean you're not exactly on vacation, can't it? Here are some tried-and-true ways to make your trip as stress-free as possible.

From a kid's point-of-view

Before you board the plane or pack up the car, sit down with your family unit and this book and go over the sights and activities listed in Chapters 16 and 17. Let your kids choose three to six things to see and do (based on the number of days you plan to stay in San Francisco), and then have them rate their choices in order of preference. You do the same for the places you want to visit. Next, plot a worksheet (see the Appendix) with the days or times you plan to do a kid activity and the times you plan to do something more adult oriented, such as enjoying the Museum of Modern Art (see Chapter 16) or scheduling a walking tour (see Chapter 18). Block out time for eating, snacking, resting, and dropping by neighborhood parks.

Keep in mind that kids turn cranky when exhaustion sets in, so don't pull them in a hundred different directions. You don't need to see everything in one day. A long afternoon in Golden Gate Park watching the squirrels may be more memorable than dashing from one site to the next. Bring along books, paper, crayons, and pencils, perhaps an inexpensive camera, a Walkman, or any other unobtrusive, portable toys and games your children enjoy that they can easily carry in their backpacks. Kids need to have their own copy of the itinerary that your family worked out together, to remind them that their time will come.

Kid-friendly sleeps, eats, and entertainment

Most hotels are more than happy to accommodate your entire clan. "Family Ties: Hotel Strategies for Traveling with Kids," in Chapter 6, also offers tips for figuring out what kind of accommodations are right for you and yours.

Chapter 17 describes various places to go and things to do — divided into age-appropriate sections. But if you'd still like more direction, consider my "San Francisco with Kids" itinerary in Chapter 20. And, don't forget to look out for the Kid Friendly icon to point you toward hotels, restaurants, and attractions that might especially appeal to kids. You'll have no trouble planning the perfect trip for tots, teens, and in-betweens.

Finding a babysitter

There may be times when you and your spouse or a friend may want to go out on the town without the little, or not-so-little, ones in tow. If you're comfortable hiring a baby-sitter, you can find a handful of agencies that will send a carefully screened sitter to your hotel. You'll find that rates vary, as do add-ons, such as transportation and agency fees, but you can expect to pay at least $43 for an evening out without the kids. **A Bay Area Child Care Agency** (☎ **650-991-7474**) used by many of the downtown hotels, charges $9 per hour (4-hour minimum) for two siblings and $7 carfare. Hotel concierges can make arrangements for you, or you can call directly at least a day in advance.

Traveling Seniors

People over the age of 60 are traveling more than ever before, and being a senior citizen entitles you to some terrific travel bargains. Become a member of AARP (American Association of Retired Persons) and save even more! For starters, you can get discounts on car rentals and hotels. Contact AARP at 601 E St. NW, Washington, DC 20049 (☎ **202-434-AARP**) for information on joining.

A popular resource for seniors, *The Mature Traveler* is a 12-page monthly newsletter on senior citizen travel. Subscribe for $30 a year by writing to GEM Publishing Group, Box 50400, Reno, NV 89513-0400. GEM also publishes *The Book of Deals,* a collection of more than 1,000 senior discounts on airlines, lodging, tours, and attractions around the country. You can order it for $9.95 by calling ☎ **800-460-6676.** See also the helpful publication *101 Tips for the Mature Traveler,* available from Grand Circle Travel, 347 Congress St., Suite 3A, Boston, MA 02210 (☎ **800-221-2610** or 617-350-7500; Fax: 617-350-6206).

Seniors get automatic discounts on public transportation fares in San Francisco. Just show identification showing your age for reduced admission at movies, museums, and many other attractions. Many tour companies also offer a discount for those over 62.

Getting the Scoop for Travelers with Disabilities

Don't let a disability stop you from traveling! There are more resources out there than ever before. Check out many of these resources with *A World of Options,* a 658-page book of resources for travelers with disabilities. For $45 you can find out about adventures from biking trips to scuba outfitters. Order it from Mobility International USA, P.O. Box 10767, Eugene, OR 97440 (☎ **541-343-1284,** voice and TDD; Internet: www.miusa.org). For more personal assistance, call the Travel Information Service at ☎ **215-456-9603** or **215-456-9602** (for TTY).

If you are a traveler with a disability, you can also consider joining a tour that caters specifically to travelers with your needs. Check out Flying Wheels Travel, 143 West Bridge (P.O. Box 382), Owatonna, MN 55060 (☎ **800-535-6790**), which offers escorted tours and cruises, as well as private tours in minivans with lifts. Another great find is FEDCAP Rehabilitation Services, 211 W. 14th St., New York, NY 10011. Call ☎ **212-727-4200** or Fax: 212-721-4374 for information about membership and summer tours.

If you are a vision-impaired traveler, contact the American Foundation for the Blind, 11 Penn Plaza, Suite 300, New York, NY 10001 (☎ **800-232-5463**) for information on traveling with Seeing-Eye dogs.

Touring on wheels

If you are a wheelchair user, you'll find San Francisco's public areas quite accessible. All sidewalks have curb cuts, and ramps for easy on/off access have been erected throughout the municipal railway system (Muni). You can find some buses equipped with wheelchair lifts as well. For specific information on public transportation accessibility, request a free copy of the *Muni Access Guide* from Muni's Accessible Services Program by phoning ☎ **415-923-6142** or writing the program at 949 Presidio Ave., San Francisco, CA 94115. If you need a ramped taxi, phone **Yellow Cab** at ☎ **415-626-2345** — at no extra charge!

Many of the major car rental companies now offer hand-controlled cars for drivers with disabilities. Avis can provide such a vehicle at any of its locations in the U.S. with 48-hour advance notice; Hertz requires between 24 and 72 hours of advance reservation at most of its locations. **Wheelchair Getaways** (☎ **800-873-4973;** Internet: www.blvd.com/wg.htm) rents specialized vans with wheelchair lifts and other features for travelers with disabilities in more than 100 cities across the U.S.

Staying accessible

The Americans with Disabilities Act requires hotels built within the past 15 years to be much more handicapped-friendly.

However, lodgings that are housed in old buildings may have entry stairs, tiny elevators, narrow hallways, and minuscule bathrooms, making them unsuitable for anyone having to maneuver in a wheelchair.

You can enjoy the **Tuscan Inn** near Fisherman's Wharf (see Chapter 8), which is a somewhat newer property that's fully accessible. Also, look for the chain hotels, such as the **Embarcadero Hyatt** (see Chapter 8), that are equipped to provide certain services such as TDD (Telephone Device for the Deaf) phones.

Let the reservation clerk at your hotel know what your needs are when making reservations to make your stay more comfortable, be it TDD phones or grip bars.

All newly built or restored restaurants should also be up-to-date on meeting requirements for accessible bathrooms and entrances. If you have any doubts about access, ask when you call for a table.

Getting to the sights

You won't have any problem accessing the main sites in San Francisco. **Golden Gate Park** is completely accessible, as are the museums, the Exploratorium, and many other sites. Some attractions are not very accessible, though; for example, places that have a series of stairs, such as the **Filbert Street Steps. Fort Point** has a wheelchair ramp, and its first floor is easily maneuverable; a walk above **Fort Funston** is also accessible for travelers with disabilities.

Advice for Gay and Lesbian Travelers

San Francisco remains an important and historic destination for gay travelers. The **Castro,** the heart of San Francisco's gay community, is the area around which the majority of gay bars and inns are located. The lesbian community resides mostly in portions of **Noe Valley** and the **Mission District** (with Valencia Street as the main drag).

Check out these great Web sites for your trip planning: www.gay.net and Citysearch (www.bayareacitysearch.com), which has a complete section devoted to gay and lesbian nightlife and an interesting history of the Castro. Also take a look at these handy print guides: ***Betty and Pansy's Severe Queer Review of San Francisco,*** which is updated yearly, and ***The Official San Francisco Gay Guide.*** You can order these books through A Different Light bookstore, 489 Castro St., San Francisco, CA 94114 (☎ **415-431-0891**) or by contacting their New York store (☎ **800-343-4002**) or Web site (www.adlbooks.com). When you get to the city, pick up a copy of the ***Bay Area Reporter*** for comprehensive entertainment listings. It's free and available in coffee houses, bookstores, and around the Castro.

For information on specific hotels that cater to gay visitors, check out *Frommer's San Francisco.* But there aren't any compelling reasons to plunk yourself down in such a hotel unless you don't intend to leave the Castro. And if that's the case, you'll be missing out on the alternative gay scene **South of Market** (see Chapter 22).

Part II
Ironing Out the Details

In this part . . .

Back in his student days, my husband was the kind of
traveler who would blithely show up in some foreign
destination without any notion of where he would sleep,
expecting that something would come along. I, however,
prefer the security of knowing a pillow, an airplane, or a
theater seat has my name on it — so go ahead and guess
which one of us does the travel planning?

The hard truth, especially for people like my devoted
spouse who aren't, shall we say, detail-oriented, is that
you need to consider a lot of things when it comes to planning a vacation, and most of them arise before you step
foot off the airplane. This part of the book lays out your
traveling options, including which airport to use if you're
flying — an important decision whether you use a travel
agent or let your fingers do the walking over your key-
board. You're also prodded to think about what you
require in accommodations so you can make a good
match with a hotel or motel. The other particulars —
renting a car, reserving theater or sightseeing tickets,
even what to pack — are covered as well.

Chapter 5

Getting to San Francisco

● ●

In This Chapter

▶ Using a travel agent

▶ Making travel arrangements on your own

▶ Traveling by air, car, or train

▶ Taking a look at escorted and package tours

● ●

*T*he Internet has made it possible for anyone to play travel agent. You want to compare flight schedules, ticket prices, and meal service? You want to take a virtual tour of a hotel? You want to purchase theater tickets online, instead of waiting to see whether they'll be available at the half-price ticket booth? Or would you rather let your local travel agent make the calls? If you do use a travel agent, make sure the agent has in-depth knowledge of the destination. Relatives of mine who shall remain nameless actually let their travel agent recommend the hotel on their last trip to San Francisco, which turned out to be a dump. The sad look on their faces made me want to hit them over the head with a book — a guidebook of course.

Using a Travel Agent

Word-of-mouth is the best way to find a good travel agent — use the information someone else has already gone through the trouble of finding out! Any travel agent can help you find the basics: airfare, hotel, and rental car. A good travel agent stops you from ruining your vacation by trying to save a few dollars. The best travel agents have actually been to the destination and can tell you how much time you need to budget for a certain destination, find you a reasonable flight that doesn't require you to leave at 3:30am and change planes in Dallas and Denver, get you a better hotel room for about the same price, arrange for a competitively priced rental car, and even give you tips on where to eat.

Take advantage of all your travel agent has to offer (and find out how much he or she really does have to offer about a destination), by starting out with your own research first. Read about San Francisco (you've already made a sound decision by buying this book) and choose some accommodations and attractions you are interested in. You can do more research by getting a more comprehensive travel guide like *Frommer's San Francisco.* If you have access to the Internet, check prices on the Web in advance to get an idea of the price ranges (see the section, "Getting the best airfare" later in this chapter for ideas). Then take your guidebook and Web information with you to the travel agent and ask them to make the arrangements for you. Travel agents have access to more resources than even the most complete Web travel site; therefore, they should be able to get you a better price than you could get by yourself. And they can issue your tickets and vouchers on the spot. If they can't get you into the hotel of your choice, they can recommend an alternative, and you can look for an objective review in your guidebook right there and then.

Travel agents work on commission. What's good about that is that *you* don't pay the commission; the airlines, accommodations, and tour companies do. What's bad about that is that unscrupulous travel agents may try to persuade you to book the vacations that bring in the most money for them in commissions. Recently, some airlines and resorts have begun to limit or eliminate travel agent commissions altogether. The immediate result has been that travel agents won't take the time or trouble to book certain services unless the customer specifically requests them. Some travel agents have started charging customers for their services. When that practice becomes more commonplace, the best agents should prove even harder to find.

The Independent Planner

Now let's talk about planning your own trip without the aid of a travel agent!

Getting the best airfare

Competition among the major U.S. airlines is unlike that of any other industry. A coach seat is virtually the same from one carrier to another, yet the difference in price may run as high as $1,000 for a product with the same intrinsic value.

Business travelers who need the flexibility to purchase their tickets at the last minute, change their itinerary at a moment's notice, or who want to get home before the weekend pay the premium rate, known as the full fare. Passengers who can book their ticket long in advance, who don't mind staying over Saturday night, or who are willing to travel on a Tuesday, Wednesday, or Thursday pay the least, usually a fraction of the full fare. On most flights, even the shortest hops, the full fare is close to $1,000 or more, but a 7-day or 14-day advance purchase ticket can be closer to $200 or $300. Obviously, it pays to plan ahead.

The airlines also periodically run fantastic sales where they lower the prices on their most popular routes. These fares have advance pur-chase requirements and date-of-travel restrictions, but you can't beat the price — usually you'll pay no more than $400 for a cross-country flight. Keep your eyes open for these sales as you are planning your vacation. The sales tend to take place during the off-seasons, when travel volume is low. Don't plan on seeing a sale around the peak summer vacation months — July and August — or around Thanksgiving or Christmas, when people have to fly regardless of the air fares.

Consolidators, also known as bucket shops, are a good place to check for the lowest fares. They can offer prices that are much better than the fares you can get yourself, and are often even lower than what your travel agent can get you. Scan the Sunday travel section — you can find their ads in the small boxes at the bottom of the page. Here are some of the most reliable consolidators:

- ✔ **Cheap Tickets** (☎ **800-377-1000;** Internet: www.cheaptickets. com), and 1-800-FLY-CHEAP (www.flycheap.com)
- ✔ **Travac Tours & Charters** (☎ **877-872-8221;** Internet: www.the travelsite. com)
- ✔ **Council Travel** (☎ **800-226-8624;** Internet: www.counciltravel. com). This one caters to young travelers, but their great prices are available to people of all ages.

Booking your ticket online

Surf the Internet to find the cheapest fare. Put your PC to work by letting it search through millions of pieces of data for the information you want, in the order you want. The number of virtual travel agents on the Internet has increased exponentially in recent years.

Too many travel booking sites exist out there to list here, but check out a few of the more respected (and more comprehensive) ones:

- ✔ **Travelocity:** www.travelocity.com
- ✔ **Microsoft Expedia:** www.expedia.com
- ✔ **Yahoo! Travel:** http://travel.yahoo.com

Each site has its own unique quirks, but all provide variations of the same service. All you do is enter the dates you want to fly and the cities you want to visit, and the computer looks for the lowest fares. Several other features have become standard to these sites: the ability to check flights at different times or dates in hopes of finding a cheaper fare; e-mail alerts when fares drop on a route you have specified; and a database of last-minute deals that advertise super-cheap vacation packages or airfares for those who can get away at a moment's notice.

You can get great last-minute deals directly from the airlines themselves through a free e-mail service called **E-savers.** Each week, the
airline sends you a list of discounted flights, usually leaving the upcoming Friday or Saturday, and returning the following Monday or Tuesday.
You check out the deals on all the major airlines at the same time by
logging on to **Smarter Living** (Internet: www.smarterliving.com), or
you can simply go to each individual airline's Web site. These Internet
sites offer schedules and information on late-breaking bargains, and
allow you to book tickets.

- ✔ **Air Canada:** www.aircanada.ca
- ✔ **Alaska Airlines:** www.alaskaair.com
- ✔ **America West:** www.americawest.com
- ✔ **American Airlines:** www.americanair.com
- ✔ **British Airways:** www.british-airways.com
- ✔ **Continental Airlines:** www.continental.com
- ✔ **Delta:** www.delta-air.com
- ✔ **National Airlines:** www.nationalairlines.com
- ✔ **Northwest Airlines:** www.nwa.com
- ✔ **Southwest Airlines:** www.iflyswa.com
- ✔ **TWA:** www.twa.com
- ✔ **United Airlines:** www.ual.com
- ✔ **US Airways:** www.usairways.com

You can fly into two airports in the Bay Area: **San Francisco
International** (SFO), which is 14 miles south of downtown, and
Oakland International Airport, which is across the Bay Bridge off
Interstate 880. SFO is closer, and more airlines fly into this major hub.
Oakland, on the other hand, is smaller and easier to get in and out of,
although you'll pay about 50 percent higher for cab fares and shuttle
fees. You can sometimes get a lower fare or a more convenient flight
flying into Oakland, so always compare fares and travel times for each
airport. Oakland also generally enjoys better weather than San
Francisco. Flights are frequently delayed due to foggy conditions at
SFO, a fact worth remembering as you mull over just how much reading material to bring with you on the plane.

Using other ways to get from there to here

Don't like to fly? The following provides some other alternatives to getting to San Francisco.

Getting on the highway

You can get to San Francisco by car along two major highways. **Interstate 5** runs through the center of the state. If you drive this route, you'll hit **Interstate 80,** which goes over the Bay Bridge into the city. It takes about 6 to 8 hours to reach San Francisco from Los Angeles along Interstate 5. The other major route you can take is **Highway 1,** which goes up from Los Angeles through San Francisco to Marin County, Napa/Sonoma, and other points north. Highway 1 is a more scenic coastal route that takes you closer to Monterey and Santa Cruz and is a much more beautiful route. But the trip up from Los Angeles takes approximately 8 to 10 hours.

Going by train

Amtrak (☎ 800-872-7245 or 800-USA-RAIL) doesn't stop in San Francisco proper, but does stop in Emeryville, a small town just south of Berkeley. Passengers then ride a regularly scheduled Amtrak bus from Emeryville to the Ferry Building or the CalTrain station in downtown San Francisco. (The Ferry Building is more convenient to the hotels recommended in this chapter.)

Traveling by train may seem romantic, but don't assume it's cheaper than flying. At this writing, the lowest round-trip fare from Los Angeles is $120, which is still more expensive than a 14-day advance purchase ticket from one of the airlines serving the L.A.–S.F. corridor. The trip by rail from New York (through Chicago) takes almost 4 days and costs anywhere from $320 to $582. But consider taking the train for the experience of chugging across the country, if you have the time, or if you're like my mother-in-law who flunked a workshop on getting over one's fear of flying. (She wouldn't take the graduation flight the last day of class.)

Evaluating Escorted Tours: Freedom or Confinement?

Do you like to let a bus driver worry about traffic while you sit in comfort and listen to a tour guide explain everything? Or do you prefer to rent a car and follow your nose, even if you don't catch all the highlights? Do you like to have events planned for each day, or would you rather improvise as you go along? The answers to these questions will determine whether you should choose the guided tour or travel à la carte.

Some people love escorted tours. The tour company takes care of all the details and tells you what to expect at each attraction. You know your costs up front, and there aren't many surprises. Escorted tours can take you to the maximum number of sights in the minimum amount of time with the least amount of hassle.

Other people need more freedom and spontaneity. They prefer to discover a destination by themselves and don't mind getting caught in a thunderstorm without an umbrella or finding that a recommended restaurant is no longer in business. That's just part of the adventure.

If you decide you want an escorted tour, think strongly about purchasing travel insurance, especially if the tour operator asks to you pay up front. But don't buy insurance from the tour operator! If they don't fulfill their obligation to provide you with the vacation you've paid for, there's no reason to think they'll fulfill their insurance obligations either. Get travel insurance through an independent agency (see "Buying Travel and Medical Insurance," Chapter 9).

When choosing an escorted tour, ask a few simple questions before you buy:

- ✔ **What is the cancellation policy?** Do you have to put a deposit down? Can the company cancel the trip if there aren't enough people? How late can you cancel if you're unable to go? When do you pay? Do you get a refund if you cancel? If the company cancels?

- ✔ **How jam-packed is the schedule?** Do they try to fit 25 hours into a 24-hour day, or will you have ample time to relax by the pool or shop? If getting up at 7am every day and not returning to your hotel until 6 or 7pm at night sounds like a grind, certain escorted tours may not be for you.

- ✔ **How big is the group?** The smaller the group, the less time you'll spend waiting for people to get on and off the bus. Tour operators may be evasive about this, because they may not know the exact size of the group until everybody has made their reservations. But they should be able to give you a rough estimate. Some tours have a minimum group size and may cancel the tour if they don't book enough people.

- ✔ **What exactly is included?** Don't assume anything. You may have to pay to get yourself to and from the airport. A box lunch may be included in an excursion, but drinks might cost extra. Beer might be included but not wine. How much flexibility do you have? Can you opt out of certain activities, or does the bus leave once a day, with no exceptions? Are all your meals planned in advance? Can you choose your entree at dinner, or does everybody get the same chicken cutlet?

Booking Package Tours: Wrap It Up, I'll Take It

Package tours are not the same as escorted tours. They're simply a way of buying your airfare and accommodations at the same time.

Package tours save money!

For popular destinations like San Francisco, package tours can be the smart way to go. In many cases, a package that includes airfare, hotel, and transportation to and from the airport will cost less than just the hotel alone if you booked it yourself. That's because packages are sold in bulk to tour operators, who resell them to the public.

Finding the best package for you

Some package tours offer a better class of hotels than others. Some offer the same hotels for lower prices. Some offer flights on scheduled airlines; others book charters. In some packages, your choice of accommodations and travel days may be limited. Some let you choose between escorted vacations and independent vacations; others will allow you to add on just a few excursions or escorted day trips (also at discounted prices) without booking an entirely escorted tour.

Each destination usually has one or two packagers that are better than the rest because they buy in even bigger bulk. The time you spend shopping around will be well rewarded.

The best place to start looking is the travel section of your local Sunday newspaper. Also check the ads in the back of national travel magazines like *Travel & Leisure, National Geographic Traveler,* and *Condé Nast Traveler.* **Liberty Travel** (☎ 888-271-1584 to find the store nearest you; Internet: www.libertytravel.com) is one of the biggest packagers in the Northeast, and usually boasts a full-page ad in Sunday papers. **American Express Vacations** (☎ 800-346-3607; Internet: http://travel.americanexpress.com/travel/) is another option.

Another good resource is the airlines themselves, which often package their flights together with accommodations. When you pick the airline, you can choose one that has frequent service to your hometown and the one on which you accumulate frequent-flyer miles. And although disreputable packagers are uncommon, they do exist; but by buying your package through the airline, you can be pretty sure that the company will still be in business when your departure date arrives. Among the airline packages, your options include: **American Airlines Vacations** (☎ 800-321-2121; Internet: www.aavacations.com); **Continental Airlines Vacations** (☎ 888-898-9255; Internet: www.coolvacations.com); **Delta Vacations** (☎ 800-872-7786; Internet: www.deltavacations.com); and **US Airways Vacations** (☎ 800-455-0123; Internet: www.usairwaysvacations.com). American in particular tends to have good packages to San Francisco, since it's one of the airline's hubs.

The biggest hotel chains also offer packages. If you already know where you want to stay, call the hotel itself and ask if it offers land/air packages.

Chapter 6

Deciding Where to Stay

· ·

In This Chapter

▶ Deciding which to stay in: hotels, motels, or B&Bs

▶ Getting the rundown on the city neighborhoods

▶ Picking out the best room for your family

▶ Securing accommodations that are right for you at the right price

· ·

*R*emember, in a city like San Francisco, accommodations take the biggest bite out of your travel budget. If you don't have lots of experience sleeping in hotels, you may not know what you require in the way of service or a room until you find yourself less than pleased with one or the other after your arrival. While you may find it difficult to anticipate your needs in advance, consider, among other variables, whether or not you really care if your room resembles something out of a *Condé Nast Traveler* magazine, overlooks the bay, has enough natural light and windows that open, is vulnerable to street noise, or has a bathtub large enough for you and a close friend. Will you feel despondent if the hotel can't supply a cup of herbal tea or a snack at 10pm? How long are you willing to wait for the valet to bring you your car? Make a list of questions to ask the reservations desk, and make sure, to the extent that you are able, that your chosen hotel is going to add to the pleasure of your stay.

In this chapter you can find descriptions of the various kinds of accommodations available, what the various city neighborhoods are like in San Francisco, descriptions of what you get in the different room rate price ranges, and a listing of accommodations, their range of room rates, and what neighborhoods they are located in. Take a look at the index at the end of the chapter to get a fast idea of the hotel names you want to initially check out. Go to Chapter 8 for a detailed description of each hotel.

Determining the Kind of Place That's Right for You

If you've started budgeting for your trip, you may have an idea how much you're willing to pay for a room. Hotels come in many shapes and sizes — you have hotels, motels, and bed-and-breakfast inns of all styles and price ranges. You have chain hotels and independent hotels, and hotels that serve business travelers rather than vacationers. So what is the difference between these various accommodations?

Staying in chain hotels or independent hotels

Hotels belonging to huge chains, such as Holiday Inn, Sheraton, Marriott, and Hyatt, tend to be monolithic structures that are impersonal and, to put it bluntly, boring. They resemble fast-food outlets — the burger you get at one McDonald's is going to be pretty much the same at every other McDonald's. But, there's a comfort in that. For travelers who like the assurance of a well-known brand name, chains are a fine choice. In San Francisco, business people and conventioneers are often the guests at these hotels. Chapter 8 describes a few of the most noteworthy chain hotels, but you can find many other reliable choices in the city. The Appendix at the back of this book contains a list of toll-free telephone numbers for the major chain hotels.

Independent hotels (also called boutique hotels) may be run by private companies that manage groups of properties, or may be family owned and operated. These accommodations are smaller in scope than other types of hotels and motels. They often target travelers who desire a more unique, perhaps quaint, atmosphere with a local flavor. Some appeal to older couples seeking quiet and cozy budget lodgings, while other independents seek to attract a hipper traveler with hip furnishings and wild color schemes. San Francisco is currently the leader of the boutique hotel scene, with a great assortment to choose from. People who want more intimate surroundings, where their fellow guests may be movie fans, literati, musicians, or shopaholics, would probably enjoy a stay in an independent hotel.

Make sure you know what you're getting into, though — boutique hotels are not for everyone. The needs of a business traveler are typically not met at an independent hotel, and you don't always find a staff person available to answer questions or provide services. Room service is also rarely available.

The difference between a hotel and a motel, for the hundredth time

Both chain and independent hotels offer services and amenities — at a price. Motels, on the other hand, are hardly eye-catching and basically consist of rooms with beds. You won't find much in the way of extras other than soap, towels, and maybe a coffeemaker. Motels are kind to your pocketbook, however. You usually find free parking, for example. Travelers who want a room solely to lay down their weary heads may find motels quite acceptable.

Do I really get breakfast in bed? — B&Bs

B&Bs, or bed-and-breakfast inns, can come in the form of an extra bedroom or two in a private home to a house renovated for the purpose of providing accommodations to visitors. Some B&Bs are lavishly decorated with antiques and extravagant fabrics where the management or owner pride themselves on serving gourmet breakfasts and afternoon sherry. Other owners put less effort into the business, keeping some food in the fridge and engaging in casual conversation with guests about the local sites, rather than providing any official tour guidance. Accommodations at a B&B usually come with a continental or full breakfast. You may have to share the bathroom with fellow guests. Rooms at B&Bs are usually more economical than hotel accommodations, but in general, the more you pay, the more comfort and service you get. For travelers who like the idea of being guests in a private home, B&Bs are a great way to go.

Some small hotels advertise as B&Bs. In general, these properties have a dozen or so bedrooms, include continental breakfast with the room, and often offer wine in the afternoon.

I recommend only a few stellar B&Bs in this book, but there are plenty more in the city. For more information on bed-and-breakfasts and lists of properties, the following resources can help.

- ✔ **Bed & Breakfast International** (☎ 800-872-4500 for reservations or 415-696-1690 for information; Internet: www.bbintl.com/).

- ✔ **California Association of Bed and Breakfast Inns**, 2715 Porter St., Soquel, CA 95073 (☎ 408-464-8159; Internet: www.InnAccess.com). Their directory ($4 by mail) advertises B&Bs throughout California.

- ✔ **Bed and Breakfast Inns of Napa Valley** for your trip to Napa Valley (☎ 707-944-4444; Internet: www.napavalley.com/ napavalley/lodging/bandb/bbnv/index.html).

Family Ties: Hotel Strategies for Traveling with Kids

Are you taking your kids along on your trip? Then you know you're either going to share a room with them, rent two rooms, or rent a suite.

Sharing a room with your family means reserving a double/double — one room with two double beds. Double/doubles are the least expensive option and work best for a family of four with kids too young to have a room of their own. If you come to terms with the fact that you won't be staying up late, won't be sleeping in, and will be revolving around the kids' needs, you can have a stress-free holiday.

If you think your kids are responsible enough to stay in their own room, renting two rooms that are either connected by an interior door or are adjacent to each other is a great choice. Although you end up spending twice the money, renting two rooms ensures that you can get some R & R from the rigors of parenting, if only for a few hours. This is a particularly smart choice for larger families.

Reserving a suite may seem like an extravagant way to give yourself a little space while keeping a close eye on the children, but it's a clever way to enjoy a high-quality hotel experience. Look at it this way: $250 buys you two rooms at a budget hotel on Union Square, but $275 sets the nuclear family up in a two-room suite complete with a stereo system, compact kitchenette, and continental breakfast in the relaxed environs of Nob Hill.

All about Location

No matter where you stay in San Francisco, you're no more than 20 minutes by cab from all the major sites, shopping areas, and restaurants. Most of the hotels are located in a few of the main, central neighborhoods of the city.

This book covers the best accommodations in the most convenient neighborhoods in terms of sightseeing, dining, shopping, and nightlife. Pick the neighborhood you want to stay in based on your interest and needs — for example, are you planning to be in shopping heaven? Are you an enthusiastic museum-goer? Do you hope to find peace and quiet? Or do you crave the noise and clamor of a big city? Whatever your lodging preferences, this chapter can help you find the perfect accommodation for you and your family. (Please see the index at the end of the chapter for hotel recommendations in each neighborhood.)

If you prefer to lodge outside of the central part of the city, in the Richmond District, for example, refer to *Frommer's San Francisco* for suggestions on accommodations in neighborhoods not covered here, or surf Citysearch on the Internet (www.bayareacitysearch.com), where you can search for hotels by area and price.

The following section gives you a general outline of
neighborhoods to tour and lodge in and the advant
tages of staying in each. See Chapter 10 for more de
these neighborhoods and the accommodations ava
see Chapter 16 for more on the major attractions in ......

Union Square

Union Square is about as convenient as it gets. You can find theatres,
lots of great restaurants, fancy department stores, boutiques, and the
greatest concentration of hotels in the city of varying price ranges,
all within a few blocks of Union Square. Chinatown and the Financial
District are within easy walking distance, as well. Transportation can
take you just about anywhere you want to go from Union Square.
Buses, Muni, BART, and the Powell Street cable cars all run through the
area. You can even hail a cab from the street corners in Union Square,
whereas in other parts of town you usually need to call for one. You're
right in the center of it all in Union Square.

The square is a welcome bit of green space that tops the very first
underground garage ever built in the U.S. Planted with grass, flowers,
and a sparse number of trees, this four-square-block park attracts its
fair share of pigeons, homeless folk, and salesclerks enjoying a slice-of-
pepperoni-to-go during their lunch break.

On the down side, be prepared for heavy traffic during the week. The
hotel rooms are generally quiet, but you can often hear emergency
vehicle sirens piercing through the walls, and some hotel lobbies draw
in the street noise more than others. Most of the hotels are in older
buildings, which lends a lot of charm to them; however, this means that
the rooms and baths often seem somewhat small. Parking in the area is
also expensive; expect to pay from $18 to $25 a day.

Although Union Square sits next to the Tenderloin, a low-income
neighborhood of immigrant families, druggies, and the down-and-out,
the area is basically safe, as are most neighborhoods in San Francisco
(see "Safety" in the Appendix, "Quick Concierge"). Because of the many
locals and tourists out and about, you do see plenty of street people
and vagrants looking for handouts, and lots of people sleeping in door-
ways. Pickpockets aren't a big problem in the area, but women should
avoid walking around unescorted at night. Certain sections of the
Tenderloin should be avoided any time of the day or night.

Watch out for the multitude of hucksters operating sleazy electronics/
camera, luggage, and gift shops on certain blocks of Mason, Powell, and
Market streets. Out-of-town customers have been known to discover
inflated charges on their credit cards after shopping at these places, so
buyer beware.

Union Square in a nutshell:

- ✔ Chinatown is around the corner.
- ✔ You have dining, shopping, and the nightlife right there.
- ✔ Public transportation is excellent.

But . . .

- ✔ You're right near the Tenderloin.
- ✔ The traffic is horrendous.
- ✔ The panhandling can get on your nerves.

Nob Hill

Just above Union Square is Nob Hill, which boasts beautiful, upper-crust residential apartments and the majestic Grace Cathedral. You can find the swanky Pacific Heights neighborhood (home to the Gettys and author Danielle Steele) just west of the Hill. A small selection of plush hotels cascades down the hill toward the Financial District, along with the California Street cable car line.

Nob Hill accommodations are pricey, with good reason. They offer a quiet, sophisticated atmosphere that contrasts with the hussle and bussle of areas such as Union Square. Here you see well-dressed business travelers and tourists going about their business, in contrast to the panhandlers and down-and-outers of other areas. Nob Hill is also quite safe, even at night. You endure a bit less traffic, and instead enjoy a more residential atmosphere. Although you may be walking up and down very steep grades (evaluate your physical fitness before you tackle these!), Nob Hill is really just a short stroll from Union Square. Muni buses and the California Street cable car, which are very reliable, provide any needed public transportation connections. And access to some of the city's finest bars and restaurants is often just an elevator ride away. Nob Hill streets also offer breath-taking views of downtown.

Nob Hill in a nutshell:

- ✔ The area is very safe.
- ✔ It's more peaceful and residential than Union Square.

But . . .

- ✔ You need to be in good physical condition to walk up and down the hills.
- ✔ It's very expensive.
- ✔ Fewer shops and restaurants exist close by the area.

SoMa

The George Moscone Convention Center, on Howard
Third and Fourth, pioneered the renaissance of a ma
downtown. South of Market Street, or SoMa for short, particularly
between Second and Fifth Streets, has exploded in the past 10 years
and is only becoming bigger and better.

Moscone Center is one part of the larger Yerba Buena Gardens. An
entertainment hub set among lovely landscaping and fountains, it was
recently fortified by the opening of Sony Corporation's Metreon (see
Chapter 16); Zeum, an extremely cool technology center for older kids;
an indoor ice-skating rink; and a bowling alley. San Francisco's Museum
of Modern Art on Third Street (see Chapter 16), the Cartoon Art
Museum on Mission and Fourth Streets (see Chapter 17), and the Ansel
Adams Museum of Photography on Howard (see Chapter 17) add a
dollop of culture to the festivities. Restaurants can't seem to debut fast
enough.

Still, vestiges of the old neighborhood remain, even as lodging and
attraction construction gussie up formerly empty lots and abandoned
buildings. Nearby Sixth Street is the purview of seedy residential hotels
and corner stores specializing in extremely cheap wine. Market Street
itself is pretty depressing west of Sixth Street, a combination of low-
rent tourist shops, strip clubs, and check-cashing counters, combined
with a few legitimate theaters (although that is positioned to change as
dot.com companies move into the area). The farther south you venture
toward I-80, the more industrial things get. And you're competing for
space in hotels with thousands of guys wearing plastic nametags and
rushing to Moscone for that panel discussion on skeletal malocclusions.

SoMa in a nutshell:

- ✔ It's the trendiest area of town (at the moment).
- ✔ You can find lots of worthy ways to spend time.
- ✔ You can find some great restaurants and clubs.

But . . .

- ✔ It still has a fringe element about it.
- ✔ The hotel choices are limited.
- ✔ You get lots of convention traffic.

The Embarcadero

Once surrounded by the cement jungle of the Embarcadero Freeway, which
was damaged by the 1989 Loma Prieta earthquake and subsequently
torn down, the Embarcadero is now a long stretch of road and walkway
along the shoreline that wraps around the northeast side of the city. It
glows in the light reflected off the waters of the bay. The views from

this area are some of the best in the city — the Bay Bridge soars above, Alcatraz seems a mere stone's throw away, and on sunny weekends sailboats blissfully glide around the bay. Office workers from the nearby Financial District picnic on the grass at Justin Herman Plaza at the foot of Market Street, and on Saturdays, the extravagant Ferry Plaza Farmers' Market sets up shop in a parking lot a few blocks from the Ferry Building (where the commuter ferries to Sausalito and Tiburon board).

This is a very safe area and is generally quiet in the evenings, except during rush hour, when it's a major thoroughfare for rush-hour traffic. The most popular activities at the Embarcadero consist of promenading slowly down Herb Caen Way, (a stretch of sidewalk near the Ferry Building named for the *San Francisco Chronicle's* legendary "three-dot" columnist for over 50 years — he separated his gossip and inside item paragraphs with three dots), jogging, biking, skateboarding, and any number of other outdoor activities. Be cautious of the joggers and skateboarders, who find the sidewalks enticing obstacle courses, especially on the weekends. You won't feel the pulse of the town as distinctly as you do at Union Square, but don't think there isn't a good time to be had. Some of the hottest kitchens around town are based here, and you can find music and nightlife in unexpected venues.

Locals trek to the Embarcadero Center, a collection of five multi-use buildings connected by bridges and walkways with excellent parking, to check out the upscale chain stores and movie theaters. Catch BART and Muni streetcars from the Embarcadero underground station to just about anywhere. A Muni extension from the Embarcadero to the CalTrain station rolls down past the magnificent new downtown ballpark, and charming old streetcars now breeze all the way down Market Street to Fisherman's Wharf and back. As for accommodations, the Hotels are quite expensive and few and far between. And the neighborhood's popularity means continued building and remodeling around the waterfront, which, unfortunately, adds noise and confusion along the boulevard.

The Embarcadero in a nutshell:

- ✔ It has beautiful bay views.
- ✔ It's a great location for strollers and joggers.
- ✔ It's convenient to shopping and dining.

But . . .

- ✔ Rush hour traffic is heavy and road construction adds to the congestion.
- ✔ Hotel choices are limited (and expensive).
- ✔ Walks to other neighborhoods are relatively long, though public transportation options are excellent.

North Beach/Fisherman's Wharf

The contrast of these two districts, North Beach and Fisherman's Wharf, is as distinct as night and day, though they are just a few blocks from each other. North Beach has all the charm of a quaint area — one I'd like to wake up in more than in any other neighborhood in the city. You can step into a cafe for a latté, choose a pastry from any number of Italian bakeries, watch elderly Chinese practicing t'ai chi in Washington Square Park — it's a heavenly way to pass the morning. Stores sell products you haven't already seen a thousand times, and the food is divine and diverse.

A distance of a few blocks away is Fisherman's Wharf. I suppose 13 million tourists can't all be wrong, but just between you and me, I don't get it. Once it was the center of the city's harbor and waterfront industries. Now, no authentic waterfront life takes place, but rather it's exclusively a tourist attraction. Locals, mostly, do not venture here. A group of hotels offer rooms on Northpoint Street, about two blocks off the Hyde Street cable car turnaround. Their selling point is location, but that's a question of taste. Walk west along the waterfront, through the most tourist-oriented section of town, and you get to Aquatic Park, which is delightful. But beware of what you pass along the way: the gauntlet of T-shirt emporiums, fast-food eateries, knickknack shops, and beggars, one of whom camouflages himself with branches and jumps out at unsuspecting pedestrians — I kid you not.

As you may guess, prices are slightly lower in both North Beach and Fisherman's Wharf, but so is the safety factor. Be careful, particularly around Fisherman's Wharf. Watch your wallet. Auto break-ins are also a problem. Depending on the weather, North Beach can be raucous during the evenings, and blocks of Broadway pulsate with bars and go-go clubs. Parking in either district is useless; you probably will only find parking in an expensive garage. You may want to consider leaving your car at home anyway — you don't need one in San Francisco!

Fisherman's Wharf/North Beach in a nutshell:

✔ Sightseers can navigate their way through either location on foot.

✔ You can find plenty of great meals in North Beach.

✔ You have access to convenient public transportation.

But . . .

✔ You're surrounded by tourists on Fisherman's Wharf.

✔ The parking is a nightmare.

✔ Hotel choices are limited.

The Marina/Cow Hollow

If you're driving to San Francisco or renting a car while you're here, this neighborhood has its advantages. People love the location here. It's much nicer than staying downtown. Most, but not all, of the accommodations here include free parking, which saves quite a bundle, depending on how long your visit is. Many of the great sites are within walking distance of the Marina/Cow Hollow, including the Exploratorium, the Palace of Fine Arts, the Presidio, and even the Golden Gate Bridge. Nearby Union Street, with its trendy shops, offers a decent assortment of good restaurants and a movie theater, and Chestnut Street is only a block away, with more of the same. This is a good neighborhood for families because the prices are more reasonable than in the other nice areas.

The downside of staying here is the traffic. Although a few charming B&Bs call the neighborhood home, most of the lodgings in the area are motels along Lombard Street, a four- to six-lane conduit to the Golden Gate Bridge and Van Ness Avenue and the busiest street in the city. Most visitors find the traffic horrendous in this area. You always have the possibility of staying somewhere just off this street, but you'll have a hard time finding anything. Also, as soon as you leave Lombard, you're once again stuck with paying parking fees.

The Marina/Cow Hollow in a nutshell:

- ✔ Near Chestnut and Union Street shopping.
- ✔ Hotel/motel parking is usually free.
- ✔ Within walking distance of the Marina and the Golden Gate Bridge.

But . . .

- ✔ Accommodation choices limited to motels and B&Bs.
- ✔ Traffic is heavy on Lombard Street.
- ✔ Immediate surroundings are less scenic.

What It's Going to Cost You

Every hotel, motel, and B&B that we recommend in this book we mark with one of four $ signs. Here's a quick breakdown of the price categories. All rates are for a standard double room, excluding taxes.

- ✔ **$ ($75–$125)** Accommodations in this category are often in older buildings that may show their age. Room service, valet parking, and porters do not come with the package; but the rooms are carefully tended, and the properties themselves exhibit some charm. The least expensive rooms may not have their own bathrooms. If sharing a shower isn't your idea of a good time no matter how much money you save, double-check when you make your reservation to make sure your room has a private bathroom.

The rooms I recommend in this price category tend to be on the "cozy" side and are typically furnished with inexpensive bedspreads, towels, and curtains. You won't find hair dryers, little toiletries, or robes in the bathroom. Air-conditioning is also considered a luxury, although you should rarely need it in mild San Francisco. While a concierge won't be at the ready to cater to your every whim, most desk clerks are delighted to help you arrange tours, rental cars, tickets for shows, and dinner reservations. Many of the budget hotels recommended in this book offer a free continental breakfast, making them especially good deals.

✔ **$$ ($125–$175)** In this price category, amenities and overall quality begin to improve. I recommend some wonderful hotels in this range, charming places with stylish (but still small) rooms, handsome lobbies, and good to great service. Antique armoires and marble-tiled bathrooms are standard-issue in a few picks, but in general, these properties are for leisure travelers with minimal demands beyond comfort and an appealing decor. A separate concierge desk is not always available, but the front desk staff is usually willing to make reservations and book tours. Parking is sometimes valet, but more often it's self-parking at lots up to three blocks away. Room service is usually nonexistent. Make sure to inquire about extras such as bathrobes and hair dryers, if these things are important to you. Often the more expensive suites are well-equipped, but the low-end rooms won't have that all-important stuff unless you ask for it.

✔ **$$$ ($175–$250)** At this price, expect attentive service — including valet parking and porters — and larger rooms with finer fabrics and decor. Many properties in this range also have on-site Stairmasters, and at least one has a pool. At the Embarcadero and on Nob Hill, you pay a premium for the location. Although at the low end of this scale you may not find hand-milled soaps in the bathroom, at the high end, you will feel pretty pampered.

When you're willing to pay this kind of money for a hotel, you probably have certain expectations. Make these expectations known when you make your reservation. Don't wait until check-in to ask if you can receive faxes or if valet parking actually means a bellhop is going to fetch your car for you at 6am. Research ahead of time what you want the hotel to deliver and ask questions when you make your reservations.

✔ **$$$$ ($250+)** Your big bucks buy views, personal service, and tasteful decor. Be prepared to be royally pampered by the well-trained staff. Large rooms feature hair dryers and thick terry robes in the mirrored bathroom, an iron in the closet, art work on the walls, and in some cases, umbrellas and flowers. Honor bars and baskets of over-priced goodies are also standard. For this much money, it would be a shame if you didn't spend some quality time in the hotel, fingering the drapes and calling down to the concierge desk for a weather report. Again, room rates are tied to location, with Nob Hill and the Embarcadero charging whatever the market will bear.

Hotel index by location

Union Square

Andrews Hotel ($)

Campton Place ($$$$)

Chancellor Hotel ($$)

The Clift Hotel ($$$$)

Commodore Hotel ($)

Golden Gate Hotel ($)

Handlery Union Square
Hotel ($$)

Hotel Beresford ($$)

Hotel Bijou ($)

Hotel Monaco ($$$)

Hotel Rex ($$$)

Hotel Triton ($$$)

Inn at Union Square
($$$)

The Juliana Hotel ($$$)

Kensington Park Hotel
($$$)

King George Hotel ($$)

The Maxwell ($$$)

Petite Auberge ($$)

Sir Francis Drake Hotel
($$$)

The Warwick Regis ($$)

Westin St. Francis
($$$$)

White Swan Inn ($$$)

Nob Hill

Huntington Hotel ($$$$)

Nob Hill Lambourne
($$$)

Ritz-Carlton ($$$$)

SoMa

The Argent ($$$$)

Hotel Milano ($$$)

W ($$$$)

The Embarcadero

Embarcadero Hyatt
Regency ($$$$)

Harbor Court Hotel
($$$$)

Hotel Griffon ($$$)

North Beach/
Fisherman's Wharf

Hotel Bohème ($$)

San Remo Hotel ($)

Tuscan Inn ($$)

Washington Square Inn
($$)

The Marina/
Cow Hollow

Edward II Inn ($)

Hotel Del Sol ($$)

The Marina Inn ($)

The Marina Motel ($)

Union Street Inn ($$$)

Chapter 7

Your Guide to a Room with a View

*T*his chapter covers a few strategies for obtaining a better room for your money. Frankly, you can get all the service and style you want if price is no object. But when it is, as is usually the case, a little advice for chatting up the reservations desk is always handy. Charm is useful; being completely clear about your expectations is just as important.

Getting the Best Room Rate

Make sure you cover all the bases. Reserving a room through the hotel's 800-number may result in a lower rate than if you called the hotel directly. On the other hand, the central reservations number may not know about discount rates at specific locations. For example, local franchises may offer a special group rate for a wedding or family reunion, but they may neglect to tell the central booking line. Your best bet is to call both the local number and the 800-number and see which one gives you a better deal.

 And, don't forget about any hidden fees and extra costs. It's best to know things up front instead of getting stuck later. The following sections discuss expenses to look out for.

Uncovering rack rates

The rack rate is the maximum rate that a hotel charges for a room. If you walked in off the street and asked for a room, the rack rate is the amount you would be charged. The hotel sometimes posts the rate on the back of your door, along with the fire/emergency exit diagrams.

Hotels will be happy to charge you the rack rate, but you don't have to pay it! The best way to avoid paying the rack rate is surprisingly simple: Just ask for a cheaper or discounted rate. You may be pleasantly surprised.

A travel agent may be able to negotiate a better price with certain hotels than you can yourself. (This is because often the hotel gives the agent a discount in exchange for steering his or her business toward that hotel.) In all but the smallest accommodations, the rate you pay for a room depends on many factors — chief among them being how you make your reservation.

Dealing with high-taxed items

A hotel room that costs $99 a night actually will end up closer to $114 because of the 14 percent hotel tax tacked onto the bill. It's steep, but it's unavoidable. Room service charges can also escalate your final room tab. Local phone calls, minibars in your room, enticing baskets of goodies on an end table — none of these are gratis. If you like to snack in bed, buy your favorite goodies at a nearby market or convenience store and bring them up to your room.

Also be aware that some hotels tack on a fee for merely dialing out on the phone in your room. This starts at 75¢ and increases depending on what the market will bear. This is, of course, in addition to the charges for making a long-distance phone call from your hotel room. For dinner reservations or event tickets, let your hotel concierge do the talking.

Selecting the right season

Officially, the low season in San Francisco is from November to March, but one highly experienced downtown concierge joked that the low season was the weekends. While it's true that more tourists visit between spring and early fall, your actual concerns should center around business travelers. The San Francisco Convention and Visitors Bureau keeps a calendar of major conventions, and I'd check with them before finalizing your plans (see Chapter 10). Hotels and restaurants around **Union Square** and **SoMa** are always crowded when **Moscone Center** is booked.

Generally, you'll get your best rate on a room in the winter, on weekends when the suits go home, and around holidays when you're actually supposed to be at Cousin Seymour's and not gallivanting around here. Don't let that discourage you from arriving whenever it's convenient for you, however. Just make your reservations far in advance (see also Chapter 2).

As room rates change with the season, occupancy rates rise and fall. A hotel is less likely to extend discount rates if it is close to full, and it may be willing to negotiate if it's close to empty. Resorts usually offer discounted rates for midweek stays since they're usually most crowded on weekends. The reverse is true for business hotels in downtown locations. Rates listed in this book may be different than the actual rate you are quoted when you make your reservation because room prices are subject to change without notice. Don't forget to ask about discounts for membership in AAA, AARP, frequent-flyer programs, and any other corporate rewards programs when you call up to make your reservation. You never know when you can save a few dollars off your hotel room bill.

Getting the Room You Deserve

After you've made your reservation, asking one or two more pointed questions can go a long way toward making sure you have the best room in the house.

- ✔ **Is there a corner on the market?** Ask for a corner room. They're usually larger, quieter, closer to the elevator, and have more windows and light than standard rooms, and don't always cost any more.

- ✔ **What's that noise?** Inquire about the location of the restaurants, bars, and discos in the hotel — these could all be a source of irritating noise. Also, ask if the hotel is renovating; if it is, request a room away from the jackhammers.

- ✔ **Does this room come in another color?** If you aren't happy with your room when you arrive, talk to the front desk. If they have another room, they should be happy to accommodate you, within reason.

- ✔ **Mind if I smoke?** You can smoke outside in San Francisco to your heart's content, but be aware that the city has stringent anti-smoking laws inside public buildings, restaurants, and even bars. A sizable number of hotels, especially the smaller ones, are completely smoke-free. Other hotels only have smoking rooms on designated floors. Common courtesy in the Golden Gate city is to ask before getting ready to light a cigarette; you'd be surprised at the number of people who are allergic to smoke. If a smoking (or no-smoking) room is important to you, let the reservations desk know when you call.

Surfing the Web for Hotel Deals

The Web can be a good resource for hotel deals, but in my humble opinion, you usually get the best rate and the most accurate information by calling the hotel directly. No matter what assurances you receive from online agencies, hotel agency Web sites cannot guarantee specific rooms (unless, perhaps, you asked for the bridal or presidential suite), and they really know very little about the hotel they are selling. As shocking as this may be, not everything you read on the Web is up-to-date or accurate. Another problem recently brought to my attention is the difficulty in getting a refund from some of these reservation services if you have to cancel your stay. It's the service, not the hotel, that has your money until they settle with the hotel sometime after you've checked out. Finally, there may be a difference between the amount of dough you pay the agency for your room and the amount the agency pays the hotel (that's the profit motive for you). If you don't like the place, again, you're stuck negotiating for a refund from the online room purveyor.

Having said all that, you can sometimes get a good deal by booking through a lodging agency Web site. While the major travel Web sites (such as Travelocity, Expedia, Yahoo! Travel, and Cheap Tickets) offer hotel booking, it's often best to use a site devoted primarily to lodging, because you may find properties that aren't listed with more general online travel agencies. Some lodging sites specialize in a particular type of accommodation, such as bed-and-breakfasts, which you won't find on the more mainstream booking services. Others, such as TravelWeb (see the following list), offer weekend deals on major chain properties, which cater to business travelers and have more empty rooms on weekends.

Check out these hotel lodging sites on the Web:

- ✔ The name **All Hotels on the Web** (www.all-hotels.com) is something of a misnomer, but the site *does* have tens of thousands of listings throughout the world. Bear in mind each hotel has paid a small fee (of $25 and up) to be listed, so it's less an objective list and more like a book of online brochures.

- ✔ **hoteldiscount!com** (www.180096hotel.com) lists bargain room rates at hotels in more than 50 U.S. and international cities. The cool thing is that hoteldiscount!com pre-books blocks of rooms in dvance, so sometimes it has rooms — at discount rates — at hotels that are "sold out." Select a city, input your dates, and you get a list of best prices for a selection of hotels. This site is notable for delivering deep discounts in cities where hotel rooms are expensive. The toll-free number is printed all over this site (☎ 800-96-HOTEL); call it if you want more options than are listed online.

- ✔ **InnSite** (www.innsite.com) has B&B listings in all 50 U.S. states and more than 50 countries around the globe. You can find an inn at your destination, see pictures of the rooms, and check prices and availability. This extensive directory of bed-and-breakfasts only includes listings if the proprietor submitted one (it's free to get an inn listed). The descriptions are written by the innkeepers; and many listings link to the inn's own Web sites. Try also the Bed and Breakfast Channel (www.bedandbreakfast.com).

- ✔ **Places to Stay** (www.placestostay.com) lists one-of-a-kind places in the U.S. and abroad that you might not find in other directories, with a focus on resort accommodations. Again, listing is selective — this isn't a comprehensive directory, but it can give you a sense of what's available at different destinations.

✔ **TravelWeb** (www.travelweb.com) lists more than 26,000 hotels in 170 countries, focusing on major chains, and you can book almost 90 percent of these online. TravelWeb's Click-It Weekends, updated each Monday, offers weekend deals at many leading hotel chains.

Traveling without Reservations

I am constantly amazed at how many vacationers come to San Francisco without hotel reservations, believing that a fabulous $30 a night room is awaiting them in a fancy hotel. They usually end up sleeping in the no-tell motel in a dicey neighborhood because that's all that was available. Or they spend the better part of a day looking for accommodations, wasting valuable vacation time searching for a bargain, or just a room, when there are none to be had. Don't be one of them. Plan your vacation lodgings ahead of time.

But if you do disregard my advice to make advance reservations, you can still try the following resources if you get stuck with no room:

✔ Call a free reservation service such as **SF Reservations** (☎ **888-782-9673** or 415-974-4499 outside of North America) or **California Reservations** (☎ **415-252-1107**).

✔ Make your way to a full-service boutique hotel and hope the desk clerk takes pity on you. Most of the boutique properties in town are part of small, independent chains, and a good-hearted staff person may be willing to make some calls to sister hotels to help you secure a room.

✔ Find a friendly concierge you can leave your luggage with so you can look for a room in the neighborhood unencumbered. If the town appears to be booked solid (ask the desk clerk's opinion), don't be picky or cheap if you find a room you don't love or that's over your budget. You can always move the next day if something better opens up.

Chapter 8

Your Home Away from Home

. . . .

In This Chapter

▶ Finding the perfect San Francisco hotel

▶ Finding a room when there's no room anywhere else

. . . .

So, you're ready to make San Francisco your home, for a brief period of time at least. You probably have an idea of how much money you want to spend (if not, check out Chapter 3), and you may have an idea what neighborhood suits your fancy (see Chapter 6 for neighborhood descriptions). Other features and amenities may be important to you, too. Take a look at the following reviews to discover which hotel is the one for you.

The hotel selections in this chapter are the best accommodations in San Francisco in my opinion — based on character, comfort, location, and price. Each one has a distinct style I believe you'll find memorable and pleasing. And none of them are below par. For those obsessed with your frequent-flyer miles, you won't find listings of most of the big, impersonal chain hotels. And I've left out most hotels on less desirable blocks, as well as places that aren't where the action is. (For a more complete rundown of places to stay, check *Frommer's San Francisco*, published by IDG Books Worldwide, Inc.)

The rack rates I've given do not include the 14 percent hotel tax. Those outrageous garage prices are per day. And parking is self-park except where otherwise noted.

Hotel Highlights: From Uptown to Downtown and All Points in Between

Andrews Hotel

$ Union Square

The services and location make this hotel a deal for couples on a budget, although the rooms and baths are small in this 48-room, 1905 Victorian. You get continental breakfast and evening wine gratis, and the recently updated décor looks very nice. Amiable receptionists serve double duty as concierge staff. You won't have movie channels, AC, or many other

San Francisco Accommodations

The Andrews Hotel **23**
The Argent Hotel **35**
Campton Place **34**
Canterbury Best Western **14**
The Cartwright Hotel **17**
Chancellor Hotel **19**
The Clift Hotel **29**
Commodore Hotel **24**
Edward II Inn **2**
Embarcadero Hyatt Regency **40**
Galleria Park Hotel **37**
Golden Gate Hotel **15**
Handlery Union Square Hotel **31**
Harbor Court Hotel **42**
Hotel Beresford **22**
Hotel Bijou **32**
Hotel Bohème **9**
Hotel Del Sol **4**
Hotel Griffon **41**
Hotel Milano **33**
Hotel Monaco **28**
Hotel Rex **16**
Hotel Triton **39**
The Huntington Hotel **12**
Inn at Union Square **20**
The Juliana Hotel **38**
Kensington Park Hotel **21**
King George Hotel **30**
The Marina Inn **5**
The Marina Motel **1**
The Maxwell **26**
Nob Hill Lambourne **11**
Petite Auberge **13**
Ritz-Carlton **10**
San Remo Hotel **7**
Sir Francis Drake Hotel **18**
Tuscan Inn **6**
Union Street Inn **3**
W **36**
Warwick Regis **25**
Washington Square Inn **8**
Westin St. Francis **27**
White Swan Inn **13**

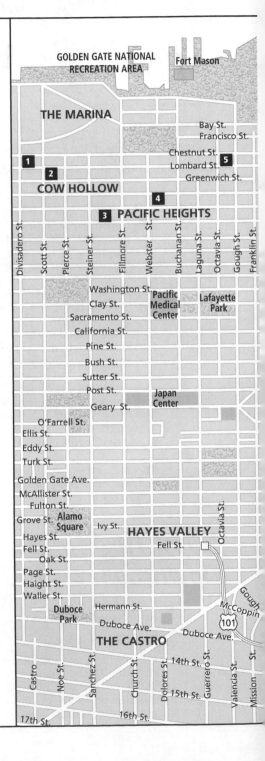

Municipal Pier
Pier 45
Pier 43 1/2
Pier 43
Pier 41
Pier 39
Pier 35
Aquatic Park
Ghiradelli Square
FISHERMAN'S WHARF
Jefferson St.
Beach St.
North Point St.
Bay St.
Pier 33
Pier 31
Pier 27
NORTH BEACH
Francisco St.
Chestnut St.
Lombard St.
Greenwich St.
Filbert St.
Union St.
Green St.
Vallejo St.
Broadway
Tunnel
Pacific Ave.
Jackson St.
Columbus Ave.
Coit Tower
CHINATOWN
NOB HILL

San Francisco Bay

Pier 23
Pier 19
Pier 17
Pier 15
Pier 9
Pier 7
Pier 5
Pier 3
Pier 1
Embarcadero
Justin Herman Plaza
Ferry Building (World Trade Center)

Van Ness Ave.
Polk St.
Larkin St.
Hyde St.
Leavenworth St.
Jones St.
Taylor St.
Mason St.
Powell St.
Stockton St.
Grant Ave.
Kearny St.
Montgomery St.
Sansome St.
Battery St.
Front St.
Davis St.
Drumm St.
Steuart St.

Rincon Center
San Francisco-Oakland Bay Bridge
Spear St.
Beale St.
Main St.
Fremont St.

Geary St.
O'Farrell St.
Eddy St.
Union Square
San Francisco Museum of Modern Art
1st St.
2nd St.

CIVIC CENTER
Market St.
Yerba Buena Gardens
Moscone Convention Center
SOMA
South Park
Delancey St.

Mission St.
Howard St.
Folsom St.
Harrison St.
4th St.
5th St.
Bryant St.
Brannan St.
3rd St.

8th St.
9th St.
10th St.
11th St.
12th St.
Townsend St.
King St.
Berry St.
Channel St.
4th St.
3rd St.
China Basin
Illinois St.

S. Van Ness Ave.
Folsom
Harrison
Alabama
15th St.
Potrero Ave.
Division St.
Alameda St.
7th St.
6th St.
280

101
6 7 8 9 10 11 12 13 14 15 16 17 18 19 20 21 22 23 24 25 26 27 28 29 30 31 32 33 34 35 36 37 38 39 40 41 42

0   1/4 mi
0   .25 km
N
80

amenities, but you can open the windows. Avoid the dark, tiny rooms ending in '08.

624 Post St., between Taylor and Jones Streets (two blocks west of Union Square). ☎ ***800-926-3739*** *or 415-563-6877. Fax: 415-928-6919. Internet:* www.andrewshotel. com. *Parking: $15 with in/out privileges. Rack rates: $92–$142 double. Low season packages available. Ask about AARP and extended-stay discounts. AE, DC, MC, V.*

The Argent Hotel

$$$$ SoMa

This is a big, run-of-the-mill hotel with nice-sized rooms and all the extras you'd better receive for the price — irons, hair dryers, quality bath products, and so on. What really earns it a place in this chapter, besides the location, are the nearly floor-to-ceiling windows with great views in rooms beyond the 14th floor. A fitness center, sauna, and pretty garden also help raise The Argent slightly beyond the ordinary.

50 Third St., near Market St. ☎ ***877-222-6699*** *or 415-974-6400. Fax: 415-543-8268. Internet:* www.destinationtravel.com. *Parking: $26 (valet). Rack Rates: $265–$305 double. Ask about weekend specials and holiday promotions. AE, DC, DISC, JCB, MC, V.*

Campton Place

$$$$ Union Square

The harpsichord music piped into Campton Place's classically decorated lobby tells you right away that this is one genteel hotel. Intimate, clubby, reserved — you'll want to use your company manners even as the valet unpacks your bags, fluffs up the bathrobes, and shows off the many luxury amenities. You can even bring your dog (if he's well-behaved). The restaurant has been the recipient of many awards and kudos — you might want to breakfast here even if you stay elsewhere.

340 Stockton St., at Post St. ☎ ***800-235-4300*** *or 415-781-5555. Fax: 415-955-5536. Internet:* www.camptonplace.com. *Parking: $26 (valet). Rack rates: $285–$375 double. AE, DC, DISC, JCB, MC, V.*

Chancellor Hotel

$$ Union Square

This 137-room hotel has been owned and managed by the same family since 1917 and offers a level of intimacy and value you just won't find in many other comparable inns. It's also right on the Powell Street cable car line, a handbag's throw from Saks Fifth Avenue. The little bathrooms are well-stocked; the petite bedrooms are brightly decorated and comfortably furnished. For views, request front rooms ending in 00 to 05. Amenities include ceiling fans (instead of A/C), homemade cookies at the front desk, and room service during restaurant hours. Smoking is not allowed.

433 Powell St., between Post and Sutter Streets. ☎ 800-428-4748 or 415-362-2004. Fax: 415-362-1403. Internet: www.chancellorhotel.com. *Parking: $19 (self); $24 (valet). Rack rates: $150 double. Inquire about special packages and AAA, AARP discounts. AE, DC, DISC, MC, V.*

The Clift Hotel

$$$$ Union Square

Has nouveau got you down? Does post-modernism leave you cold? No problem. Have a scotch in the Redwood Room, which hasn't changed much in 87 years, or a nice cup of tea in the French Room. Yes, the hallways of this venerated establishment are dowdy, but the air-conditioned rooms are large and chock-a-block with amenities, and the service is what service is meant to be. But be advised: A complete renovation, designed to drag the hotel into the twenty-first century, is on the way.

495 Geary St., at Taylor St. ☎ 800-652-5438 or 415-775-4700. Fax: 415-931-7417. Internet: www.clifthotel.com. *Parking: $25 (valet) with in/out privileges. Rack rates: $255–$305 double. AE, CB, DC, MC, V. Dogs welcome.*

Commodore Hotel

$ Union Square

Bright but small rooms and bathrooms give a boost to an older building that shows some signs of wear. And this section of Sutter Street is just close enough to the Tenderloin to put me on alert for drug dealers and prostitutes. Still, the location doesn't discourage European tourists, who appreciate the good value. It's just three flat blocks from Union Square, so food and entertainment are near at hand. There's the Titanic cafe on one side of the building and the severely trendy Red Room bar on the other. No A/C.

825 Sutter St., near Jones St. ☎ 800-338-6848 or 415-923-6800. Fax: 415-923-6804. Internet: www.sftrips.com. *Parking: $16. Rack rates: $99–$149. Inquire about seasonal packages and AAA, AARP discounts. AE, CB, DC, DISC, MC, V.*

Edward II Inn

$ The Marina/Cow Hollow

This place is a step up from other budget lodgings in the area. B&B aficionados can appreciate the intimate feel of this 1914 English-style inn, but due to its busy corner location, be prepared for noise. The small rooms are done in a pretty, British decor. A second building across the street, which is part of the hotel, has suites with whirlpool baths. Rates include continental breakfast. No A/C, no smoking. The friendly desk clerk can handle all your tour arrangements.

3155 Scott St., at Lombard St. ☎ 800-473-2846 or 415-922-3000. Fax: 415-931-5784. Internet: www.citysearch.com/sfo/edwardiiinn. *Parking: $10 at limited offsite spaces. Rack rates: $79–$225 double. AE, MC, V.*

Accommodations Near Union Square, SoMa & Nob Hill

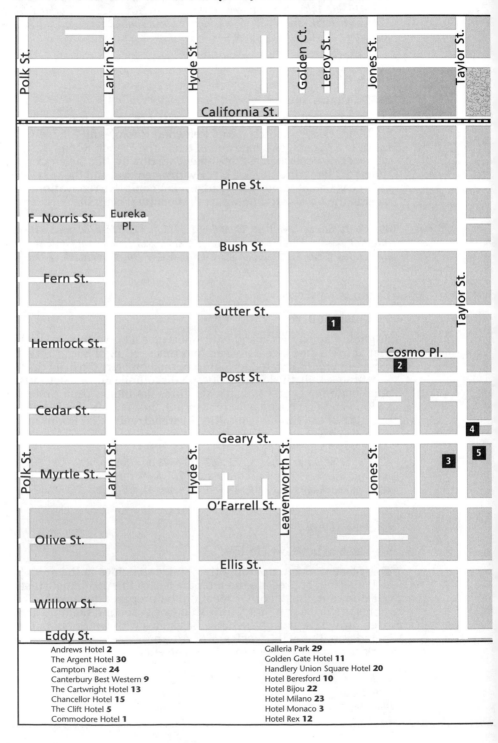

Polk St.
Larkin St.
Hyde St.
Golden Ct.
Leroy St.
Jones St.
Taylor St.

California St.

Pine St.

F. Norris St.   Eureka Pl.

Bush St.

Fern St.

Taylor St.

Sutter St.

1

Hemlock St.

Cosmo Pl.

2

Post St.

Cedar St.

Geary St.

4

Polk St.
Larkin St.
Hyde St.
Leavenworth St.
Jones St.

Myrtle St.

5

3

O'Farrell St.

Olive St.

Ellis St.

Willow St.

Eddy St.

Andrews Hotel **2**
The Argent Hotel **30**
Campton Place **24**
Canterbury Best Western **9**
The Cartwright Hotel **13**
Chancellor Hotel **15**
The Clift Hotel **5**
Commodore Hotel **1**

Galleria Park **29**
Golden Gate Hotel **11**
Handlery Union Square Hotel **20**
Hotel Beresford **10**
Hotel Bijou **22**
Hotel Milano **23**
Hotel Monaco **3**
Hotel Rex **12**

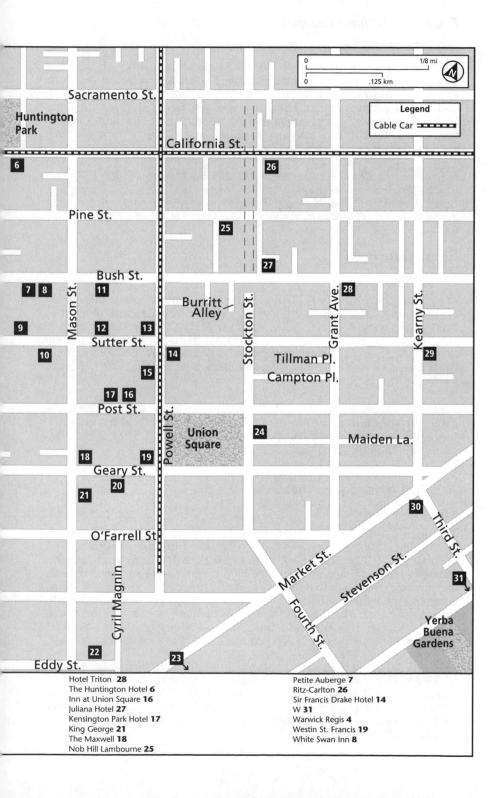

Hotel Triton **28**
The Huntington Hotel **6**
Inn at Union Square **16**
Juliana Hotel **27**
Kensington Park Hotel **17**
King George **21**
The Maxwell **18**
Nob Hill Lambourne **25**

Petite Auberge **7**
Ritz-Carlton **26**
Sir Francis Drake Hotel **14**
W **31**
Warwick Regis **4**
Westin St. Francis **19**
White Swan Inn **8**

Embarcadero Hyatt Regency

$$$$ The Embarcadero

This huge, corporate hotel at the foot of Market Street gets an honorable mention because of its tempting location. Rooms are well-equipped and spacious, and some have beautiful views. The hotel has two restaurants and an onsite fitness center. The inside glass elevators are irresistible for kids, who will surely get lost wandering the hallways in search of their room. And the hotel's revolving Equinox Bar and Restaurant are irresistible to out-of-towners, who line up at the lifts for a ride up.

5 Embarcadero Center, at Market St. ☎ *800-233-1234 or 415-788-1234. Fax: 415-398-2567. Internet:* www.sanfrancisco.regency.hyatt.com. *Parking: $30 (valet). Rack rates: $179–$320 double. Weekend packages and corporate discounts available. AE, CB, DC, DISC, MC, V; personal checks from U.S. banks. Dogs welcome.*

Golden Gate Hotel

$ Union Square

Are you flexible (or broke)? Then you can share a bathroom at this cheerful, charming, 23-room Edwardian B&B. If you're traveling with older children, you may even want to take two of the pretty, small rooms, assuring yourself some privacy. Complimentary continental breakfast and afternoon tea are served, although the rooms contain few other amenities. Great locale for cable car lovers and walkers. Because there's a big cat in the lobby, this is not the right spot if you are allergic to cats. No A/C.

775 Bush St., between Powell and Mason Streets (two blocks from the Chinatown gate). ☎ *800-835-1118 or 415-392-3702. Fax: 415-392-6202. Internet:* www.goldengatehotel.com. *Parking: A relative bargain at $12. Rates: $72 (shared bath) or $109 (private bath) double. DC, MC, V.*

Handlery Union Square Hotel

$$$ Union Square

The heated outdoor pool will attract the kids; the Nintendo will have them calling this place home. It's also a favorite with tour packagers. The normal doubles are ordinary with smallish bathrooms that may be renovated by the time you read this. If you enjoy having a dressing area, fluffy robes, newspaper delivery, and fresher décor, spend the extra dough on the larger Club Rooms located in an adjacent building (despite the longer walk to the lobby). The hotel's two-bedroom suites are also a good value. Other amenities include room service (from 7 to 10am and 5 to 10pm) and refrigerators (on request), and there's a concierge.

351 Geary St., between Powell and Mason Streets (½ block from Union Square). ☎ *800-843-4343 or 415-781-7800. Fax: 415-781-0269. Internet:* www.handlerysf@handlery.com. *Parking: $21 (valet). Rack rates: $159–$195 double. Ask about AAA discount; corporate, federal government, and senior citizen rates; and Internet specials. Romance, leisure, Christmas, and other special packages available. AE, CB, DC, JCB, MC, V.*

Harbor Court Hotel

$$$$ The Embarcadero

Once a shady neighborhood, now you're lucky to score a room, especially in this classy, romantic hotel. In addition to express check-in and concierge services, the hotel has a happenin' restaurant/bar with live entertainment. Guests have free access to the state-of-the-art Embarcadero YMCA pool and health club, which is right next door. Rooms include half-canopy beds and are spacious. Some have views of the bay, and all rooms include high-end amenities. This is quite a place!

165 Steuart St., between Mission and Howard Streets. ☎ 800-346-0555 or 415-882-1300. Fax: 415-882-1313. Internet: www.harborcourthotel.com. *Parking: $24 (valet). Rack rates: $205–$250 double. Packages sometimes available; ask about weekend rates. AE, CB, DC, DISC, MC, V.*

Hotel Beresford

$$ Union Square

For a great location and reasonable prices, the winner is . . . Hotel Beresford! The staff is friendly and a continental breakfast is included. You may have to call Martha Stewart about the wallpaper, but you probably won't complain with rates this low and rooms large enough to accommodate a family of four.

635 Sutter St., near Mason St. (about two blocks west of Union Square). ☎ 800-533-6533 or 415-673-9900. Fax: 415-474-0449. Internet: www.beresford.com. *Parking: $16. Rack rates: $115–$135 double. AARP discount. AE, DC, MC, V. Dogs welcome.*

Hotel Bijou

$ Union Square

This hotel shares the block with a sleazy strip club; so if you have a delicate nature, you won't be happy. But film buffs will get a kick out of this cinema-themed inn. In the evening, it shows San Francisco-based videos in a 10-seat screening room off the lobby. Freshly decorated rooms and baths (some with shower only) are tight and amenities few, but the staff is professional and service-oriented. A continental breakfast is included in the rates.

111 Mason St., at Eddy St. (around the corner from Hallidie Plaza). ☎ 800-771-1022 or 415-771-1200. Fax: 415-346-3196. Internet: www.sftrips.com. *Parking: Shockingly reasonable at $18 (valet). Rack rates: $109–$159 double. Inquire about packages. AE, DC, MC, V.*

Hotel Bohème

$$ North Beach/Fisherman's Wharf

Set in the heart of North Beach, this charming, intimate hotel has 15 small but beautiful rooms with iron beds and vivid wall colors. The in-room amenities are generous and even include hair dryers, while the bathrooms are equipped with showers only. The staff do not help with carrying your luggage, and the stairs are narrow and cumbersome, so pack lightly. However, an accommodating staff member will assist with tours, rental cars, and restaurant reservations. No A/C.

444 Columbus Ave., between Vallejo and Green Streets. ☎ *415-433-9111. Fax: 415-362-6292. Internet:* www.hotelboheme.com. *Parking: $23 in a garage 1 ½ blocks away. Rack rates: $159 double. AE, CB, DC, DISC, JCB, MC, V.*

Hotel Del Sol

$$ Marina/Cow Hollow

Paint, mosaic tiles, and a lively imagination can do a lot to reinvent a motel, and there's no better example than the Del Sol. You'll think you're in Southern California (once the fog lifts), but it's lots better here, because pedestrians can walk around without getting startled looks from drivers. Anyway, the heated pool and a hammock suspended between palm trees complete the hallucination. Multi-colored guestrooms and suites are way fun, too.

3100 Webster St., at Filbert St. ☎ *877-433-5765 or 415-921-5520. Fax: 415-931-4137. Internet:* www.sftrips.com. *Parking: Free! Rack rates: $119–$129 double. AE, DC, DISC, MC, V.*

Hotel Griffon

$$$$ The Embarcadero

These small rooms don't sing style — lots of beige walls and a lack of artwork equal a drab appearance. In some rooms, sink/vanity combos sit just a few feet from the bed — a juxtaposition I find unsettling. Nevertheless, the hotel has concierge services that are top-notch, and eight end rooms have unsurpassed bay views. A well-equipped YMCA (free for guests) is next door, and a new restaurant is off the lobby. Continental breakfast is included in the rates.

155 Steuart St., between Mission and Howard Streets. ☎ *800-321-2201 or 415-495-2100. Fax: 415-495-3522. Internet:* www.hotelgriffon.com. *Parking: $18. Rack rates: $220–$415 double. Ask about weekend packages. AE, DC, DISC, MC, V.*

Hotel Milano

$$$ SoMa

You see nothing flashy or exciting about this well-designed and maintained modern-Italian-themed boutique hotel, but you won't find a better value in SoMa. Amenities include one of the more spacious onsite fitness rooms, a concierge, a restaurant, and all you'd expect in the rooms, including a minibar. The multi-story San Francisco Shopping Centre is a few feet away, and Yerba Buena Gardens is just around the corner.

55 Fifth St., between Market and Mission Streets. ☎ *800-398-7555 or 415-543-8555. Fax: 415-543-5885. Internet:* www.hotelmilano.citysearch.com. *Parking: $24 (valet). Rack rates: $169–$269 double. Ask about weekend packages. AE, DC, MC, V.*

Hotel Monaco

$$$$ Union Square

Though Hotel Monaco has a sophisticated '20s décor, the hotel's clientele is largely corporate. The medium-sized rooms have modern furniture, patterned wallpaper, floral prints, and canopied beds. All the amenities, such as room service, robes, and a fitness center, are available, along with the aptly named Grand Cafe restaurant. They'll even deliver live goldfish to your room if you need some company.

501 Geary St., at Taylor St. ☎ ***800-214-4220*** *or 415-292-0100. Fax: 415-292-0111. Internet:* www.hotelmonaco.com. *Parking: $24 (valet). Rack rates: $219–$289. Ask about packages and specials. AE, CB, DC, DISC, MC, V.*

Hotel Rex

$$$ Union Square

Despite its artsy leanings, this sophisticated 94-room delight is thankfully unpretentious. Watch cable cars clank by or peruse a book from the lobby library while drinking complimentary wine. The rooms are all smartly designed and colorfully decorated, and sizes vary from smallish doubles on up. Enjoy full service here, too, including a concierge and thoughtful amenities.

562 Sutter St., between Powell and Mason Streets. ☎ ***800-433-4434*** *or 415-433-4434. Fax: 415-433-3695. Parking: $19 (self-park), $25 (valet). Rack rates: $175–$575 double. AE, DC, DISC, MC, V.*

Hotel Triton

$$$ Union Square

You'll hear rock music blaring from the lobby in this hip 'n happening place with sponge painting and mod furniture. Doubles are small here, like at most Union Square hotels, but, oh baby, are they stylish. This trendy place is heavy on attitude and amenities like a concierge, robes, hair dryers, and Nintendo. In homage to the ab gods, there's a small onsite fitness room. The fabulous location, across from Chinatown's Dragon Gate, makes standing on the sidewalk outside an exotic experience.

342 Grant Ave., at Sutter St. (across from the Dragon Gate). ☎ ***888-364-2622*** *or 415-394-0500. Fax: 415-394-0555. Internet:* www.hotel-tritonsf.com. *Parking: $24 (valet). Rack rates: $179–$305 double. AE, CB, DC, DISC, MC, V. Dogs welcome.*

The Huntington

$$$$ Nob Hill

The Boston Brahmin in you will adore this refined, quiet oasis with its subtle elegance and impeccable service. The 1924 building originally housed apartments, so guestrooms and baths are larger than average. Rooms above the 8th floor have views; the ones below are extra spacious.

Children are welcome, and the staff, concierge included, will anticipate your every need. Manicured Huntington Park, complete with a playground, is across the street.

1075 California St., at Taylor St. ☎ *800-227-4683 or 415-474-5400. Fax: 415-474-6227. Internet:* www.slh.com. *Parking: $19.50 (valet). Rack rates: $255–$375 double. AE, DC, DISC, MC, V.*

Inn at Union Square

$$$ Union Square

This small, classic hotel is just the ticket if you crave luxury, but your pocketbook cries can't handle it. You get those little extras, such as continental breakfast, newspapers, afternoon tea, fresh flowers, wine in the early evening, nice linens, 24-hour concierge, believe it or not, combined with a no-tipping policy that makes it a bit easier to part with some, but not too much, money. Tasteful rooms range from small to very large, depending on how much you're able to spend. No A/C.

440 Post St., near Powell St. ☎ *800-288-4346 or 415-397-3510. Fax: 415-989-0529. Internet:* www.unionsquare.com. *Parking: $22 per day (valet). Rack rates: $175–$350 double. AE, CB, DC, DISC, MC, V.*

The Juliana Hotel

$$$ Union Square

Perched between Nob Hill and Union Square, this hotel appeals to couples who desire the benefits of both neighborhoods and like a cozy atmosphere. It's also a reasonable choice for small families, as suites are available for around $200. The rooms are gaily decorated, complete with coffeepots, irons, and hair dryers. An evening wine reception is gratis; continental breakfast is available for an extra charge. Guests can also use the Fairmont Hotel's health club, two blocks away.

590 Bush St., at Stockton St. ☎ *800-328-3880 or 415-392-2540. Fax: 415-391-8447. Internet:* www.julianahotel.com. *Parking: $24 (valet). Rack rates: $149–$199 double. AE, DC, DISC, JCB, MC, V.*

Kensington Park Hotel

$$$ Union Square

No matter what price range you're looking in, this 86-room gem, with a theater on the second floor and a well-known restaurant next door, Farralon (which I personally do not recommend due to the unfriendly service), is a find among Union Square hotels. The larger-than-average rooms were renovated in 1998; the bathrooms were already among the handsomest in the area. One of the best amenities is the long-time employee who's both concierge and porter and couldn't be friendlier or more willing to assist guests. If you like a great view (who doesn't?) request a room above the seventh floor, either Nob Hill side or on a corner. Rates include continental breakfast and afternoon tea. Workout facilities are available.

450 Post St., between Mason and Powell Streets. ☎ ***800-553-1900*** *or 415-788-6400. Fax: 415-399-9484. Internet:* www.kensingtonparkhotel.com. *Parking $22 (valet). Rack rates: $185–$225 double. AE, CB, DC, DISC, JCB, MC, V.*

King George Hotel

$$ Union Square

Pictures of British statesmen and royalty (pre-Diana) decorate this quaint, old-fashioned hotel, which was built in 1913. The decor's been updated as recently as 1998, but there's not much wiggle room. Expect teeny baths and tiny bedrooms with only one small window to provide natural light. However, conscientious and helpful staffers will assist with every request, and room service is round-the-clock. The Windsor Tea Room serves a traditional afternoon tea service.

334 Mason St., between Geary and O'Farrell Streets. ☎ ***800-288-6005*** *or 415-781-5050. Fax: 415-391-6976. Internet:* www.kinggeorge.com. *Parking: $18. Rack rates: $140–$170 double. AAA, AARP discounts and seasonal packages. AE, DC, DISC, MC, V.*

The Marina Inn

$ The Marina/Cow Hollow

Those who are looking for value and grace, in the form of a plainer, quieter atmosphere outside Union Square, are in luck. A two-story arched entrance gives this inexpensive 40-room Victorian inn an air of quiet grandeur. The furnishings are simple: armoires, wooden beds, and small tables. If you're looking for lots of light, the street-side rooms are bright but noisy; inside rooms are quieter, but natural light comes from a light well. A continental breakfast is included in the room rates; rack rates vary with the size of the room. The desk staff will make restaurant, tour, and airport shuttle reservations on request.

3110 Octavia, at Lombard St. ☎ ***800-274-1420*** *or 415-928-1000. Fax: 415-928-5909. Internet:* www.marinainn.com. *Parking: $9.50 at the nearest public garage. Rack rates: $65–$125 double. AAA, AARP discounts. AE, MC, V.*

The Marina Motel

$ The Marina/Cow Hollow

Originally an apartment building, 15 of the rentals in this funky courtyard-style budget motel have fully equipped kitchens. A granddaughter of the original owner is refurbishing the medium-sized guest rooms with Italian bathroom tiles, Mission-style furniture, and pretty quilts. Although some rooms still need an update, all are clean and neat. This is one of the few places on Lombard Street with even a hint of charm. Surprisingly, considering the location, rooms off the street are remarkably quiet. The front desk clerk will arrange tours or rental cars at your request.

2576 Lombard St., near Divisadero St. ☎ ***800-346-6118*** *or 415-921-9406. Fax: 415-921-0364. Internet:* www.marinamotel.com. *Parking: Free in little garages on the premises. Rack rates: $69–$129 double. AE, MC, V. Dogs welcome.*

The Maxwell

$$ Union Square

If you're a serious shopper, you'll like this hotel's neat shopping resources, such as its *Shopologist* newsletter. The guest rooms, which are either spacious and art deco–chic or somewhat dark and smallish (depending on your pocketbook), lie off an intimate, theatrical lobby. During a recent remodeling, designers thoughtfully didn't alter original bathroom tile and the deep bathtubs. Max's on the Square provides room service from 7am to 10pm.

386 Geary St., at Mason St. ☎ *888-734-6299 or 415-986-2000. Fax: 415-397-2447. Internet:* www.ammax@jdvhospitality.com. *Parking: $18 at a nearby garage. Rack rates: $155–$215 double. Ask about corporate discounts and special shopping packages. AE, DC, DISC, MC, V.*

Nob Hill Lambourne

$$$$ Nob Hill

The Lambourne, an intimate 20-room hotel, is relaxed and soothing, with spacious rooms that have compact kitchenettes and many amenities. You won't find a better deal on Nob Hill. If you're with your family, try the family suite — it's a beauty. Massages and other on-site spa treatments can be scheduled by the front desk staff. No smoking. Continental breakfast is included in the rates, and a basket of fruit is always in the hallway for your pleasure.

725 Pine St., at Stockton St. ☎ *800-274-8466 or 415-433-2287. Fax: 415-433-0975. Internet:* www.sftrips.com. *Parking: $24 (valet). Rack rates: $200–$325 double. AE, CB, DC, DISC, MC, V.*

Petite Auberge

$$ Union Square

Romantics will find happiness here among the florals and French country effects. The high-end rooms are enormous; the less expensive are cozy and have showers only, but are equally comfortable. Along with a full breakfast served downstairs in the homey dining room, there is complimentary tea, wine, and hors d'oeuvres in the afternoon. This B&B is wellknown and exceedingly popular, so if you want to experience the charms of a Provençal inn, book way ahead of time.

863 Bush St., between Mason and Taylor Streets. ☎ *800-365-3004 or 415-928-6000. Fax: 415-775-5717. Internet:* www.foursisters.com. *Parking: $19 (valet). Rack rates: $120–$165 double. AE, DC, MC, V.*

Ritz-Carlton

$$$$ Nob Hill

Okay, big spenders, here's your hotel. The Ritz takes posh to the extreme. It's for those who want to be waited on hand and foot. Settle into your beautiful, spacious room; then you can swim in the indoor pool, exercise, shop without ever leaving the cushy confines, and eat in a nationally renowned restaurant. Where the mantra is "Instant guest pacification will be ensured by all," how can you not love it?

600 Stockton St., between Pine and California Streets. ☎ *800-241-3333 or 415-296-7465. Fax: 415-291-0288. Internet:* www.ritzcarlton.com. *Parking: $30 (valet). Rack rates: well, if you have to ask . . . oh, $365–$575 double. Special occasion packages available. AE, CD, DC, DISC, MC, V.*

San Remo Hotel

$ **North Beach/Fisherman's Wharf**

Think of staying in this 1906 building as bunking at a pal's home: Because you have to share the bathrooms, it's the best attitude to have. Rooms are small but adorable. All the hotel guests are relaxed and friendly, thrilled to have found such a bargain close to the bay. Ambiance from the low-income housing project on the next block may not be the sort you crave. Laundry facilities are available. No A/C.

2237 Mason St., near Chestnut Street (two blocks from the Cannery). ☎ *800-352-7366 or 415-776-8688. Fax: 415-776-2811. Parking: $12 at a garage two blocks north. Rack rates: $60–$80 double. AE, DC, MC, V.*

Sir Francis Drake Hotel

$$$ **Union Square**

You will be enamored of this place as you walk into this historic building, past uniformed valets, into the elegant lobby. The medium-sized, up-to-date rooms won't immediately impress you, but the view from a corner room above the 10th floor will. An excellent restaurant, cafe, small workout facility, and nightclub are on-site. Services, including concierge, are superlative.

450 Powell St., at Sutter (one block north of Union Square). ☎ *800-227-5480 or 415-392-7755. Fax: 415-391-8719. Internet:* www.sirfrancisdrake.com. *Parking: $24 (valet). Rack rates: $179–$269 double. Packages available. AAA and AARP discounts. AE, CB, DC, DISC, MC, V.*

Tuscan Inn

$$ **North Beach/Fisherman's Wharf**

The Tuscan is a welcome change compared to the rest of the chain hotels on Fisherman's Wharf. Personality doesn't abound, but the rooms are fairly large by local standards, and kids like the location. The concierge is enthusiastic and friendly, and all the amenities you expect are available. In warm weather, enjoy dining al fresco at the hotel restaurant.

425 North Point, between Mason and Taylor Streets. ☎ *800-648-4626 or 415-561-1100. Fax: 415-561-1199. Internet:* www.tuscaninn.com. *Parking: $18 (valet). Rack rates: $148–300 double. Packages available. Ask about AAA, corporate, and senior discounts. AE, CB, DC, DISC, MC, V.*

Union Street Inn

$$ The Marina/Cow Hollow

This B&B has six richly appointed rooms and a choice location on a prime shopping street. If you want a bit less urban color, this is a fantastic retreat. The charming managers serve as concierge and cook a full breakfast as part of the deal. Rooms are large, but beware of the steep stairs to the front door, which make this an impractical choice for anyone who has difficulty walking.

2229 Union St., between Fillmore and Steiner Streets. ☎ *415-346-0424. Fax: 415-922-8046. Internet:* www.unionstreetinn.com. *Parking: $12 at a lot 1½ blocks away. Rack rates: $135–$245 double. AE, MC, V.*

W

$$$ SoMa

Ultra modern and light on the frou-frou, W precisely aims its glossy high-style and service at hip business travelers. Of course, they generally head for the airport on Fridays, leaving the vaguely masculine, moderate-sized rooms available to the rest of us. Marvel at the handsome chrome-and-frosted-glass bathroom, the deluxe amenities, the CD player, and the dataports. A lap pool, fitness room, restaurant, cafe, bar, room service, and well-trained staff add heft to an already solid package.

181 Third St., at Howard St. ☎ *877-946-8357 or 415-777-5300. Fax: 415-817-7860. Internet:* www.whotels.com. *Parking: $27 (valet). Rack rates: $239–$319 double. Ask about promotional rates. AE, DC, DISC, JCB, MC, V. Dogs welcome.*

The Warwick Regis

$$ Union Square

This is the closest we get to a French chateau downtown. If circa Louis XVI armoires, brocade fabrics, crown-canopied beds, and marble-tiled bathrooms get your heart racing, you're going to adore this hotel. Guests are privy to big hotel services — twice-daily housekeeping, fresh flowers, great amenities, a restaurant/bar — in an intimate, classy atmosphere, and 24-hour room service for an unbelievably reasonable price. Twelve of the beautiful suites contain two bathrooms; all the rooms, ranging from tiny to generous, are blissfully quiet.

490 Geary St., at Taylor St. ☎ *800-827-3447 or 415-928-7900. Fax: 415-441-8788. Internet:* www.warwickhotels.com. *Parking: $23 (valet). Rack rates: $135–$165 double. Inquire about packages. AE, DC, DISC, JCB, MC, V.*

Washington Square Inn

$$ North Beach/Fisherman's Wharf

The elegant yet homey atmosphere in North Beach makes this hotel a fine choice, if you don't require much in the way of hand-holding. The rooms that are in the lower end of the price range are small, but amenities such as continental breakfast, afternoon tea, and evening wine and hors d'oeuvres in the antiques-filled lobby are available to all guests. The staff will help you with your bags, but otherwise, the front desk service isn't so impressive.

1660 Stockton St., at Filbert St. (across from Washington Square Park). ☎ *800-388-0220 or 415-981-4220. Fax: 415-397-7242. Internet:* www.wsisf.com. *Parking: $20 per day (valet — vital in North Beach). Rack rates: $125–$210 double. AE, DC, DISC, JCB, MC, V.*

Westin St. Francis

$$$ Union Square

It's the location, pal. That and the glittering, bustling lobby that gives the historic St. Francis its air of excitement. But this is a really big, impersonal hotel — albeit one with 24-hour room service, concierges, shops, and dining opportunities. In any case, stick to the original (main) building. Its moderate-sized standard doubles are furnished with gorgeous reproductions and romantic antique chandeliers, although bathrooms are on the small side.

335 Powell St., across from Union Sq. ☎ *800-937-8461 or 415-397-7000. Fax: 415-774-0124. Parking: $30 (valet). Rack rates: $229–$360 double. AE, DC, DISC, JCB, MC, V.*

White Swan Inn

$$ Union Square

The 26 guest rooms in this Englishy B&B are designed to be lingered in. You'll certainly want to take every advantage of the four-poster beds and fireplaces in the spacious rooms. A full breakfast is included in the rates, as is afternoon tea and sherry served downstairs in the parlor. You'll think you're visiting a well-to-do British aunt. Back rooms are sunnier; the queen rooms have showers only. Just as in the White Swan's sister inn, Petite Auberge, advance reservations are imperative here.

845 Bush St., between Mason and Taylor Streets. ☎ *800-999-9570 or 415-775-1755. Fax: 415-775-5717. Internet:* www.foursisters.com. *Parking: $19 (valet). Rack rates: $165–$180 double. AE, DC, MC, V.*

If You Need a Room When There Are No Rooms Available . . .

Having trouble finding a room? If the hotels listed earlier in this chapter are booked, try booking at some of the following accommodations. They may have saved you some room.

Canterbury Best Western

$$ Union Square

Just slightly farther from the action around Union Square, the Canterbury's bedrooms are somewhat hotel-generic but absolutely comfortable and clean. The convenient restaurant has a new chef, and the food is reputed to be pretty good.

750 Sutter St., between Mason and Taylor Streets. ☎ *800-227-4788 or 415-474-6464. Fax: 415-474-0831. Internet:* www.canterbury-hotel.com. *Parking: $22 (valet). Rack rates: $39–$179 double. Special value rates and discounts. AE, CB, DC, DISC, MC, V. Restaurant, fitness room, smoking lounge, city views bayside above seventh floor, room service during restaurant hours.*

The Cartwright Hotel

$$ Union Square

Quiet and elegantly appointed with antiques in most rooms, families will be delighted with any of the two bedroom suites.

524 Sutter St., at Powell St. ☎ *800-227-3844 or 415-421-2865. Fax: 415-983-6244. Internet:* www.cartwrighthotel.com. *Parking: Self-park $18; valet $24. Rack rates: $139–$259 double. AAA, AARP discounts. AE, CB, DC, DISC, MC, V. Health club privileges at the Monaco.*

Galleria Park Hotel

$$$ Union Square

This is a terrific, small hotel in a clever location close to Chinatown, the Financial District, and Union Square. Unlike most downtown properties, this one has on-site parking, handy for travelers who need quick access to their automobile. The hotel's experienced concierge is a gold mine of information and assistance.

191 Sutter St., at Kearny St. ☎ *800-792-9639 or 415-781-3060. Fax: 415-433-4409. Internet:* www.galleriapark.com. *Parking: valet $25. Rack rates: $189–$289 double. Inquire about holiday and weekend packages. AE, CB, DC, DISC, MC, V. Workout room, rooftop garden, room service until 9pm.*

Chapter 9

Little Things Mean A Lot: Last-Minute Details to Keep in Mind

● ●

In This Chapter

▶ Buying travel insurance — or not

▶ Being sick away from home

▶ Deciding whether to drive

▶ How to find out what's going on in the city before you get there

▶ Getting your hands on tickets

● ●

*N*ow that you know how to get to San Francisco and know where you can stay, it's time to take care of details such as transportation and entertainment. In this chapter, I discuss these and a few other issues for you to ponder.

Buying Travel and Medical Insurance

The three primary kinds of travel insurance are trip cancellation insurance, medical, and lost luggage.

If you have paid a large portion of your vacation expenses up front, you may want to get trip cancellation insurance.

However, for most travelers, the other two types of insurance — medical and lost luggage — aren't really necessary. Your existing health insurance should cover you if you get sick while on vacation (double-check that your HMO fully covers you in this instance). If your luggage gets stolen, your homeowner's policy should cover it. Double-checking your existing policies before buying additional coverage can save you a lot of money. The airlines are responsible for $2,500 on domestic flights (and $9.07 per pound, up to $640, on international flights) if they lose your luggage; if your valuables are worth more than that, keep them in your carry-on bag.

Automatic flight insurance against death or dismemberment in case of an airplane crash is offered by many credit cards, including American Express and some gold and platinum Visa and MasterCards. If you still feel you need more insurance, try one of the following companies. Keep in mind, though, that paying for more insurance than you need is a waste of money. For example, if you only need trip cancellation insurance, don't purchase coverage for lost or stolen property. You should pay no more than approximately 6 to 8 percent of the total value of your vacation for trip cancellation insurance. Some of the reputable issuers of travel insurance include the following:

- ✔ **Access America,** 6600 W. Broad St., Richmond, VA 23230; ☎ **800-284-8300;** Fax: 800-346-9265; Internet: www.accessamerica.com

- ✔ **Travel Guard International,** 1145 Clark St., Stevens Point, WI 54481; ☎ **800-826-1300;** Internet: www.travel-guard.com

- ✔ **Travel Insured International, Inc.,** P.O. Box 280568, 52-S Oakland Ave., East Hartford, CT 06128-0568; ☎ **800-243-3174;** Internet: www.travelinsured.com

- ✔ **Travelex Insurance Services,** 11717 Burt St., Ste. 202, Omaha, NE 68154; ☎ **800-228-9792;** Internet: www.travelex-insurance.com

Getting Sick Away from Home

Getting sick away from home is no fun, so make sure you pack all your medications, as well as a prescription for more in case you run out or lose a bottle. Packing an extra pair of contact lenses in case you lose one as well as a pair of glasses is a good idea, too. And bring along some over-the-counter medications for common travelers' ailments like upset stomach or diarrhea.

If you have health insurance, check with your provider to find out the extent of your coverage outside of your home area. Be sure to carry your identification card in your wallet. And if you worry that your existing policy won't be sufficient, purchase medical insurance (see the section, "Buying Travel and Medical Insurance" earlier in this chapter) for more comprehensive coverage.

If you suffer from a chronic illness, talk to your doctor before taking the trip. For such conditions as epilepsy, diabetes, or a heart condition, wearing a Medic Alert identification tag will immediately alert any doctor to your condition and give him or her access to your medical records through Medic Alert's 24-hour hotline. Membership is $35, with a $15 renewal fee. Contact the **Medic Alert Foundation,** 2323 Colorado Ave., Turlock, CA 95382; ☎ **800-432-5378;** Internet: www.medicalert.org.

Ask your hotel concierge to recommend a local doctor if you get sick. A recommendation from a real person is probably better than any you'd get from an 800 number. If you can't get a doctor to see you promptly, see whether the local hospital ER has a walk-in clinic for non-life-threatening emergencies. You may have to wait a while, but it'll be cheaper than a typical emergency room visit, which usually runs about $300, not including treatment or medications.

Renting a Car (Or Six Reasons Why You Shouldn't)

If lots of traffic, steep hills, no parking spaces, one-way streets, crazy bike messengers, and the occasional threat of a tow don't bother you, then having access to a car would be good for you. If you'd rather not deal with those kind of hassles, plenty of professionals are around to cart you all over the city.

However, San Francisco doesn't have one of those enviable public transportation systems found in other cities; a bus can take you just about anywhere, but San Francisco's municipal railway system (Muni Metro) is fairly limited. The Muni streetcars can get you close to where you want to go, but often you'll still need to catch a bus or cab or walk to get to many places. However, because San Francisco neighborhoods are small and distinct, and because you'll find beautiful or bizarre happenings around every corner, walking around is delightful.

One reason why you should rent a car

If you plan on any out-of-city excursions, perhaps to go wine tasting (if you don't like escorted tours, that is), you probably want to rent a car. However, by waiting until the day you plan to do your driving to take possession of your rental, you can save yourself a lot of hassle and parking garage charges. Most rental car companies, including Enterprise Rent-A-Car (☎ **800-325-8007**) can pick you up and drop you off right at your hotel.

To get from the airport to your hotel, just take the shuttle instead of renting a car or taking a cab (see Chapter 10). Look for these vans at designated areas outside the departure terminals at San Francisco International and Oakland International airports.

Getting the best rate

As much as airline fares vary, car-rental rates vary even more. How much you pay is determined by the car size, how long you keep it, where and when you take possession of it and drop it off, where you take it, and tons of other factors.

One tip that could save you some cold hard cash is to ask a few key questions, including the following:

✔ Are weekend rates lower than weekday rates? For example, ask whether picking up the car Friday morning is cheaper than picking it up Thursday night.

✔ Can I get the weekly rate if I'm keeping the car five or more days?

✔ Will I be charged a fee for not returning the car to the same renting location? Some companies assess a drop-off charge in this instance; others, such as National, do not.

✔ Is it cheaper to pick up the car at the airport or at a location in town?

✔ Are any specials running right now? Or, if you see an advertised price in your local newspaper, be sure to ask for that specific rate; otherwise, you may be charged the standard (higher) rate.

When making your rental reservations, don't forget to mention membership in AAA, AARP, frequent-flyer programs, and trade unions. These usually entitle you to discounts ranging from 5 to 30 percent. Ask your travel agent to check any and all of these rates. And most car-rentals are worth at least 500 miles on your frequent-flyer account!

Comparing rates on the Web

As with other aspects of planning your trip, using the Internet can make comparison shopping for a car-rental much easier. All the major booking sites — Travelocity (www.travelocity.com), Expedia (www.expedia.com), Yahoo! Travel (www.travel.yahoo.com), and Cheap Tickets (www.cheaptickets.com), for example — have search engines that can dig up discounted car-rental rates. Just enter the size of the car you want, the pickup and return dates, and the city where you want to rent, and the server returns a price. You can even make the reservation through these sites.

Taking care of insurance, gas, and other charges

In addition to the standard rental prices, other optional charges can raise the cost of your car-rentals. For example, if you choose to add the Collision Damage Waiver (CDW), you may pay an added fee of as much as $10 per day! Some states have made this charge illegal. Plus, many credit-card companies already offer this insurance option when you charge the car-rental to that credit card. Before you go on vacation, call your credit-card company to inquire whether it offers this insurance option so you can avoid paying the large fee to the car-rental company.

Another optional charge is additional liability insurance (which covers you if you're in an accident where others are injured), personal accident insurance (if you or your passengers are injured), and personal effects insurance (if someone steals your luggage from your car). The insurance on your car at home probably covers you for most of these unlikely events. If your own insurance doesn't cover you for rentals, or if you don't have auto insurance, consider getting the additional coverage on your rental. car-rental companies are liable for certain base amounts, varying from state to state.

As for putting gas in your car, you have the option of paying for a full tank of gas up front. In this package, the gas price is average compared with local prices, but you don't get reimbursed for gas you leave in the tank after your trip. Your other option is to pay only for the gas you use, but you have to return the car with a full tank of gas, or the company will charge you $3 to $4 a gallon for the deficiency. If you don't want to bother filling up the tank at the last minute, then go with the package deal. If you know you won't be rushed, then don't bother.

Getting the Jump on Dinner Reservations and Tickets for Events and Attractions

Finding out what cool stuff will be going on in San Francisco during your stay is easy. Check out the quality entertainment listing of local publications and Web sites listed in the next section. If you know of a music concert scheduled during your stay that you'd like to go to, you can easily find out the details in time to get tickets.

You can even buy tickets ahead of time for special events, theatre performances, or even a baseball game at Pacific Bell Park. Many Web sites, including those for the ballet, opera, and the Giants baseball team enable you to purchase tickets online. Or you can call **BASS TicketMaster** (☎ **800-225-2277** outside California, or ☎ 510-762-2277) or check out the local Ticketron.

The concierge at the hotel where you'll be staying (or the desk staff if the hotel doesn't have a separate concierge desk) can usually help you acquire tickets to events and shows after you make your hotel reservations. Take advantage of their services.

For **Alcatraz tours,** reserve tickets at least two weeks in advance during the summer. Call ☎ **415-705-5555** to charge tickets by phone with a credit card. A $2.25 service charge will be added to each ticket. Your tickets will be mailed to you, or you can pick them up at the ticket booth at the pier.

Finding events via publications and the Web

Check out the following local publications for the latest happenings around town:

  ✔ *The Bay Guardian:* This weekly is a favorite of locals because of its up-to-date entertainment listings and yearly "Best Of" awards. Issues cost $3 by mail; call ☎ **415-255-3100.**

  ✔ *The San Francisco Chronicle:* Check out the "Datebook" section for information about the arts. To save on the high cost of postage, don't order a copy by mail; order the paper from your local newsstand instead.

  ✔ *San Francisco:* Our very own monthly magazine is chock-full of arts and entertainment information. You can find it on newsstands in all major cities, or you can order a single copy for $2.95 by calling ☎ **415-398-2800.**

  ✔ *SF Weekly:* This alternative paper contains entertainment listings and investigative reporting. Call ☎ **415-541-0700** to request a copy.

If you prefer to surf for entertainment information, general city information, and current event listings, check out the following Web sites:

  ✔ www.athand.com: This site is operated by Pacific Bell and contains San Francisco restaurant reviews and hotel listings.

  ✔ www.bayarea.citysearch.com: Citysearch not only lets you search on your specific interests, but it also directs you to restaurants and points of interest close to wherever you plan to be.

  ✔ www.sfbay.yahoo.com: Yahoo!, the Web search engine, publishes this guide to San Francisco.

  ✔ www.sfbayconcerts.com: Check out this site for a complete concert listing.

  ✔ www.sfbg.com: You can find *The Bay Guardian's* complete entertainment listings online.

  ✔ www.sfgate.com/eguide: The *San Francisco Chronicle's* entertainment Web site.

Checking out sports on the Web

In addition to the following specific sites, you can also swing by the Bay Area's general sports site at www.bayinsider.com.

  ✔ **Golden State Warriors:** www.nba.com/warriors/

  ✔ **Oakland Raiders:** www.oaklandraiders.com

  ✔ **San Francisco 49ers Football:** www.sf49ers.com

  ✔ **San Francisco Giants Baseball:** www.sfgiants.com

Surfing for performing arts information

Check out the following sites for all your performing arts needs:

  ✔ **American Conservatory Theater:** www.act-sfbay.org

  ✔ **Best of Broadway theater info:** www.bestofbroadway_sf.com

> ✔ **Lamplighters light opera company:** www.lamplighters.org
>
> ✔ **San Francisco Ballet:** www.sfballet.org
>
> ✔ **San Francisco Opera:** www.sfopera.org
>
> ✔ **San Francisco Symphony:** www.sfsymphony.org

Museums on the Web

Find out what San Francisco's museums have to offer at the following Web sites:

> ✔ **Asian Art Museum:** www.asianart.com
>
> ✔ **California Academy of Sciences:** www.calacademy.org
>
> ✔ **The Exploratorium:** www.exploratorium.edu
>
> ✔ **M. H. de Young Memorial Museum and California Palace of the Legion of Honor:** www.thinker.org
>
> ✔ **Museum of the City of San Francisco:** www.sfmuseum.org
>
> ✔ **San Francisco Museum of Modern Art:** www.sfmoma.org

Getting a table at 8:00

San Francisco has thousands of restaurants, but if you don't make dinner reservations — sometimes way in advance — you may not get to eat where you want. For dinner seating (7 to 9pm) at some of the award-winning restaurants, such as Charles Nob Hill, Gary Danko, Hawthorne Lane, Boulevard, and Jardinière, you will need to make reservations several weeks in advance. Even some of the slightly lower profile, but equally fabulous restaurants that attract more locals and fewer tourists, such as Slanted Door and Delfina, get booked up quickly. Make your reservations as much as four weeks in advance if you have a particular restaurant in mind.

You can also tell your hotel to make dinner reservations for you. Restaurants like to stay on good terms with hotel concierges — which means you may have better luck obtaining that hard-to-get table at 8 at the oh-so-trendy bistro if the concierge calls for you. It doesn't always work, but it's worth a try.

You can also make reservations over the Web. A fair number of good local restaurants now belong to www.opentable.com, a Web site that can help you find and reserve a table at dozens of places around the Bay Area. If you choose this option, the cautious side of me suggests that you confirm directly with the restaurant when you get here.

Packing Strategies

Start your packing by taking everything you think you'll need and laying it out on the bed. Then get rid of half of it.

I recommend this strategy not because the airlines won't let you take it all — they will, within limits — but because you don't want to hurt yourself by toting half your earthly belongings around with you.

No matter what time of year you visit San Francisco, don't forget to bring along a coat or warm jacket; the weather can change almost instantly from sunny and warm to windy and cold. Also don't forget to pack the following: good walking shoes, a camera, a versatile sweater and/or blazer, a belt, toiletries and medications (pack these in your carry-on bag so you'll have them if the airline loses your luggage), and pajamas. Unless you'll be attending a board meeting, a wedding, or one of the city's finest restaurants, you probably won't need a suit or a fancy dress. A pair of jeans or khakis and a comfortable sweater will be more useful to you. (See the following packing list for other packing wisdom.)

Choose a suitcase that fits the type of traveling you plan to do. If you plan to walk a lot on hard floors or on the sidewalk, get a suitcase with wheels. However, they won't do you much good if you'll be going up and down stairs with your luggage. A foldover garment bag helps keep more formal attire from wrinkling but isn't well adapted for frequent packing and unpacking. Hard-sided luggage provides more protection for fragile items but weighs a lot more than soft-sided bags.

Pack big, hard items like shoes first, then fit smaller items in and around them. Pack breakable items in between several layers of clothes, or keep them in your carry-on bag. Put items with the potential to leak, like conditioners, lotions, and so on, in resealable bags. Use a small padlock (available at most luggage stores, if your bag doesn't already have one) on your luggage to discourage thieves, and put an identification tag on the outside.

Call your airline to find out how many pieces of carry-on luggage you can bring. Remember that both must fit in the overhead compartment or under the seat in front of you. In your carry-on, pack a book, any breakable items you don't want to put in your suitcase, a personal headphone stereo, a snack in case you don't want what the airline's serving that day, any vital documents you don't want to lose in your luggage (like your return tickets, passport, wallet, and so on), and space to put your sweater or jacket if you get warm in an overheated terminal.

Checking off items on your packing list

- ✔ Bathing suit (if your hotel has a pool or spa)
- ✔ Belt
- ✔ Camera (don't forget the film; it can be very expensive when you're traveling)
- ✔ Coat and tie or a dress (only if you plan to go some place fancy in the evening)
- ✔ Medications (pack these in a carry-on bag so you'll have them even if you lose your luggage)

- ✔ Pants and/or skirts

- ✔ Shirts or blouses

- ✔ Shoes (only bring two or three pairs, including a good pair of walking shoes)

- ✔ Shorts

- ✔ Socks

- ✔ Sweaters and/or jackets

- ✔ Toiletries (a razor, toothbrush, comb, deodorant, makeup, contact lens solutions, hairdryer, extra pair of glasses, sewing kit)

- ✔ Umbrella (you never know when you'll need one)

- ✔ Underwear

Dressing like the locals

It's a tradition to scoff at tourists in cargo shorts wandering around Union Square in the dead of summer (when temperatures rarely top 70°F and a chilling fog rolls in most mornings and evenings). Avoid the snickers (and catching cold) by dressing in layers — you know, a T-shirt under a sweater under a jacket. Sure, you'll end up tying the jacket and the sweater around your waist mid-afternoon, but at least we'll think you're one of us.

The city is known for informality, but it still has style. Men who don't want to be considered rubes ought to pack a sports coat for an evening at the theater, symphony, opera, or even a really nice restaurant. For women, a good pair of lightweight wool slacks and a sweater set will take you anywhere. Anyone planning on heading to dance clubs will want to dress on the trendy side, which usually means wearing black.

Part III
Settling into San Francisco

The 5th Wave   By Rich Tennant

SAN FRANCISCO'S AMAZING CABLE CARS

Travelers can ride from Market Street to the Financial District, through the Rocky Mountains and on to Denver all for the price of one Muni Passport.

In this part . . .

This part gets you from the airport to the city, introduces you to the neighborhoods, and explains how to use San Francisco's handy public transportation system. If you're driving, you can flip directly to the tips for upping your parking karma quotient — you need it around San Francisco.

Chapter 10

Orienting Yourself in San Francisco

You can't really glean much about a town from its airports and roadways. Plus, until you check in to your hotel, change into comfortable attire, stretch your limbs, and head out the door, you can't really focus on your surroundings. The industrial sites and parking lots you pass through gradually become the neighborhoods and landmarks you may have seen or heard about from films, magazines, or some other traveler's postcard to you. Suddenly, you happily realize that you are on an adventure in a tantalizingly new and wonderfully exciting place. San Francisco welcomes you.

Getting around San Francisco International Airport

You may at first be overwhelmed by how big and busy **San Francisco International** (SFO) is, but it's easier to navigate than it looks. The airport, which is undergoing major construction, currently consists of three main terminals: North, South, and International. After you get off your plane, follow the signs to the baggage terminal on the first floor. The baggage level of each terminal also houses information booths. Bank of America operates a branch on the mezzanine level of the North and International terminals, and you can find ATMs on the upper level of all three terminals.

You can call the airport's toll-free telephone hot line (☎ 800-736-2008) weekdays from 8am to 5pm (PST) for information on how to get into the city from the airport. The traveler's information desk in each of the three main terminals can also give you this information. You can also go to the Web site at `www.ci.sf.ca.us/sfo/` for more about the airport and ground transportation.

To get to your hotel by cab, exit from the baggage claim area and line up for a cab. To get to it by shuttle bus or a rental car van, exit from upstairs and wait for the appropriate vehicle. Here are the specifics:

✔ Taxis line up for passengers at well-marked yellow columns on the center island outside the lower level of the airport. Expect to pay around $30 plus tip to go downtown, and the 14-mile trip takes 30 minutes or so depending on traffic and time of day.

✔ If you can stand to wait 10 to 20 minutes for one heading to your neighborhood, shuttle vans offer door-to-door service from the airport. However, the shuttle may make up to three stops before you get to where you're going. You can find the shuttles by exiting the airport from the upper level and heading to the center island outside the ticket counter nearest you. A guide will direct you. Look for exact shuttle fares posted throughout the terminals; most charge between $10 and $12. **Super Shuttle** (☎ **415-558-8500**) is my personal favorite. You don't need to make advance reservations.

✔ Also traversing the upper level is a free minibus marked **Cal Trains SFO Shuttle,** which takes passengers to the Millbrae Cal Train Station, a few miles from the airport. From there, you can board a Cal Train to the depot at 4th and King Streets in San Francisco. The fare is a bargain at $2, and the ride takes under 30 minutes. For the train schedule, go to `www.transitinfo.org` or call ☎ **800-660-4287.**

✔ If you're renting a car, a free bus will transport you to the vast building where all the counters and cars are located. Catch the bus from the upper level center islands outside the terminals.

Unless the construction is finished by the time you retrieve your car, getting to the freeways can be confusing. Head west and follow the signs until you locate the entrance to Highway 101 and Highway 280. Stay toward the left, so you don't end up on 280, which will take you to the city but not as efficiently as 101. If you want to go to Union Square, exit 101 north at Fourth Street. Traffic is manageable until rush hour, from 3 to 7pm.

Getting around Oakland International Airport

Landing at **Oakland International** (☎ **510-577-4000**) is similar to landing at San Francisco International (see the preceding section) except all ground transportation is on one level. A shuttle service called Bayporter Express (☎ **415-467-1800**) picks up passengers from Terminal 1 at the center island, and from Terminal 2 around the corner from baggage claim. The fare to San Francisco is $26 for one person,

$36 for two people in the same party, and $5 for kids under 12. You'll have an easier time if you make reservations for the 45- to 90-minute ride. To take a cab downtown, expect to pay around $40; the trip takes 30 to 40 minutes, depending on traffic. You can find ATMs in the airport.

If you don't want to take a shuttle or a cab, take **BART** — Bay Area Rapid Transit — (☎ **510-464-6000**) into the city. The **AirBART** shuttle (☎ **510-430-9440**) runs in front of Terminals 1 or 2 every 15 minutes. The cost is $2 for the 10-minute ride to the Oakland Coliseum BART station. From there, take a BART train into the city. How much your fare is depends on where you're going; the cost to get downtown is around $2.45. You can buy your ticket from well-marked kiosks inside the airport or at the BART station. If you're staying around Union Square, take BART to the Powell Street station, a 23-minute ride.

All the major rental car company counters are inside the terminals, and the cars are a short walk away. If you're driving into San Francisco, exit the airport on Hegenberger Road. Follow it north to Highway 880 toward San Francisco. From there follow the signs to Highway 80 to San Francisco. When you reach the Bay Bridge, you'll have to stop at the tollbooths and pay $2 to cross. After you enter San Francisco, exit on 5th Street to reach Union Square.

Arriving Some Other Way

The following sections explain what to do if you get into town via a way other than flying.

By train

You can't actually take an Amtrak train to San Francisco; you actually arrive in Emeryville, just north of Oakland. You can catch one of the regularly scheduled buses to take you the rest of the way to downtown San Francisco. The buses stop at the CalTrain station, where there's a new Muni streetcar line to the Embarcadero (and thus, into downtown) and at the Ferry Building. The Ferry Building is more convenient to the hotels recommended in this book, and from there you can take a taxi to Union Square or wherever.

By automobile

Drivers arriving from east of town will eventually find their way across the Bay Bridge into downtown. It's the neighborhood with all the tall buildings on your right. You can't miss it. Cars coming from the south on Highway 101 will discover the same view a few miles past 3-Com (or Candlestick) Park. Anyone making the journey along Highway 101 coming from the north will enter San Francisco from the Golden Gate Bridge. After you pass the toll booth (it's $3 coming into the city), exit along the bay to Van Ness Avenue.

Encountering the Neighborhoods

San Francisco is perfectly situated at the end of a 32-mile long peninsula between the Pacific Ocean and the San Francisco Bay. You may be surprised to find out that the city itself covers just seven square miles. Streets are laid out in a traditional grid pattern, except for two major diagonal arteries, Market Street and Columbus Avenue. Market cuts through town from the Embarcadero up toward Twin Peaks. Columbus runs at an angle through North Beach, beginning near the Transamerica Pyramid in the Financial District and ending near the Hyde Street Pier. You can find numbered *streets* downtown, and numbered *avenues* in the Richmond and Sunset Districts southwest of downtown. Other important thoroughfares include Van Ness Avenue, which begins in the Mission District as South Van Ness and ends at Aquatic Park, and Geary Street, which begins at Market and meanders through the city to Ocean Beach.

San Francisco neighborhoods, which are no more uniform than puzzle pieces, are as diverse and interesting as their inhabitants. Of course, you'll have no trouble distinguishing Union Square from Chinatown or even the Financial District. But even if you amble through largely residential neighborhoods, you'll notice distinct differences in the makeup of the locals and the commercial establishments. In the Mission District (above Mission Street), hip habitués frequent the latest restaurants and bars, while 10 blocks away in Noe Valley, stroller-strapped mammas sip mochas with their play-group pals. Over the hill in the Castro, muscular young men walk their Chihuahuas oblivious of the SUV-wielding Pacific Heights matrons vying for parking spaces a few miles away on Fillmore Street.

You can immerse yourself in one culture or another merely by taking a walk, dropping into the local coffeehouse or bookstore, or sitting at a cafe table and taking it all in. The following sections tell you where to start.

The Castro

An active gay community is the Castro's claim to fame. Visitors can admire the beautifully restored Victorian homes, visit the Castro Theater, and shop in the superb men's clothing stores. For shopping and people-watching, head to **Castro Street,** between Market and 18th Streets.

China Basin

This neighborhood is not new, but B.S. (before the PacBell baseball stadium), visitors had no reason to come here. Boy, have things changed. King Street from Third Street to the Embarcadero is the main drag; here is where you can find restaurants, bars, and the boys of summer.

Chinatown

The borders of Chinatown are in a state of flux, but you can generally find this densely packed area roughly between Broadway, Taylor, Bush, and Montgomery Streets. It is every bit as vivid and fascinating as advertised. The Dragon Gate entrance on Grant Avenue leads to touristy shops, and you'll swear you're in another country after you wander up Stockton and through the abundant number of alleyways.

The Civic Center

If you're looking for the New Main Library; the Ballet, Symphony, and Opera buildings; and City Hall, which underwent a spectacular renovation a few years ago, then the Civic Center is where you want to head. City Hall's resplendent black and gold dome makes for a fabulous landmark. Van Ness and Golden Gate Avenues, and Franklin, Hyde, and Market Streets border the area. This area also attracts a large homeless population. If you see a performance or are in one of the area's many restaurants at night, you may feel more at ease taking a cab to the next place on your itinerary.

Cow Hollow

Between Broadway, Lyon, and Lombard Streets, and Van Ness Avenue is Cow Hollow, a residential utopia. You can find the famous Union Street here, popular among locals and tourists alike. Here you'll find a trendy cloister of shops, restaurants, and young, urban professionals. Architecture and history fans can regard the Octagon House (ca. 1861) at 2645 Gough St. (at Union). It's open to the public.

The Embarcadero and the Financial District

The Embarcadero and Financial District take up a great bay location from Bay Street to Market Street east of Montgomery Street. This area is home to major corporations, as well as the Transamerica Pyramid, a skyline landmark, located on Montgomery and Clay Streets. Antiques hounds hunt through Jackson Square's exclusive shops.

Fisherman's Wharf

Many tourists flock to Fisherman's Wharf, located on Bay Street between Powell and Polk Streets, but the former working piers have been stripped of their glory and are now filled with the sounds of cash registers. Pass by Pier 39 and the plethora of shlock shops to the Hyde Street Pier and Ghirardelli Square to discover a few legitimate reasons to spend some time here. Don't forget to visit Aquatic Park and the Maritime Museum.

San Francisco Neighborhoods

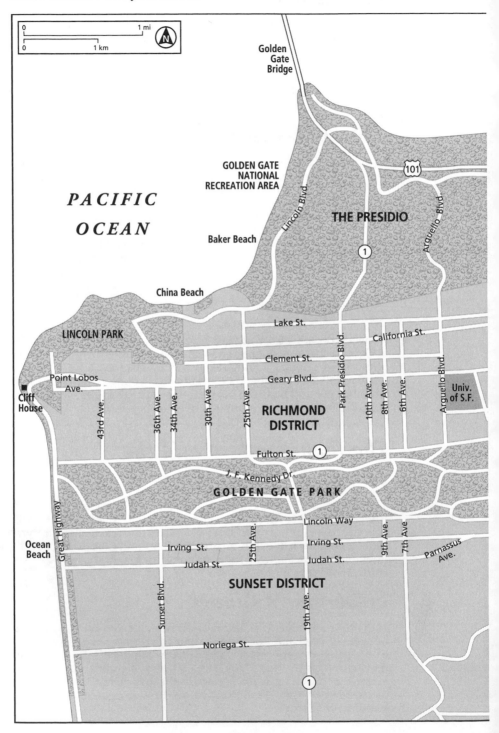

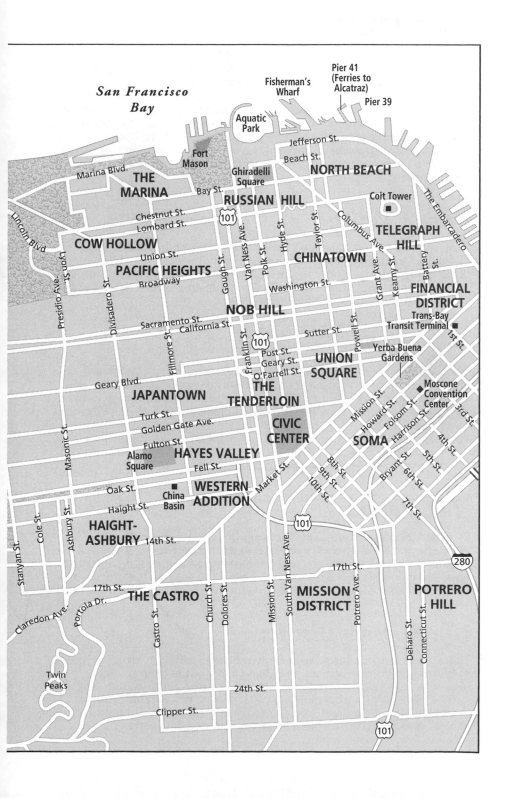

Haight-Ashbury

Often referred to as just The Haight, Haight-Ashbury is surrounded by Stanyan Street to the east, Divisadero Street to the west, Fulton Street to the north, and Waller Street to the south. The area still hasn't fully recovered from what must have been a real bummer to some of its residents — the demise of the '60s. You can find most of the action on Haight Street, which continues to hold a magical appeal over scruffy groups of youngsters campaigning for handouts. If nostalgia or curiosity overtake you, swing by some of the many used-clothing stores that compete for space with all kinds of commercial endeavors, most of which are perfectly legit.

Hayes Valley

You can find Hayes Valley just west of Civic Center surrounded by Franklin Street to the east, Webster Street to the west, Grove Street to the north, and Page Street to the south. Here you'll find many places to shop and a few quality restaurants. This chic area is a bit pricey, but it's definitely worth your time visiting here.

Japantown

Off Geary, between Webster and Laguna Streets, is Japantown and rather ugly indoor shopping centers. Contrary to its appearance, you can find some good, inexpensive noodle restaurants and some interesting shops housed in the dismal gray buildings attached by a pedestrian walkway. Check out the AMC-Kabuki movie theaters here, or have a massage and a soak at the Kabuki Hot Springs. Across Sutter Street (between Fillmore and Webster), look for Cottage Row, the last remaining bit of the real Japantown before the neighborhood got redeveloped.

The Marina

On the Marina's commercial blocks on Chestnut Street between Franklin and Lyon Streets, you can find a full array of coffeehouses, restaurants, and shops targeting the sleek and the slender. This is the neighborhood of choice for newly arrived singles. Tourists stop by to see Fort Mason Center, the Palace of Fine Arts, and the Exploratorium.

The Mission District

Located in the area from Cesar Chavez Street to Market Street between Dolores and Potrero Streets, the Mission District is a busy, largely Hispanic community. Check out Mission Dolores, Dolores Park, and 24th Street, along with a plethora of affordable restaurants and eye-catching building murals. You can find a multitude of restaurants on Valencia and Guererro Streets between 16th and 23rd Streets.

Nob Hill

One of the city's more recognized areas, Nob Hill envelops California Street from Leavenworth to Stockton and overlooks the Financial District. Grace Cathedral and a selection of expensive apartments and hotels leave quite the impression.

North Beach

North Beach isn't an actual beach; it's the old Italian neighborhood next to Chinatown. Head here to sit around various cafes, to browse bookstores and other shops, and to sample the selections at the various delis and pastry shops. Columbus Avenue is the main drag, but you can find family-style restaurants and crowded bars along the streets from Washington to Grant. The XXX-rated clubs stick together on Broadway.

Telegraph Hill is just to the east of North Beach, behind Coit Tower and the Filbert steps. Russian Hill is just to the northwest, where you'll find the wiggly part of Lombard Street and Macondry Lane, immortalized in Armistead Maupin's book *Tales of the City.*

Pacific Heights

Pacific Heights, which is bordered by Broadway, Pine, Divisadero, and Franklin Streets, is where the wealthy lounge around in their extravagant and tastefully decorated homes. You can visit the **Haas-Lilienthal House,** an 1886 Queen Anne Victorian at 2007 Franklin St. (at Washington), and stare at *Mrs. Doubtfire's* fictional digs on the corner of Broadway and Steiner.

The Presidio

On the westernmost point of the city on 1,500 some-odd acres is the Presidio. Not so long ago, the area used to belong to the U.S. Army, but now it's part of the Golden Gate National Recreation Area. If you are in the mood for a hike, go to the visitor's center for maps and suggestions. The views and landscape are sensational. If you'd rather bowl, a great little bowling alley is also located here.

The Richmond District

The Richmond District is largely residential but includes Golden Gate Park (see Chapter 16) at one edge and the Pacific Ocean at another. Lincoln Park, Land's End, the California Palace of the Legion of Honor museum, and the Cliff House are all located in this rather large neighborhood. Clement Street is another Chinatown, and on Geary Boulevard, you can find authentic Russian food.

South of Market (SoMa)

South of Market, or SoMa for short, continues to have growth spurts. The area below Market Street between 10th, King, and Steuart Streets used to be an industrial truck stop but now offers a variety of things. Clubs have multiplied around Folsom Street; restaurants and bars are thick from Howard Street down to the tiny South Park neighborhood. The Rincon Center near the bay, the Museum of Modern Art on 4th Street, and Yerba Buena Center are all worthy of your attention. Avoid 6th and 7th Streets below Market, however, because this area is rife with unsavory clientele.

The Tenderloin

The Tenderloin isn't a tourist magnet. The blocks bounded by Sutter and Mason Streets and Van Ness and Golden Gate Avenues are a section of town currently home to low-income immigrant families attempting to live their lives alongside flop houses, bars, massage parlors, and people sub-siding on the fringes of society. A slim rectangle of space from roughly O'Farrell to Market Streets between Larkin and Polk is dangerous at night and rough during the day. The only place worth visiting in the Tenderloin is the Glide Memorial Church for Sunday services.

Union Square

Union Square, surrounded by Neiman Marcus, Macy's, Saks Fifth Avenue, and the Westin St. Francis Hotel, is the shopping core of the city. The area surrounding the actual square has the city's highest concentration of shopping, dining, theater, and nightlife options.

The Western Addition

I mention this old neighborhood between Geary and Haight, Gough and Divisidero Streets not because there's much here to see — outside of Alamo Square — but because people studying their maps often believe it's an easy walk from Civic Center to Golden Gate Park by way of Oak or Fell Streets. That's not entirely accurate. First, it's hilly. Second, while the area has improved, it's still not the safest section of town.

Getting Information After You Arrive

Your hotel concierge or desk clerk can be a virtual fount of information. You may be inundated with material. But, if you need more, stop by the **Convention and Visitors Bureau Information Center** on the lower level of Hallidie Plaza, 900 Market St. (at Powell), or call ☎ **800-220-5747** or 415-391-2000. The office is open Monday through Friday from 9am to 5:30pm, on Saturday from 9am to 3pm, and on Sunday from 10am to 2pm. It's closed Thanksgiving Day, Christmas Day, and

New Year's Day. If you're in the Fisherman's Wharf area, stop by the **Visitors Information Center of the Redwood Empire Association** on the second floor of the Cannery, 2801 Leavenworth, or call ☎ **800-200-8334** or 415-543-8334; it's open Monday through Saturday from 10am to 6pm.

Look for a free *Bay Guardian* or *SF Weekly* from sidewalk kiosks or coffee-houses for listings of city events and entertainment. The Convention and Visitor's Bureau also operates a 24-hour events line at ☎ **415-391-2000.**

Chapter 11

Getting around San Francisco

• •

In This Chapter

▶ Using your feet

▶ Using MUNI and BART

▶ Riding the cable cars

▶ Driving and parking tips

• •

*A*s you may have gleaned from other chapters, having a car in the city isn't highly advised and isn't necessary most of the time. San Francisco really caters to walkers, putting benches in excellent spots and building cafes in perfect places for a break. Getting around on a bus or Muni metro streetcar is hassle-free and cheap. In the rare instance that you do need a car, renting one from downtown is easy.

This chapter contains everything you need to know about cruising around the city sans car. It even includes some inside tips on parking should you decide to throw caution to the wind and join the legendary drivers — and I don't mean that in a good way — gracing our city's roads and highways. (See Chapter 9 to find out about car-rental companies in SF, where you can get your wheels!)

 The one-stop shopping number for local traffic or public transit information is ☎ 415-817-1717. This number connects callers to whatever they need — be it BART and Muni routes, or traffic conditions.

Heading Out on Foot

Walking is not only the best way to travel for those not in a rush, but it's also the only way to really see and enjoy the neighborhoods. Take one of the many walking tours given around town to see details of the neighborhoods that you would never even catch a glimpse of in a car. I recommend some walking tours in Chapter 18.

 Use caution, as there have been a rash of vehicle/pedestrian accidents lately. Be alert at all times. Watch for drivers running red lights or turning right on a red light; make sure bus drivers see you entering the crosswalk (avoid jaywalking); and be especially wary of bike messengers, who show no mercy for anyone.

Among the best neighborhoods for walkers are **Chinatown, North Beach,** and **The Embarcadero.** If you're in good shape and don't mind a little wind, a walk across the **Golden Gate Bridge** is much more satisfying than a drive, especially if you're the one who has to keep your eyes on the road.

Traveling by Streetcar

Walking probably won't take you everywhere you want to go. But getting around by public transportation is easy once you know a few basics. The San Francisco Municipal Railway, known as "Muni" (☎ 415-673-6864), is much maligned by locals for inefficiency, but tens of thousands of commuters rely daily on its buses and electric streetcars for a lift to the office. The fare is $1 for an adult and 35¢ for seniors and children to ride a bus or streetcar anywhere in the system; exact change is required. Muni Passports, accepted on buses, streetcars, and even cable cars, are a bargain for visitors planning to take public transportation extensively. A one-day passport is $6, a three-day pass is $10, and a seven-day pass is $15. These passes can be purchased at the **Convention and Visitors Bureau Information Center** at Hallidie Plaza, at the Union Square TIX Bay Area booth, and at the cable car booth at Sutter and Hyde Streets. You can find public transit schedules on the Web at www.ci.sf.ca.us/muni.

Citypass, a booklet of discounted tickets to six major attractions, including the major museums and a one-hour bay cruise, now includes a seven-day Muni Passport, making it quite a bargain for those who are ambitious enough to use all the coupons. It's $33.25 for adults and can be purchased at the participating attractions, at Hallidie Plaza, and over the Internet at www.citypass.net.

You can also save two dollars by purchasing a roll of 10 Muni tokens for $8. Tokens are available at the cable car booth at Powell and Market and at the ticket booths inside the Montgomery and Embarcadero stations. Don't buy tokens from anyone hawking them on the street. For a complete listing of token vendors, check the Web site.

At the underground Muni stops from Civic Center to the Embarcadero, the fare boxes (which are located at the entry point prior to reaching the escalators) only accept coins or tokens, an important point to remember if you're in a hurry and have only dollar bills in hand. There are change machines on the walls next to the BART ticket dispensers.

Muni streetcars run underground downtown and above ground in the outlying neighborhoods from 6am until 1am, although I did attempt to take Muni home late in the evening once, only to discover that the station entrance was gated shut. The five Muni Metro streetcar lines — the J, K, L, M, and N — make the same stops as BART (see the discussion later) along Market Street, including Embarcadero Station, Montgomery and Powell Streets (both near Union Square), Civic Center and Van Ness Avenue. Past Van Ness Avenue, the routes go off in different directions. The N-Judah line services the Haight-Ashbury and parallels Golden Gate Park on its way down Judah Street to the ocean. The J-Church line passes close to Mission Dolores and the Castro.

The L-Taraval line travels through the Sunset district within walking distance of the San Francisco Zoo.

Another line, the F-Market, is made up of a collection of vintage streetcars. It runs along Market Street to the Castro Street station and back. The F line was recently extended, allowing these rejuvenated antiques to continue from Market Street over to Mission Street and down the Embarcadero to Fisherman's Wharf. Muni cars marked Mission Bay end their journey at the CalTrain Station on King Street, just past the new Giants baseball park.

Spend the $3 to get the Official San Francisco Street and Transit MUNI Map. It is invaluable for public transportation users. It shows all bus, streetcar, cable car, and BART routes and stations. You can buy the maps at the Convention and Visitors Bureau Information Center. You can also call ☎ 415-673-MUNI for route information.

Trekking by Bus

The Muni buses are clearly numbered on the front and run through the city from 6am to midnight (however, I don't recommend taking them too late at night). Street corner signs and painted yellow bands on utility poles and on curbs mark bus stops. Buses come by every 5 to 20 minutes, depending on where you want to go and the time of day. They aren't the most rapid way to travel, but with 80 transit lines, they are the most complete. Muni metro streetcars are faster, but the buses cover a wider area. Expect the buses to be extremely crowded during commute rush hours (from 7 to 9am and 4 to 6pm).

Exact change is required on the buses, like the streetcars (for information on fares, see the previous section "Traveling by Streetcar"). The driver will likely hand you a paper transfer, which is good for a second ride within two hours. If you plan on riding another bus or streetcar within the time limit, make sure to get a transfer.

Befriending BART

BART (☎ 650-992-2278), which stands for Bay Area Rapid Transit, is not Muni. Tourists often get the two systems mixed-up because they share the same underground stations downtown. You won't get into too much trouble if you get the systems confused within the city limits. BART, however, runs all over the Bay Area, and if you are inattentive, you may end up in a place far different from where you expected to be. More than one unsuspecting traveler has ended up in Fremont when he intended to exit at the Embarcadero. If BART is what you want, check the signs carefully in the stations and pay attention to the cars themselves. The sleek silver and blue BART trains do not resemble Muni electric streetcars in the least. You purchase tickets for BART from machines at the station. Fares to and from any point in the city are $1.10 each way; outside the city, fares vary depending on how far down the line you go. You can't use Muni transfers, tokens, or passes on BART.

Getting Around by Cable Car

As a traveler to San Francisco, you simply must ride a cable car at least once. Three lines cross the downtown area. If you're in the mood for some scenery, take the **Powell-Hyde line,** which begins at Powell Street and ends at the turnaround across from Ghirardelli Square. The **Powell-Mason line** goes through North Beach and ends near Fisherman's Wharf. The **California Street line,** the least scenic, crests at Nob Hill and then makes its way to Van Ness Avenue. (The lines for the California Street cable cars are usually much shorter because the route isn't as twisty.) Rides are $2 one way, so buy a Muni Passport and take all three as often as you like. The pass is worth every penny. You may only board a cable car at specific, clearly marked stops.

Cable cars operate from 6:30 am to 12:30am, but I suggest taking one early in the day if you want to have a little elbow room as you ride; otherwise, as the day goes on, tourists jam-pack the cars. (See Chapter 26 for more on cable cars.)

Cable Car Routes

Catching a Taxi

You can easily get a taxi downtown, especially in front of hotels, but you have to call a cab to retrieve you almost anywhere else. Unfortunately, reaching the taxi companies by phone can take a while. Keep these numbers handy:

- ✓ **Desoto Cab** — ☎ **415-673-1414**
- ✓ **Luxor Cabs** — ☎ **415-282-4141**
- ✓ **Pacific** — ☎ **415-986-7220**
- ✓ **Veteran's Cab** — ☎ **415-552-1300**
- ✓ **Yellow Cab** — ☎ **415-626-2345**

Rates are about $2 for the first mile and $1.80 for each additional mile.

Motoring Around by Car

Drivers unfamiliar with the area often have a difficult time navigating the heavy downtown traffic and multitude of one-way streets. Add to these problems the lack of parking and heavy-handed metermaids, and leaving your car outside the city limits makes sense. However, if you plan to go over the Golden Gate or Bay bridges, or south to Monterey and Santa Cruz, a car may be useful.

Dealing with Rush Hour

During the week, traffic backs up on bridge approaches throughout the Financial District and downtown from 3pm until about 7pm. North Beach is usually busy from the late afternoon into the evenings, and because the streets bump into Columbus Avenue, navigating the area can be confusing. On the weekends, Lombard Street and Van Ness Avenue take the brunt of all the cars inching their way toward the Golden Gate Bridge. Getting through Chinatown's narrow, crowded streets by car is basically impossible during waking hours. If you must cross town, I suggest taking California Street past the Financial District.

For sanity's sake, avoid traveling north on the Golden Gate or Bay bridges between 3 and 7pm weekday afternoons. If you plan to drive to Point Reyes or the Wine Country, do not leave on a Friday after 2pm if at all possible. Traffic across the Golden Gate Bridge is generally awful on weekends, especially if the weather is nice. Leave before 10am if you must leave at all.

Driving by the rules

California law requires that both drivers and passengers wear seat belts. You may turn right at a red light (unless otherwise indicated) after yielding to traffic and pedestrians, and after making a complete stop. Cable cars and streetcars always have the right-of-way, as do pedestrians, especially if they use intersections and crosswalks. On Market Street, one lane is exclusively for buses unless you're making a right turn. Heed the signs.

Being cautious with red lights

Although turning right on a red light (unless marked otherwise) is allowed, be extremely careful when crossing on the green. San Francisco drivers have a wretched tendency to run red lights, so count to three slowly before entering an intersection just after the light has changed, and check oncoming traffic carefully.

Parking the car

I'm not going to take up space discussing the many parking regulations; just take my advice: Park in a garage. They are expensive, but they could save you some money in the long run because parking tickets start at $25!

Legal street parking spaces are next to unpainted curbs. Yellow, white, green, and red painted curbs are all off limits in general — the only exception being commercial zones (yellow curbs), which are okay to park in after delivery hours. Pay attention to the signs liberally posted on the streets. Be very aware of tow-away zones. You can't park on most streets downtown between 4pm and 6pm without running the high risk of having your car towed. Never park in front of a driveway. Otherwise, you'll find your rental at the **City Tow Lot** at 375 7th St., between Harrison and Folsom Streets (☎ **415-621-8605**), faster than you can blink. If your car isn't where you thought you left it, call ☎ **415–553-1235** to find out whether your vehicle has been towed or merely stolen. If your car has been towed to the city tow lot, you need to go there in person to pay the ticket and the storage charges (which vary depending on how long the car has been there). This misadventure will cost you at least $130, cash or credit card only.

Legal parking spots are hard to come by. If you're driving, park in a public garage or use the services of a valet — don't keep circling your prey hoping someone will drive off, unless you have a lot of time to spare. And if you do happen to find a legal space within walking distance of your destination, grab it immediately. By my calculations, walking distance is about four blocks, not two doors down.

Tips for improving your parking karma

Here are some tips for improving your parking karma:

- ✔ Carry quarters. Most parking meters accept nothing else.

- ✔ Watch the clock. Many crosstown downtown streets do not allow parking from 4 to 6pm. Get to the Financial District, Union Square, SoMa, or Nob Hill area a few minutes before 6pm to grab a great street parking space.

- ✔ Spring for valet parking. The extra money now may be worth avoiding the headache of finding a parking spot later.

- ✔ Check out public parking garages. Public parking garages are cheaper than privately owned ones. In North Beach, park in the garage on Vallejo Street (between Kearny and Green). In Chinatown, park at the Portsmouth Square garage on Kearny Street.

- ✔ Make note of street sweeping times. If you find street parking places galore in some outlying neighborhood, check posted signs for street sweeping times. That's generally the real reason for your good luck. Don't park without carefully checking the signs, unless you want to give the Department of Traffic a $25 donation.

- ✔ Stop "runaway" car syndrome. To keep your car from rolling away while you're parked on a hill, follow these easy steps: Put the car in gear, apply the hand brake, and *curb your wheels* — turn your wheels toward the curb when facing downhill and away from the curb when facing uphill. Curbing your wheels is the law!

Chapter 12

Keeping Track of Your Cash

* *

In This Chapter

▶ Getting cash in San Francisco

▶ What to do if your wallet is stolen

▶ Adding up the taxes

* *

*B*ring money. It costs a lot to vacation in San Francisco. Recent
Convention and Visitors Bureau statistics show that the average
daily per capita spending for all visitors, including those who stay with
relatives or friends, is a substantial $130.40. The major cost is for lodg-
ing, while food takes the next largest bite out of one's pocketbook.

There are always ways to keep costs down. By using public transportation rather than renting a car, you can save a small fortune, even if you
splurge on cabs now and then. As for food, there's such a wide variety
of low-cost ethnic restaurants and inexpensive cafes around town that
you can save some dough and still eat like a frugal gourmet. Two can
spend as little as $75 per night for a pleasant hotel room, depending on
the level of comfort and privacy you require.

Finding Cash in San Francisco

You're never far from an ATM on most commercial streets, and most
machines accept cards from any network. It's a good idea to withdraw
only as much money as you need every couple of days, so that you
don't have to carry a large amount of cash. Note, however, that a fee
ranging from 50¢ to $3 is imposed by just about every bank every time
you use the ATM in a different city. Your own bank may also charge you
a fee for using ATMs from other banks.

In San Francisco, **Bank of America, Wells Fargo Bank,** and **California
Federal Bank** have the largest ATM networks. They all charge fees —
$1.50 seems to be the going rate. Watch out for privately owned ATMs
at convenience stores, in shopping centers, or in non-bank businesses.
These machines usually charge more than bank ATMs.

Some people like to carry traveler's checks because they can be
replaced if lost or stolen, and they offer a sound alternative instead of
carrying a lot of cash at the beginning of the trip. ATMs have made

traveler's checks unnecessary, but if you prefer the security of traveler's checks, you can get them at almost any bank. **American Express** offers checks in denominations of $20, $50, $100, $500, and $1,000. You pay a service charge ranging from 1–4 percent, though AAA members can obtain checks without a fee at most AAA offices. You can also get American Express traveler's checks over the phone by calling ☎ **800-221-7282. Visa** (☎ **800-227-6811**) also offers traveler's checks, available at Citibank locations across the country and at several other banks. The service charge ranges between 1.5 and 2 percent; checks come in denominations of $50, $100, $500, and $1,000. **MasterCard** also offers traveler's checks; call ☎ **800-223-9920** for a location near you.

A safe way to carry money and provide a convenient record of all your travel expenses is with credit cards. You can even get cash advances with your credit card at any bank. And if you don't like waiting for a teller, you can get a cash advance at the ATM if you know your PIN number. If you need your PIN number (or didn't even know you had one), call the phone number on the back of your credit card and ask the bank to send it to you. It usually takes five to seven business days. Some banks will do it over the phone, although this transaction usually requires that you give them personal information to verify that you are the owner of the credit card in question.

Another hidden expense to contend with: Interest rates for cash advances are often significantly higher than rates for credit-card purchases. More importantly, you'll start paying interest on the advance *the moment you receive the cash.* On an airline-affiliated credit card, a cash advance does not earn frequent-flyer miles.

Dealing with the Nightmare of a Stolen Wallet

While it's pretty unlikely that you'll be the victim of a crime while on vacation, there are some talented pickpockets roaming the streets of San Francisco. And I can tell you from personal experience, it's not thrilling to discover that your wallet has magically disappeared, leaving you with only the change that's fallen to the bottom of your purse. So here's a reminder: Don't carry your wallet in a back pocket. If you must carry a handbag, hold it in front of you, not dangling from your shoulder. Don't leave your pocketbook or backpack unattended. Carry only as much cash as you need in a day and consider keeping your credit cards and driver's license in an inside pocket.

If the worst does happen and your wallet or purse is stolen, call the credit card company's emergency 800 number. In many cities, the company can get you an emergency credit card within a day or two. Some may also be able to wire you a cash advance off your credit card right away. The issuing bank's 800 number is usually on the back of the card, but that doesn't help much if the card was stolen. Write down the phone and credit-card numbers before you leave, and keep them in a safe place just in case. **Citicorp Visa's** U.S. emergency number is ☎ **800-645-6556. American Express** cardholders and traveler's check holders should call ☎ **800-221-7282** for all money emergencies. **MasterCard** holders should call ☎ **800-307-7309.**

If your wallet is stolen, chances are that you won't be seeing it again, and it's unlikely to be recovered by the police, either. Be sure to inform the police anyway, though, because you may need the police report number for credit-card or insurance purposes later.

Taxing Your Wallet

Along with the more obvious expenses, such as souvenir bridges and such, you have those little extras called taxes that add up. In our fair city, sales tax of 8.5 percent is added to just about everything but snacks and take-out food. Additionally, a hotel tax of 14 percent is added to the cost of your room. The good news is, most of it goes to fund local arts organizations, which makes it a bit more palatable, I hope.

Part IV
Dining in San Francisco

"OK Cookie-your venison in lingonberry sauce is good, as are your eggplant soufflé and the risotto with foie gras. But whoever taught you how to make a croquembouche should be shot!"

In this part . . .

An entire section devoted to food? You betcha. If not in a book devoted to the culinary center of the universe, or at least a good three-quarters of the U.S., then where? Read these chapters and you'll soon be able to discuss the intricacies of the local food scene as if you spend all your weekends dining in these parts. And if you prefer to eat and run, you'll get a head start with a chapter on food to go, and I don't mean fast food.

Chapter 13

Making the Scene: The Ins and Outs of Dining in San Francisco

● ●

In This Chapter

▶ Dining trends

▶ Getting the local flavor

▶ Remembering reservations

▶ Dressing the part

● ●

*W*hether you are a genuine gourmet, a fledgling foodie, or just a picky eater, San Francisco has more culinary options than you can shake a credit card at. But no matter where you rank yourself on the scale of adventuresome eating, there's no excuse to waste a meal in this city. Fast-food counters, chain restaurants, marketing enterprises masquerading as dining establishments — you will find them here, but a brand name doesn't guarantee quality eats. Instead, take advantage of the fresh food and skilled chefs around here, and I guarantee you'll dine to your heart's content.

Turning up the Heat

Restaurants debut in this town with great hoopla, but what's hot today may be cool or even out of business by the time you turn this page. At the moment, going out to dinner has as much to do with entertainment as with food. Eye-catching décor plays mightily in this trend, as does music — restaurants here keep many a clarinet player, not to mention jazz pianist, employed. There's even a hip dinner house that projects films on a patio wall, in case, I suppose, you haven't much to say to your date. On the other hand, the neo-nostalgic supper clubs that popped up all over town a few years ago had a hard time finding steady customers and have gone the way of creamed chicken and taffy pulls. But you're on vacation, so if dining and dancing sounds appealing, I'm still happy to oblige. See Chapter 14 for more restaurant suggestions.

The trendiest tables

San Francisco has no lack of sizzling white-tablecloth restaurants. It's still tough to get last-minute reservations at **Jardinère** (call ☎ 415-861-5555 if you want to try) or at two of the city's even more sophisticated purveyors of fine dining, **Fifth Floor** (☎ 415-348-1555) and **Gary Danko** (see Chapter 14). Call ahead, way, way ahead, if you have your heart set on supping at either of these bastions of chic. It can be equally challenging to wrangle a table at the intimate **Charles Nob Hill** (see Chapter 14) ever since Charles' chef and kitchen god Ron Siegel bested the Japan television phenom, "Iron Chef." For a romantic night on the town, however, it's worth giving it a shot.

Cooking up San Francisco cuisine

When it comes to cuisine, Asian influences continue to make themselves at home on Bay City menus. This is not odd considering the ethnic makeup of the city's population, but it may throw you for a loop the first time you see East meeting West on your dinner plate, such as when Ahi tuna brushed with wasabi butter is paired with rosemary-mashed potatoes. This cuisine is called fusion, not to be mistaken with confusion, and it's all the rage.

California cuisine, which is beginning to sound quaint, continues to have a presence here as well, although it's being usurped by "Modern American" or "New American" cuisine. California cuisine features fresh seasonal ingredients prepared in simple and light ways. It differs from traditional American-style cooking in method and presentation — in other words, you'll get an herb-roasted chicken, rather than a fried one. New American cuisine, on the other hand, also uses seasonal, American ingredients, but the preparations are influenced by whatever foreign cuisines interest the chef. Although the subtleties may be lost on those of us who don't deconstruct our meals, I mention this because many new restaurants describe their cooking in these terms. I fervently hope the lingo won't interfere with anyone's enjoyment of a meal.

Another welcome dining trend has to do with accommodating those of us who are organizationally challenged. Many excellent restaurants in town, including **3 Ring** and **Neo** (see Chapter 14) in the **Mission District,** and even **Gary Danko,** have counter seats for walk-ins. Others serve in their bar areas. This is the most opportune way to eat where you want to eat without reservations — but if there are more than two in your party, conversation may be limited to those sitting next to you.

Where the Locals Eat

With the exception of Fisherman's Wharf restaurants, which make gobs of money off the tourist trade, the locals are eating everywhere. It's amazing how often people go out to eat around here, but much of the population is young and gainfully employed, and they don't want to go home and cook for themselves after a long day designing Web pages or presenting to venture capitalists. And that's why visitors and residents alike must follow the rules and. . . .

The dining zones

Cafés and restaurants often congregate on certain blocks, making it easy to stroll down the street until an enticing odor, inviting menu, or open table calls out to you. One of my absolute favorite dining blocks is **Belden Place** in the **Financial District,** a one-block alley closed to traffic off Bush and Pine Streets between Kearny and Montgomery. The many restaurants packed together serve lunch and dinner indoors and out, depending on the weather. Two standouts on multicultural Belden are **Plouf,** a delightful French restaurant specializing in fish and shellfish, and **B-44,** a Spanish newcomer specializing in paella and Catalan dishes. All the establishments on Belden close on Sundays.

North Beach is awash in Italian cafes, Italian restaurants of all persuasions, and even a Southern French bistro, **Bandol,** on the corner of Stockton and Columbus. The family-style **La Felce** (1570 Stockton at Union) and **Capps Corner** are among the last of the breed, where complete meals are no understatement. You order a bottle of Chianti and watch as your table fills with an antipasti, then a tureen of minestrone, followed by huge platters of spaghetti, chicken cacciatore, and spumoni for dessert.

The **Mission District** gourmet zone is booming, but 16th Street between Valencia and Dolores is particularly chock-a-block with cafes, including the highly popular creperie **Ti Couz,** and a new, moderately priced Italian trattoria, **Il Cantuccio.** Mexican-food lovers should try **Pancho Villa,** which draws a crowd with its inexpensive and fresh burritos, tacos, and specialty platters. The mood in this neighborhood is casual and urban; it's populated by students, techies, a large Hispanic community, and a fair number of street people. Parking isn't easy, but there's a BART stop at 16th and Mission — a station to exit from quickly.

You can take the **N-Judah** streetcar to Irving Street and Ninth Avenue near Golden Gate Park to find another great couple of blocks of moderately priced and high quality restaurants. The **House** has a location here (see Chapter 14) as does **Chow** (see Chapter 14), and you can't go wrong at **P.J.'s Oyster Bar** on Irving Street at Ninth. There are also some good Japanese and Thai restaurants nearby, including **Hana Sushi,** 408 Irving St. between 5th and 6th Avenues.

Off-the-beaten-track restaurants

Restaurants are mining new territory as well, as evidenced by the dozens of places opening in neighborhoods most visitors would have shunned once upon a time. The blocks around **Dolores, Valencia,** and **Guerrero Streets** in the **Mission District** from 16th to 23rd Streets are just one example. Storefronts and former corner markets have become the domain of chefs hoping to create the next big thing food-wise, and some are succeeding to the point that there's always a line to snag a table (unless you've made reservations, and even then you'll probably have to wait). The popular **Slanted Door** (see Chapter 14) is one of the area's stars, while **Delfina** (see Chapter 14), a relatively new up-and-comer, had to quickly expand into the building next door in order to keep up with the multitudes who were begging for a taste from the Tuscan-Italian menu.

A section of **SoMa** that edges **Potrero Hill** is also drawing lots of interest from professional eaters and cooks. Mosey around **Florida** and **Mariposa Streets** for a taste of high style American cooking at **Gordon's House of Fine Eats** (see Chapter 14), but call for reservations first and take a cab, as the parking is either valet or impossible. But if there is one thing San Franciscans support with loyal fervor, it's their favorite neighborhood restaurant, no matter which neighborhood it's in.

San Francisco's Ethnic Eats

Certain neighborhoods in San Francisco are hubs for particular regional cuisines, as is the case in other big cities. You can find several ethnic enclaves, although Chinatown is the most obvious example. Head to North Beach, full of trattorias and bakeries, for authentic Italian. Not to be outdone, the Mission District serves up terrific, inexpensive taquerias and you can see Central American cafés alongside new gourmet restaurants. The tasty, authentic fare is worth the trip beyond downtown.

Head over to the **Richmond District** (see Chapter 10) where you'll notice a clutch of Russian bakeries, delicatessens, and restaurants, most notably **Katia, A Russian Tea Room,** 600 Fifth Ave., at Balboa Street (☎ **415-668-9292,** open Tuesday through Sunday for lunch and dinner). You can also find many more Asian and Chinese eateries in the **Richmond District.** Another excellent local Asian favorite, farther out in the fogbelt, is the **Mayflower,** 6255 Geary Blvd., near 27th Avenue (☎ **415-387-8338;** open daily for excellent dim sum, lunch, and dinner; call for evening reservations).

Japantown (see Chapter 10) is bargain-town when it comes to dining. Inside the **Japan Center** on Post Street (at Webster Street) are a number of noodle houses and sushi bars with more across the way. **Mifune** (☎ **415-922-0337**), upstairs in the Japan Center, is a perennial favorite for big bowls of udon noodles in broth with slices of beef or chicken and a smattering of vegetables competing for space. It's open until 10pm every day. **Isuzu,** at 1581 Webster (☎ **415-922-2290**), is a great spot for sushi or tempura.

All Dressed Up and Everywhere to Go

Most restaurants do not enforce a dress code nowadays, but if they do, they usually keep a small stock of ties on hand for gentlemen. For most places in town, casual wear is the norm. But among those who pay attention to such things, the trend is to dress up for certain venues with specific types of delicacies, such as any place that has a cheese course or a wine steward. Actually, there seem to be lots of hipster types who, when out on the town, look down on jeans in favor of a ventless sports coat or the vintage little black dress. While I doubt you will encounter attitude even in rooms once known for attitude (and I did my best to keep 'em out of this book), dressing the part never hurts. Besides, an element of formality is added when you change for dinner that makes an occasion out of a meal. In general, however, wearing trousers and a handsome sweater or jacket will do for any culinary spot your taste buds want to go.

Tips for Saving Money

Do not head to the nearest fast-food joint! Even if your travel budget doesn't allow for a $75 dinner for two every night. But you can limit the stress on your credit card and save your waistline if you share an appetizer and dessert, or order beer instead of wine, or better yet, skip the alcohol entirely. (The mark-up on wine is usually outrageous!) If you read all about a certain restaurant you're dying to try that's way too expensive, have lunch there instead of dinner, if it's open; the same quality food will be offered, but for less money. Or you can eat brunch or have an inexpensive picnic lunch and contribute your savings toward a really nice dinner. See Chapter 15 for places to get a quick but delicious meal or snack.

You can eat for under $10 per person at any of the ground floor restaurants at the Metreon on Mission and 4th Streets. There are four informal cafes serving sushi, salads, grilled meats, and Asian noodle dishes for lunch and dinner. Another $8.50 will get you into a movie upstairs. Another good choice for inexpensive, flavorful dishes is to try out one of the city's many ethnic restaurants. Head to the Mission District for cheap Mexican, Salvadoran, and Cambodian food; to Geary and Clement streets in the Richmond District for excellent Vietnamese, Chinese, and Thai; and to Japantown for tempura and noodles. Your wallet will thank you and your taste buds will still be satisfied.

Make Reservations

Am I repeating myself? I don't mean to, but I really want you to be able to experience some of the great restaurants while you're in town, and that might not be possible unless you reserve a table before you get here. It's not that the host or hostess takes pleasure in turning you away on a Friday night at 7pm. It's that they don't know whether a table is going to magically open up in the next 10 minutes, and did you notice all the other people drinking in the bar who also thought they could just amble in and get a table?

Besides picking up the phone, you can contact a number of restaurants through the Web site www.opentable.com. You might also put your hotel to work by requesting that they assist you with dinner reservations. Of course, you absolutely can waltz in the door and winsomely request a table, but be prepared to nurse your glass of chardonnay for an hour on a busy night. You could also show a little chuzpah like my friend Josie, who has been known to march up to the host, look him or her in the eye and announce she has reservations, even when that's not entirely accurate. The caveat here is to make sure your dining partners don't sweat under pressure.

Chapter 14

San Francisco's Fine Food Fare

In This Chapter

▶ Breaking down restaurants by price, location, and cuisine

▶ Finding a great meal

So, what are you in the mood for? Chinese? California-Mediterranean? Catalan tapas? Do you want to dine near your hotel or venture farther afield? Are you looking to rekindle a little romance? Do you need to satisfy a range of tastes? There's no reason to go hungry seeking the right restaurant. Read the listings below, and when you start to salivate, then it's time to make reservations. Actually, the recommendations below only scratch the surface of my favorite places to dine in San Francisco. What you have here is a representative cross section of the best the city has to offer, in a variety of price ranges and neighborhoods.

 While I've tried to peer into the future and only include those eateries I believe will be in business when you arrive, confirm your reservations or call before heading over with your stomach growling. I'd rather you be briefly disappointed by a disconnected number than a deserted storefront.

Finding a Restaurant by Price, Location, and Cuisine

The following indexes give you a brief overview of my dining picks. Each restaurant is categorized according to location, price, and cuisine — and unless the kitchen is having an off night, there isn't a lemon in the bunch.

The dollar signs attached to the restaurant recommendations give you an idea how much you'll have to shell out for dinner for one person, including appetizer, main course, dessert, one drink, tax, and tip. If a place is marked with $, a meal there will run under $25. At $$ places, expect to spend between $25 and $40. Restaurants with $$$ will cost from $40 to $50. Feel like going for broke? Expect to fork over lots more than $50 at places with $$$$.

Index by price

$

Bistro Aix (FRENCH, The Marina/
  Cow Hollow)
Buca di Beppo (FAMILY-STYLE ITALIAN,
  SoMa)
Chow (AMERICAN, The Castro)
Kay Cheung (CHINESE, Chinatown)
Kelly's Mission Rock (AMERICAN,
  China Basin)
Lichee Garden (CHINESE, Chinatown)
L'Osteria del Forno (RUSTIC ITALIAN,
  North Beach)
Pazzia (NORTHERN ITALIAN, SoMa)
R&G Lounge (CHINESE, Chinatown)

$$

Café Marimba (MEXICAN, The Marina/
  Cow Hollow)
Delfina (TUSCAN ITALIAN, Mission
  District)
E&O Trading Company (PAN ASIAN,
  Union Square)
Enrico's Sidewalk Cafe (CALIFORNIA/
  ITALIAN, North Beach)
Fringale (FRENCH, SoMa)
Gordon's House of Fine Eats (AMERICAN,
  Mission District)
Grand Cafe (CALIFORNIA, Union Square)
Green's (VEGETARIAN, The Marina/
  Cow Hollow)
Hayes Street Grill (SEAFOOD,
  Civic Center, Hayes Valley)
The House (CALIFORNIA/
  ASIAN, North Beach)
Il Fornaio (ITALIAN, The Embarcadero)
Kelly's Mission Rock (AMERICAN,
  China Basin)
Le Charm (FRENCH, SoMa)
Slanted Door (VIETNAMESE,
  Mission District)
Tadich Grill (SEAFOOD, Financial
  District)

Thirsty Bear (SPANISH, SoMa)
3 Ring (SOUTHERN FRENCH, Mission
  District)
Zuni Cafe (CALIFORNIA, Civic Center,
  Hayes Valley)

$$$

Alfred's (STEAK HOUSE, Financial
  District)
Foreign Cinema (NEW AMERICAN/
  FRENCH, Mission District)
Jardinière (CALIFORNIA/FRENCH,
  Civic Center/Hayes Valley)
Grand Cafe (CALIFORNIA, Union
  Square)
Kokkari (GREEK, Financial District)
Le Colonial (FRENCH VIETNAMESE,
  Union Square)
Moose's (CALIFORNIA/
  MEDITERRANEAN, North Beach)
Neo (NEW AMERICAN/
  MEDITERRANEAN, Mission District)
Oritalia (ASIAN/MEDITERRANEAN,
  Union Square)
Piaf's (FRENCH, Civic Center/
  Hayes Valley)
Rose Pistola (ITALIAN, North Beach)
Scala's Bistro (ITALIAN, Union Square)
Splendido (CALIFORNIA/
  MEDITERRANEAN, The Embarcadero)

$$$$

Boulevard (AMERICAN, The
  Embarcadero)
Charles-Nob Hill (NEW AMERICAN,
  Nob Hill)
Gary Danko (NEW AMERICAN/FRENCH,
  Telegraph Hill)
Hawthorne Lane (CALIFORNIA/
  ASIAN, SoMa)

Index by location

The Castro
Chow — AMERICAN, $

China Basin
Kelly's Mission Rock — AMERICAN, $–$$

Chinatown
Kay Cheung — CHINESE, $
Lichee Garden — CHINESE, $
R&G Lounge — CHINESE, $

Civic Center/Hayes Valley
Hayes Street Grill — SEAFOOD, $$
Jardinière — CALIFORNIA/FRENCH, $$$
Piaf's — FRENCH, $$$
Zuni Cafe — CALIFORNIA, $$

The Embarcadero
Boulevard — AMERICAN, $$$$
Il Fornaio — ITALIAN, $$
Splendido — CALIFORNIA/ MEDITERRANEAN, $$$

Financial District
Alfred's Steakhouse — STEAK HOUSE, $$$
Kokkari — GREEK, $$$
Tadich Grill — SEAFOOD, $$

The Marina/Cow Hollow
Bistro Aix — FRENCH, $
Cafe Marimba — MEXICAN, $$
Green's — VEGETARIAN, $$

The Mission District
Delfina — TUSCAN ITALIAN, $$
Foreign Cinema — NEW AMERICAN/ FRENCH, $$$
Gordon's House of Fine Eats — AMERICAN, $$

Neo — NEW AMERICAN/ MEDITERRANEAN, $$$
Slanted Door — VIETNAMESE, $$
3 Ring — SOUTHERN FRENCH, $$

Nob Hill
Charles-Nob Hill — NEW AMERICAN, $$$$

North Beach
Enrico's Sidewalk Cafe — CALIFORNIA/ ITALIAN, $$
The House — CALIFORNIA/ASIAN, $$
L'Osteria del Forna — RUSTIC ITALIAN, $
Moose's — CALIFORNIA/ MEDITERRANEAN, $$$
Rose Pistola — ITALIAN, $$$

South of Market — SoMa)
Buca di Beppo — FAMILY-STYLE ITALIAN, $
Fringale — FRENCH, $$
Hawthorne Lane — CALIFORNIA/ ASIAN, $$$$
Le Charm — FRENCH, $$
Pazzia — NORTHERN ITALIAN, $
Thirsty Bear — SPANISH, $$

Fisherman's Wharf
Gary Danko — NEW AMERICAN/ FRENCH, $$$$

Union Square
E&O Trading Company — PAN ASIAN, $$
Grand Cafe — CALIFORNIA, $$–$$$
Le Colonial — FRENCH VIETNAMESE, $$$
Oritalia — ASIAN/MEDITERRANEAN, $$$
Scala's Bistro — ITALIAN, $$$

San Francisco Dining

Alfred's **26**
Bandol **14**
Belden Place **29**
Bistro Aix **2**
Boulevard **23**
Buca di Beppo **37**
Café Marimba **1**
Capp's Corner **10**
Charles-Nob Hill **27**
Chow **4**
Enrico's Sidewalk Cafe **17**
E&O Trading Company **30**
Fringale **39**
Gary Danko **9**
Grand Cafe **33**
Green's **3**
Hawthorne Lane **34**
Hayes Street Grill **7**
The House **16**
Il Fornaio **19**
Jardinière **8**
Kay Cheung **18**
Kelly's Mission Rock **40**
Kokkari Estiatorio **20**
La Felce **12**
Le Charm **38**
Le Colonial **32**
Lichee Garden **15**
L'Osteria del Forna **11**
Moose's **12**
Oritalia **28**
Pazzia **36**
Piaf's **5**
R&G Lounge **25**
Rose Pistola **13**
Scala's Bistro **31**
Splendido **22**
Tadish Grill **24**
Thirsty Bear **35**
Yank Sing **21**
Zuni Cafe **6**

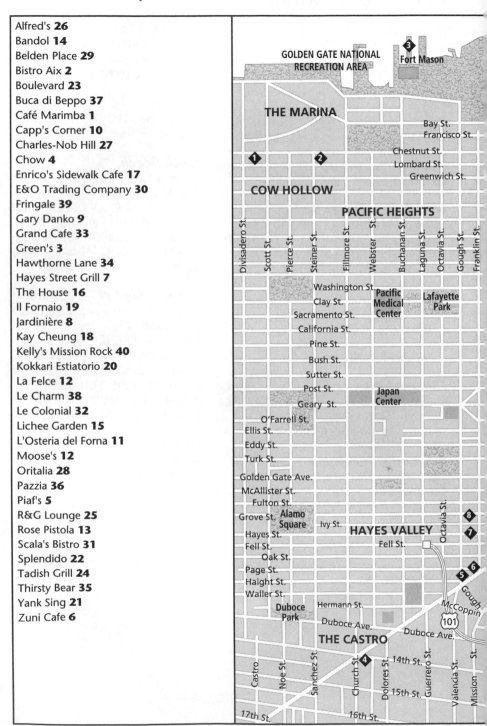

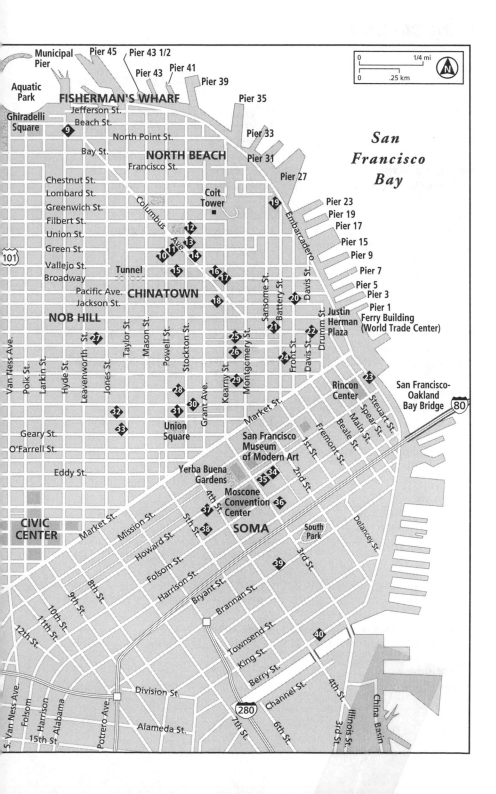

Municipal Pier
Pier 45
Pier 43 1/2
Pier 43
Pier 41
Pier 39
Pier 35
Aquatic Park
FISHERMAN'S WHARF
Jefferson St.
Beach St.
Pier 33
Ghiradelli Square
North Point St.
Pier 31
Bay St.
NORTH BEACH
Francisco St.
Pier 27
Chestnut St.
Lombard St.
Greenwich St.
Filbert St.
Union St.
Green St.
Vallejo St.
Broadway
Columbus Ave.
Coit Tower
Pier 23
Pier 19
Pier 17
Pier 15
Pier 9
Pier 7
Pier 5
Pier 3
Pier 1

San Francisco Bay

101

Tunnel
Pacific Ave.
Jackson St.
CHINATOWN

NOB HILL
Van Ness Ave.
Polk St.
Larkin St.
Hyde St.
Leavenworth St.
Jones St.
Taylor St.
Mason St.
Powell St.
Stockton St.
Grant Ave.
Kearny St.
Montgomery St.
Sansome St.
Battery St.
Front St.
Davis St.
Drumm St.

Justin Herman Plaza
Ferry Building (World Trade Center)

Geary St.
O'Farrell St.
Union Square
Eddy St.

CIVIC CENTER
Market St.
Mission St.
Howard St.
Folsom St.
Harrison St.
8th St.
9th St.
10th St.
11th St.
12th St.
7th St.
4th St.
5th St.
6th St.
3rd St.
2nd St.
1st St.
Fremont St.
Beale St.
Main St.
Spear St.
Steuart St.

San Francisco Museum of Modern Art
Yerba Buena Gardens
Moscone Convention Center
SOMA
South Park

Rincon Center
San Francisco-Oakland Bay Bridge
80

Bryant St.
Brannan St.
Townsend St.
King St.
Berry St.
Channel St.
Division St.
Alameda St.
15th St.
Delancey St.
China Basin
Illinois St.
3rd St.

280

S. Van Ness Ave.
Folsom
Harrison
Alabama
Potrero Ave.

0   1/4 mi
0   .25 km
N

Index by cuisine

American
Boulevard — The Embarcadero, $$$$
Chow — The Castro, $
Gordon's House of Fine Eats — Mission District, $$
Kelly's Mission Rock — China Basin, $–$$

Asian/Mediterranean
Oritalia — Union Square, $$$

California
Grand Cafe — Union Square, $$–$$$
Zuni Cafe — Civic Center/Hayes Valley, $$

California/Asian
Hawthorne Lane — SoMa, $$$$
The House — North Beach, $$

California/French
Jardinière — Civic Center/ Hayes Valley, $$$

California/Italian
Enrico's Sidewalk Cafe — North Beach, $$

California/Mediterranean
Splendido — The Embarcadero, $$$
Moose's — North Beach, $$$

Chinese
Kay Cheung — Chinatown, $
Lichee Garden — Chinatown, $
R&G Lounge — Chinatown, $

French
Bistro Aix — The Marina/Cow Hollow, $
Fringale — SoMa, $$
Le Charm — SoMa, $$
Piaf's — Civic Center/Hayes Valley, $$$
3 Ring — SOUTHERN, Mission District, $$

French-Vietnamese
Le Colonial — Union Square, $$$

Greek
Kokkari — Financial District, $$$

Italian
Buca di Beppo — FAMILY-STYLE, SoMa, $
Delfina — TUSCAN, Mission District, $$
Il Fornaio — The Embarcadero, $$
L'Osteria del Forno — RUSTIC, North Beach, $
Pazzia — NORTHERN, SoMa, $
Rose Pistola — North Beach, $$$
Scala's Bistro — Union Square, $$$

Mexican
Café Marimba — The Marina/ Cow Hollow, $$

New American
Charles-Nob Hill — Nob Hill, $$$$
Foreign Cinema — FRENCH, Mission District, $$$
Gary Danko — FRENCH, Russian Hill, $$$$
Neo — MEDITERRANEAN, Mission District, $$$

Pan Asian
E&O Trading Company — Union Square, $$

Seafood
Hayes Street Grill — Civic Center/ Hayes Valley, $$
Tadich Grill — Union Square, $$

Spanish
Thirsty Bear — SoMa, $$

Steak House
Alfred's — Financial District, $$$

Vegetarian
Green's — The Marina/Cow Hollow, $$

Vietnamese
Slanted Door — Mission District, $$)

Dining Near North Beach & Chinatown

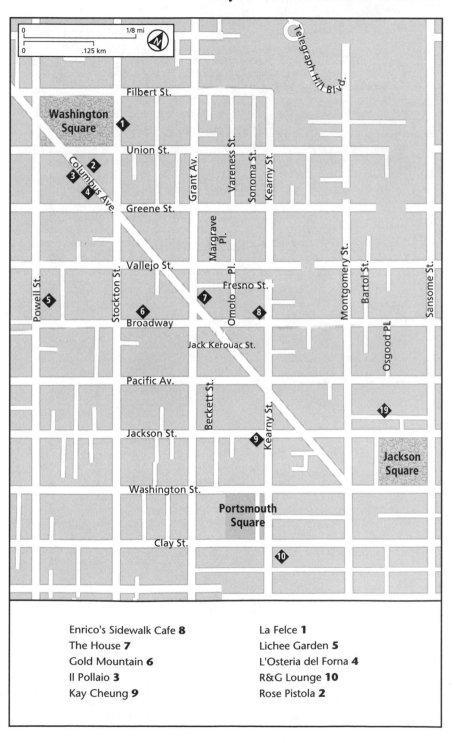

Enrico's Sidewalk Cafe **8**
The House **7**
Gold Mountain **6**
Il Pollaio **3**
Kay Cheung **9**

La Felce **1**
Lichee Garden **5**
L'Osteria del Forna **4**
R&G Lounge **10**
Rose Pistola **2**

Dining Near Union Square, SoMa & Nob Hill

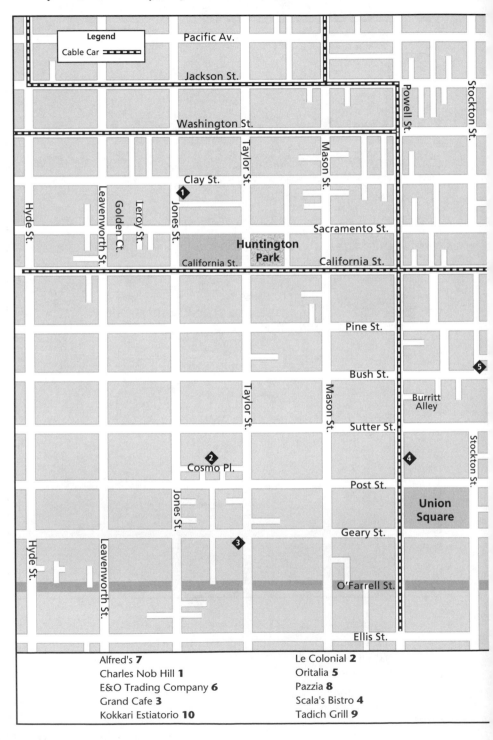

Alfred's **7**
Charles Nob Hill **1**
E&O Trading Company **6**
Grand Cafe **3**
Kokkari Estiatorio **10**

Le Colonial **2**
Oritalia **5**
Pazzia **8**
Scala's Bistro **4**
Tadich Grill **9**

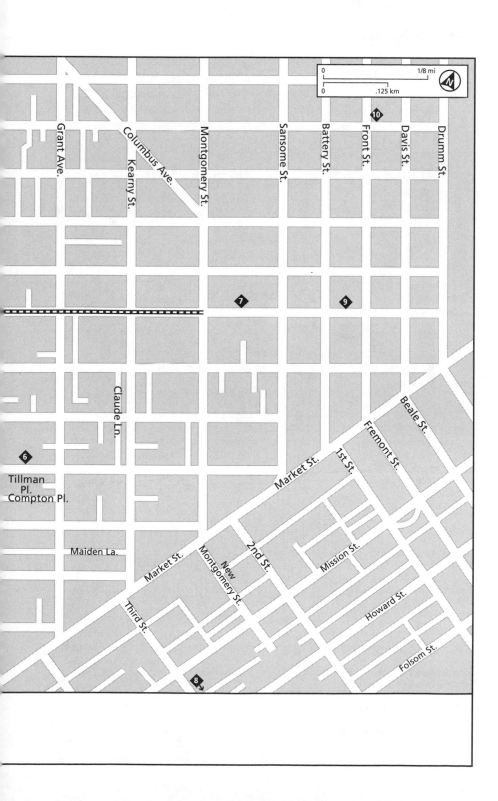

The Mission District

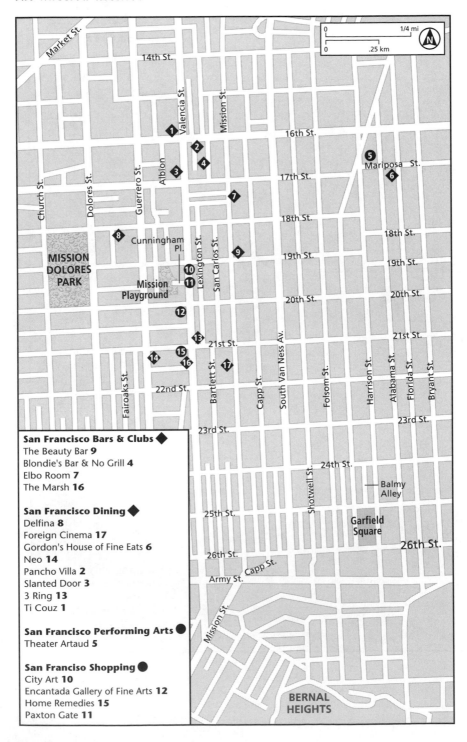

San Francisco Bars & Clubs ◆
The Beauty Bar **9**
Blondie's Bar & No Grill **4**
Elbo Room **7**
The Marsh **16**

San Francisco Dining ◆
Delfina **8**
Foreign Cinema **17**
Gordon's House of Fine Eats **6**
Neo **14**
Pancho Villa **2**
Slanted Door **3**
3 Ring **13**
Ti Couz **1**

San Francisco Performing Arts ●
Theater Artaud **5**

San Franciso Shopping ●
City Art **10**
Encantada Gallery of Fine Arts **12**
Home Remedies **15**
Paxton Gate **11**

Eating to Your Heart's Content: A Complete Listing of Restaurants

Alfred's

$$$ Financial District   STEAK HOUSE

There are a handful of excellent steak houses in town, but Alfred's is the oldest and most San Francisco-ish. The burgundy leather booths, crystal chandeliers, and aproned waiters delivering perfectly grilled steaks, baked potatoes with sour cream and chives, and lusciously creamed spinach really do make the olden days appear golden.

659 Merchant Alley between Montgomery and Kearny Streets. ☎ 415-781-7058. Reservations recommended, especially on weekends. Cable Car: California line to Kearny and walk north 3 ½ blocks, or Powell line to Washington and walk east to Kearny. Main courses: $23–$28. AE, CB, DC, MC, V. Open: lunch Tues–Fri; dinner nightly.

Bistro Aix

$ The Marina/Cow Hollow   BISTRO FRENCH

This casual French-style bistro caters to lucky neighborhood residents who don't have to look for parking. Dining alfresco is a delight during any season in the heated, covered patio out back — it's the perfect setting to enjoy tasty plates of crispy, skinned chicken, fresh pasta, grilled sirloin, and perfectly dressed salads. The $13.95 prix-fixe menu, served from 6 to 8pm Sunday through Thursday, would be a bargain even if the food were half as good.

3340 Steiner St., between Chestnut and Lombard Streets. ☎ 415-202-0100. Reservations recommended. Bus: the 22-Fillmore, 28-19th Ave., 30-Stockton, and 43-Masonic all stop close by. Main courses: $12–$14; prix-fixe menu $13.95. AE, DC, MC, V. Open: dinner nightly.

Boulevard

$$$$ The Embarcadero   AMERICAN

Housed in an elegant turn-of-the-century building with views of the Bay Bridge (from front tables only), Boulevard serves consistently excellent and generous plates of seasonal comfort food, such as tender lamb shanks accompanied by a flavorful artichoke risotto. Noisy but comfortable, the place caters to an upscale, older crowd. Counter and bar seating is available for those without reservations, but call three or four weeks in advance for a prime-time table.

One Mission St., at Steuart St. ☎ 415-543-6084. Reservations advised three weeks in advance. Muni: Take any Muni streetcar to the Embarcadero Station and walk 1 block east to Mission St. Main courses: $22–$35. AE, CB, DC, D, MC, V. Open: lunch weekdays; bistro menu 2:30–5:15pm weekdays; dinner nightly.

Buca di Beppo

$ SoMa   FAMILY-STYLE ITALIAN

Sinatra favorites compete with opera selections on the sound system of this fun, '50s-themed, family-style Southern Italian eatery. Be prepared for the huge plates of tasty pasta, chicken marsala, and salad — they're meant to be shared at tables roomy enough for six or more. A party of two may feel conspicuous surrounded by the bounty.

855 Howard St., between 4th and 5th Streets. ☎ *415-543-7673. Reservations a must unless you're content to wait. Bus: 27-Bryant or 30-Stockton. Main courses: $16–$18 (serve 4). MC, V. Open: nightly.*

Café Marimba

$$ The Marina/Cow Hollow   MEXICAN

Disregard any preconceived notions of Mexican cuisine that those Tex-Mex pretender chain restaurants have stamped on your brain. When you visit this colorful but noisy restaurant, you're in for a treat. The flavorful, fresh fish and grilled meats arrive at your table in authentic stone mortars, putting Café Marimba in a class of its own. It's a great choice for a late lunch after touring the Presidio or the Palace of Fine Arts.

2317 Chestnut St., between Scott and Divisidero Streets. ☎ *415-776-1506. Reservations recommended on weekends. Bus: 30-Stockton. Main courses: $5–$13. AE, MC, V. Open: lunch Tues–Sun; dinner nightly; brunch weekends.*

Dining and dancing

The **Top of the Mark** (☎ 415-616-6916), in the Mark Hopkins Intercontinental Hotel, 1 Nob Hill, at Mason and California Streets, has it all — views, music from 9pm, dancing, and a convivial crowd of suits. The hotel recently began serving a $39 prix-fixe dinner on Friday and Saturday nights; with 7:30 reservations, a night on the town is a done deal. **Harry Denton's Starlight Room**, in the Sir Francis Drake Hotel on Union Square, 450 Powell St., (☎ 415-395-8595), attracts tons of hotel guests and locals who appreciate the Starlight Orchestra and the adult prom night atmosphere. It's a glorious room for drinking expensive glasses of whatever, dancing, and supping. A more youthful group congregates at **Cafe du Nord**, 2170 Market St. at Sanchez (☎ 415-861-5016). This basement level club serves basic food (salad, sandwiches, chicken, steak) but the draw is the live music. Fridays are particularly popular, when jazz singer Lavay Smith and her Red Hot Skillet Lickers raise the roof.

Charles-Nob Hill

$$$$ Nob Hill   NEW AMERICAN/FRENCH

Two small, elegantly appointed dining rooms tucked inside a swanky apartment building give Charles an extra-intimate feel. Dishes are exquisitely prepared and presented, from the tiny appetizers brought gratis by the mannerly waitstaff, to the plate of miniature sweets that ends each meal. Living large? Consider the traditional caviar service, but save room for such memorable main courses as black bass served over braised short rib ravioli. Walk-ins are served in the bar, so rejoice all ye who live in the moment.

1250 Jones St., at Clay St. ☎ *415/771-5400. Reservations required four weeks in advance. Cable car: California line. Main courses: $25–$34. AE, DC, MC, V. Open: dinner Tues–Sun.*

Chow

$ The Castro   AMERICAN

If there weren't so many people eagerly waiting for a table at this noisy postmodern bar and ungrill, it might qualify as a quick bite place. But once you score a table, it's more fun to savor the straightforward pasta dishes, brick-oven roasted chicken, or thin-crusted pizzas. A great price performer, too. A second location, Park Chow, is on Ninth Street near Golden Gate Park.

215 Church St., at Market St. ☎ *415-552-2469. Reservations not accepted. Muni Metro: Take J-Church or F-Market to Church St. Main courses: $6.50–$12.95. MC, V. Open: lunch and dinner daily.*

Enrico's Sidewalk Cafe

$$ North Beach   CALIFORNIA/ITALIAN

Dining on a patio with a view of the bawdy section of Broadway would liven up any evening, but at this friendly, cosmopolitan bar/restaurant you also get live jazz and a menu of knockout seasonal fish and meat dishes. Casual and fun.

504 Broadway, at Kearny St. ☎ *415-982-6223. Reservations recommended. Cable car: Powell-Mason line. Bus: 30-Stockton. Main courses: $10–$22. AE, DC, MC, V. Open: lunch and dinner daily.*

Delfina

$$ Mission District   TUSCAN ITALIAN

This wonderfully friendly and casual newcomer defines what's incredible about the city's neighborhood restaurants. Dishes such as chianti-braised beef ravioli, quail with spring onion-chanterelle bread salad, or roasted beets with local goat cheese are full of flavor and feature the freshest ingredients, a smattering of herbs, and brilliant preparation. Make the effort to eat here.

3621 18th St. between Dolores and Guerrero Streets. ☎ 415-552-4055. Reservations necessary three weeks in advance. Muni: J-Church. Main courses: $10–$15. MC, V. Open: nightly.

E&O Trading Company

$$ Union Square PAN ASIAN

This grown-up "Tiki" room caters to a mixed bag of locals and visitors who happily munch on Southeast-Asian–style skewered meats or mushrooms, *nan* (Indian bread), and savory but not exciting main courses. The drinks are oversized (and expensive), and the beer is microbrewed. Live jazz starts around 8:30pm.

314 Sutter St., at Stockton St. ☎ 415-693-0303. Reservations recommended. Cable car: Powell-Hyde or Powell-Mason line. Main courses: $7.75–$20. AE, DC, DISC, MC, V. Open: lunch and dinner daily.

Foreign Cinema

$$$ Mission District NEW AMERICAN/FRENCH

Mission District regulars nearly lost their *empanadas* when the shiny chic Foreign Cinema opened in 1999. The expansive dining room, and outdoor patio where foreign films are screened on a concrete wall, would throw anyone at first, but an elegant plate of escargots or perhaps some oysters from the raw bar helps to lower any resistance to the inevitable changes in the neighborhood. Be advised that the bench seating outside isn't entirely comfortable. Ask for a chair.

2534 Mission St., between 21st and 22nd Streets. ☎ 415-648-7600. Reservations highly recommended. BART: 24th St. station. Main Courses: $11–$19. AE, MC, V. Open: dinner Tues–Sun; late-night menu until 1am.

Fringale

$$ SoMa FRENCH BASQUE

Set a few blocks east of Yerba Buena Center, away from the madness of Union Square and North Beach, this intimate, *très* French bistro is especially warm and welcoming on a cold night. Plates of steamed mussels, pork tenderloin confit, and rack of lamb, among other delights, are prepared with an eye toward simplicity and taste.

570 Fourth St., between Brannan and Bryant Streets. ☎ 415-543-0573. Reservations necessary. Bus: 45-Union/Stockton or 30-Stockton. Main courses: $13–$21. AE, MC, V. Open: lunch Mon–Fri; dinner Mon–Sat.

Gary Danko

$$$$ Russian Hill NEW AMERICAN/FRENCH

The ovens were barely lit at this new fine dining center before the food and wine cognoscenti descended to proclaim Danko's among the best restaurants not only in town, but in the country. You choose your own three-course (or more if you like) meal from the menu — perhaps a composed lobster salad followed by day boat scallops and ending with a magno Napoleon or selections from the cheese cart — then let the kitchen make magic. If you don't mind eating at the bar, you can actually walk in without reservations.

800 Northpoint at Hyde St. ☎ 415-749-2060. Reservations advised four weeks in advance. Cable car: Powell-Hyde line. Prix fixe menu from $51. AE, MC, V. Open: dinner nightly.

Gordon's House of Fine Eats

$$ Mission District   AMERICAN

So maybe your mom served corn flake-fried chicken, but trust me, it's nothing like the tender, moist, and savory basketful delivered at this industrial-chic trend center. The seasonal menu includes more sophisticated items, too — a perfectly executed asparagus eggroll, twice-cooked crab in black bean sauce, pork osso buco — and everything's delicious. You can sit at the counter overlooking the kitchen if you arrive without reservations.

500 Florida St. at Mariposa St. (take a cab). ☎ 415-861-8900. Reservations necessary two weeks in advance. Main courses: $8–$20. CB, DISC, MC, V. Open: Mon–Fri for lunch; dinner nightly; live music after 9pm Tues–Sat.

Grand Cafe

$$–$$$ Union Square   CALIFORNIA

Living up to its name in every respect, this vast, high-ceilinged, muraled bistro is abuzz with activity and energy. People gravitate here pre- and post-theater for brick-oven pizzas, roasts, grilled fish and chicken, and desserts. They don't have a children's menu per se, but kids get crayons and can order from the Petit Cafe offerings.

501 Geary St., at Taylor St. ☎ 415-292-0101. Reservations accepted. Cable car: Powell-Hyde or Powell-Mason line. Bus: 2-Clement, 3-Jackson, 4-Sutter, 27-Bryant, or 38-Geary. Main courses: $14–$22. AE, CB, DC, DISC, MC, V. Open: breakfast, lunch, and dinner daily; weekend brunch.

Green's

$$ The Marina/Cow Hollow   VEGETARIAN

If you haven't eaten in a gourmet vegetarian restaurant, or if your vegetarian dining has been limited to alfalfa sprouts, you're in for a marvelous new culinary experience. The Saturday evening prix-fixe menu is a deal, especially when you see the gorgeous views that come with the meal. This is a good destination for lunch if you are walking along the Marina.

Fort Mason, Bldg. A, off Marina Blvd. at Buchanan St. ☎ 415-771-6222. Reservations highly recommended at least 2 weeks in advance. Bus: Take the 30-Stockton to Laguna and transfer to the 28-19th Ave. into Fort Mason. Main courses: $10–$14; prix-fixe menu (Sat only) $38. DISC, MC, V. Open: lunch Tues–Sat; dinner Mon–Sat; Sun brunch.

Hawthorne Lane

$$$$ SoMa   CALIFORNIA/ASIAN

The chefs who made Postrio famous left a few years ago to open this classy, art-filled restaurant in a one-block alley near the Museum of Modern Art. You'll probably feel more comfortable here if you dress up a bit — to meet the elegant food on an equal footing.

22 Hawthorne Lane, off Howard St. between Second and Third Streets. ☎ *415-777-9779. Reservations recommended two weeks in advance. Muni: Any Muni streetcar to Montgomery St. Station. Bus: 12-Folsom, 30-Stockton, or 45-Union/Stockton. Main courses: $24–$30. CB, DC, DISC, JCB, MC, V. Open: lunch Mon–Fri; dinner nightly.*

Hayes Street Grill

$$ Civic Center/Hayes Valley   SEAFOOD

This is one of the better fish restaurants in the city. Whatever's been caught that morning will be prepared simply, carefully, and with integrity. The non-fish selections are equally delicious, and walk-ins can eat at the bar. The restaurant quiets down considerably around 8pm when the opera/symphony/ballet-goers dash off to the show.

320 Hayes St., between Gough and Franklin Streets. ☎ *415-863-5545. Reservations recommended. Muni Metro: Take any Muni Metro to the Civic Center Station. Main courses: $13.50–$18.25. AE, DC, DISC, MC, V. Open: lunch Mon–Fri; dinner nightly.*

The House

$$ North Beach   CALIFORNIA/ASIAN

This tiny place is casually worldly and decidedly un-Italian, despite its North Beach location. East meets West in the House kitchen, and the relationship is pleasing and harmonious. Dishes such as taro spring rolls or grilled Chilean sea bass bathed in a ginger soy sauce grace the menu, along with daily specials. The other location on Ninth Avenue, near Golden Gate Park, gives you another chance to try this fresh, seasonal cuisine.

1230 Grant St., near Columbus Ave. ☎ *415-986-8612. Reservations recommended. Cable car: Powell-Mason line. Bus: 30-Stockton. Main courses: $11–$17. AE, DC, MC, V. Open: lunch and dinner Tues–Sat.*

Il Fornaio

$$ The Embarcadero   REGIONAL ITALIAN

Although part of a small chain, this expansive, popular Italian trattoria usually hits the mark with tender pastas, thin-crusted pizzas, and savory meat dishes. Don't overlook the interesting regional specials that supplement the menu every month. A child's menu is available, and afterward the kids can run around the fountain in Levi's Plaza.

Levi's Plaza, 1265 Battery St., between Greenwich and Union Streets.
☎ *415-986-0100. Reservations recommended. Bus: 42-Downtown Loop. Main courses: $8.75–$21.95. AE, DC, MC, V. Open: breakfast, lunch, and dinner daily.*

Jardinière

$$$ Civic Center/Hayes Valley   CALIFORNIA/FRENCH

Head to Jardinière for sophisticated surroundings, a lively bar, and highly touted celebrity-chef food that exceeds expectations. (The duck confit is heaven-sent.) This is where the upscale crowd sups before the opera, ballet, or symphony. A jazz combo plays upstairs Sunday through Tuesday.

300 Grove St., at Franklin St. ☎ *415-861-5555. Reservations necessary. Muni: Any streetcar to the Civic Center Station. Main courses: $20–$28. AE, DC, DISC, MC, V. Open: dinner nightly; bar menu until midnight.*

Kay Cheung

$ Chinatown   CHINESE

For a fresh and interesting selection of dim sum or live seafood, this small, pleasant room can't be beat for quality or price. Most of the tables seat 8, so you'll probably end up sitting with Chinatown regulars — a terrific opportunity to chat up folks who really know their dumplings.

615 Jackson St., at Kearny St. ☎ *415-989-6838. Reservations accepted. Bus: 15-Third. AE, MC, V. Main courses: $6–$11. Open: dim sum, lunch and dinner daily.*

Kelly's Mission Rock

$–$$ China Basin   AMERICAN

For an inexpensive lunch of pizza, sandwiches, and salad, order at the ground floor counter and take a table dockside. Even if the sun isn't shining anywhere else, it'll be shining here. With bay views and music Thursday through Saturday afternoons, you'll have a great time. Upstairs, or "topside," the menu is fancier and more expensive. This is a great location for brunch.

817 China Basin Rd. off Third St. ☎ *415-626-5355. Reservations accepted "topside." Bus: 15-Third. Main courses: Cafe $4.95–$6; Restaurant $7.95–$24. AE, MC, V. Open: lunch Tues–Fri; brunch Sat–Sun; dinner Thurs–Sat. Cafe open daily.*

Kokkari Estiatorio

$$$ Financial District   GREEK

Your average Mediterranean shipping tycoon would feel perfectly comfortable underneath the beamed ceilings of this richly appointed "taverna." The California-meets-Greek menu does feature some familiar dishes, such as moussaka, but takes them to Mount Olympus-style heights. Order the *Yiaourti Graniti* (yogurt sorbet with tangerine ice) for dessert even if you're full.

200 Jackson St. at Front St. ☎ *415-981-0983. Reservations necessary. Main courses: $14–$27. AE, DC, MC, V. Open: lunch weekdays; dinner Mon–Sat.*

Le Charm

$$ SoMa FRENCH

Bargain-hunter alert! The Parisian-inspired 3-course prix fixe dinner for under $25 is the real deal at this popular little sponge-painted bistro. Diners choose from a menu that includes a lovely roasted quail served on salad greens, a fragrant leg of lamb with flageolet beans, and a soup of fresh apricots and cherries for dessert. Le Charm is also a winner for lunch, especially if the weather is decent and you can get a table outside in the garden.

315 Fifth St. between Folsom and Howard Streets (near Yerba Buena Center). ☎ *415-546-6128. Reservations accepted. Main courses: $11–$14. MC, V. Open: lunch weekdays; dinner Mon–Sat.*

Le Colonial

$$$ Union Square FRENCH-VIETNAMESE

Walking into this tall, whitewashed building sitting off by itself in an alley downtown, you immediately feel transported to another era. The pressed tin ceiling, the fans, the potted palms, the rattan furniture — it could all easily feel contrived, but doesn't. The look, the service, and the haute Vietnamese cuisine — starring a beautiful piece of sea bass steamed in a banana leaf — are all well executed. The enticing upstairs lounge is a great place to begin or end the evening. The clientele is unusually dressy, by the way.

20 Cosmo Place, off Taylor St. between Sutter and Post Streets. ☎ *415-931-3600. Reservations advised. Main courses: $16.50–$28. AE, MC, V. Open: lunch weekdays; dinner nightly. Live jazz Fri and Sun nights.*

Lichee Garden

$ Chinatown CHINESE

This is the Chinese restaurant of your childhood, where happy families pass platters of pork spareribs and Peking duck around a white-linen-covered table. The only difference is that the food here is really good. And as another bonus, this place is just far enough from the center of Chinatown to feel unhurried.

1416 Powell St., between Broadway and Vallejo St. ☎ *415-397-2290. Reservations accepted but not required. Bus: 30-Stockton. Main courses: $5.75–$18.50. MC, V. Open: Breakfast, lunch, and dinner daily.*

L'Osteria del Forna

$ North Beach   ITALIAN

A tiny storefront with an equally tiny kitchen, L'Osteria manages to dish up fine thin-crusted pizzas, homey pasta dishes that change daily, and a great roast pork loin cooked in milk. It's equally satisfying to make a meal of antipasti. This is one North Beach restaurant that feels and tastes authentic.

519 Columbus Ave., between Green and Union Streets. ☎ 415-982-1124. No reservations accepted. Cable car: Powell-Mason line. Bus: 30-Stockton. Main courses: $7–$11. No credit cards. Open: lunch and dinner Wed–Mon.

Moose's

$$$ North Beach   CALIFORNIA/MEDITERRANEAN

Popular with politicos, socialites, and local luminaries, the great thing about Moose's, besides the food, is that even the little people have a great time eating here. While a splendidly prepared appetizer of crab cakes followed by the filet of beef will definitely leave a draft whistling through your wallet, the smooth, professional staff and bright decor guarantees a memorable, very San Francisco meal.

1652 Stockton St. across from Washington Sq. ☎ 415-989-7800. Reservations recommended. Cable car: Powell-Mason Line. Bus: 30-Stockton. Main courses: $17–$30. AE, DC, JCB, MC, V. Open: lunch Thur–Sat; dinner Mon–Sat; Sun brunch.

Neo

$$$ Mission District   NEW AMERICAN/MEDITERRANEAN

It takes nerve to design a completely white restaurant in a town where so many people's wardrobes are comprised of nothing but black pants and jackets — one could feel like a chess piece — but it is attention-getting. The food, including tender pasta dishes, hearty veal chops, and mussels with chorizo, is both eye-catching and tongue-pleasing.

1007 Guerrero St. between 22nd and 23rd Streets. ☎ 415-643-3119. Reservations advised. Main courses: $15–$17. MC, V. Open: dinner Tues–Sun.

Oritalia

$$$ Union Square   ASIAN/MEDITERRANEAN

The regularly changing menu in this burnished and beautiful fine-dining establishment reflects the fusion of Asian and Italian cuisine in interesting yet highly accessible dishes. Tuna tartare mounded with Asian pears, meltingly yummy gnocchi and lobster, and tea-smoked pork loin are all layered with flavor. You'll be telling the folks back home about this one.

586 Bush St. at Stockton St. next to the Hotel Juliana. ☎ 415-782-8122. Reservations advised two weeks in advance. Main courses: $16–$22. AE, CB, MC, V. Open: dinner nightly.

Pazzia

$ SoMa NORTHERN ITALIAN

Have a Northern Italian moment at this colorful tiny place, a quick walk from Yerba Buena Center and the museum. The tempting pizza, delicious pasta dishes, and heartier entrees provide something to please everyone.

337 Third St. ☎ 415-512-1693. Reservations advised. Muni: Montgomery St. station. Bus: 15-Third, 30-Stockton, or 45-Union/Stockton. Main courses: $8.75–$16.95. MC, V. Open: lunch weekdays; dinner nightly.

Piaf's

$$$ Civic Center/Hayes Valley FRENCH

Fairy lights adorn branches that decorate this intimate room, where the waiters speak with French accents. There's usually a singer/pianist warbling standards on a small, raised stage. Between the music and the mood, I'm relieved to report that the food is quite good. (If scallops are on the menu, you're in for a treat.) Check the Web site (www.piafs.com) for event listings.

1686 Market St. at Gough St. ☎ 415-864-3700. Reservations advised. Muni: F-line down Market St. Main courses: $10.50–$21. MC, V. Open: dinner Tues–Sun.

R&G Lounge

$ Chinatown CHINESE

Downstairs, you get excellent Hong Kong Chinese dishes in a setting that reminds me of an airport lounge, with lackluster service. The small dining room upstairs is more attractive, so talk your way to a table up there. In either case, you'll have a chance to order live spot shrimp from the downstairs tank and fresh, crisp vegetables such as Chinese broccoli and *yin choy* (a leafy green vegetable with a red root, often boiled then braised with garlic).

631 Kearny St., between Sacramento and Clay Streets. ☎ 415-982-7877. Reservations accepted. Bus: 15-Third. Main courses: $6.50–$8.50. AE, MC, V. Open: lunch and dinner daily.

Rose Pistola

$$$ North Beach ITALIAN

Walk by the sidewalk tables covered in gaily printed cloths, and you'll immediately feel the pull of this very "in" restaurant. From the couples praying for a few bar stools to free up, to the parties sipping wine in the more private dining areas in the back, the scene is intense. But if you succumb to its great charm and style (and I'll certainly understand), don't let the kitchen get away with any goofs.

532 Columbus Ave., between Union and Green Streets. ☎ *415-399-0499. Reservations recommended two weeks in advance. Cable car: Powell-Mason line. Bus: 30-Stockton. Main courses: $9–$18. AE, MC, V. Open: lunch and dinner daily.*

Scala's Bistro

$$$ **Union Square   ITALIAN**

Even on a Monday night, Scala's pulsates with laughter and conversation from a packed house of regulars and conventioneers (who either recognize a good thing when they see it or got lucky). The seductively masculine dining room complements the well-rounded menu of favorites, including an excellent Caesar salad and flavorful local bass.

432 Powell St., between Post and Sutter Streets (next to the Sir Francis Drake Hotel). ☎ *415-395-8555. Reservations recommended. Cable car: Powell-Hyde line. Main courses: $12–$24. AE, DC, DISC, MC, V. Open: breakfast, lunch, and dinner daily.*

Slanted Door

$$ **Mission District   VIETNAMESE**

Savvy travelers and locals of every stripe come here to swoon over the buttery steamed sea bass, caramelized chicken, and plates of "shaking" beef. Even if dinner reservations are impossible to come by, show up around 6pm (they hold a few tables for walk-ins) and you might get lucky.

584 Valencia St. at 17th St. ☎ *415-861-8032. Reservations necessary. BART: 16th St. Station. Main courses: $11.50–$19.50. MC, V. Open: lunch and dinner Tues–Sun.*

Splendido

$$$ **The Embarcadero   CALIFORNIA/MEDITERRANEAN**

Request a table by the window when you make reservations, although your eyes won't leave your plate once the rustic Mediterranean dishes arrive from the kitchen. The setting is lush and romantic, but the portions are generous enough that the only thing you'll want after dessert is a nap.

Four Embarcadero Center, between Clay and Drumm Streets. ☎ *415-986-3222. Reservations recommended. Muni: Take any Muni streetcar to the Embarcadero Station. Main courses: $14–$23. AE, DC, DISC, MC, V. Open: lunch weekdays; bar menu served 2:30pm to closing; dinner nightly.*

Tadich Grill

$$ **Financial District   SEAFOOD**

If you're making the rounds of old San Francisco, lunch here is mandatory. This turn-of-the-century watering hole, with waiters to match, features a daily printed menu advertising dishes so old-fashioned (had Lobster Newburg lately?) that they're probably the next big thing (like martinis and cigars). Stick with whatever fresh fish is available and try the delicious creamed spinach.

240 California St., between Front and Battery Streets. ☎ *415-391-1849. Reservations not accepted. Muni: Take any Muni streetcar to the Embarcadero Station. Main courses: $12–$18. MC, V. Open: lunch and dinner Mon–Sat.*

Thirsty Bear

$$ SoMa   SPANISH

Tapas (Spanish appetizers) are all the rage around these parts, but no one serves small (and large) plates of authentic Catalan food like this cavernous restaurant/brewery. The original managing chef was a handsome blue-eyed Spaniard direct from one of the wine-producing regions of Catalonia, and he carefully translated the local recipes for an appreciative audience. Don't miss the fish cheeks. Really.

661 Howard St., near Third St. ☎ *415-974-0905. Reservations recommended. Bus: 12-Folsom, 15-Third, 30-Stockton, or 45-Union/Stockton. Main courses: $14–$18. AE, MC, V. Open: lunch Mon–Sat; dinner nightly.*

3 Ring

$$ Mission District   SOUTHERN FRENCH

In a neighborhood where gourmet eateries abound, 3 Ring is charming and sweet, a lot like the blue cotton candy that's brought to the table at the end of the meal. But you have to eat your dinner first, which can be a pleasure. Share a salad of beets and tatsoi judiciously dressed in a vinagrette and whatever crepe is on the menu; follow up with porcini-crusted chicken or comforting veal shortribs.

995 Valencia St. at 21st St. ☎ *415-821-3210. Reservations accepted. BART: 24th St. Station. Main courses: $10–$16. AE, MC, V. Open: dinner nightly; weekend brunch.*

Zuni Cafe

$$ Civic Center/Hayes Valley   CALIFORNIA

There's always a palpable buzz from the smartly dressed crowd hanging about Zuni's copper bar drinking vodka and snarfing oysters. Everything from the brick oven is terrific, but the roast chicken with bread salad for two is downright divine. Don't opt for an outside table, as the view on this section of Market Street isn't all that pleasant.

1658 Market St., between Franklin and Gough Streets. ☎ *415-552-2522. Reservations recommended. Muni Metro: F-Market to Civic Center. Main courses: $16–$20. AE, MC, V. Open: lunch and dinner Tues–Sat; Sun brunch and dinner.*

Dim sum for dummies

I wasn't sure what to expect the first time I entered a Chinese restaurant for the sole purpose of trying dim sum. I'll admit — and only because you were kind enough to buy this book — that I was a little nervous. I wasn't born an adventuresome diner, and the idea of eating these little Chinese dumplings filled with ingredients I couldn't identify without actually taking a bite, was a bit scary. I am delighted to report that I quickly overcame my initial wariness and now love dim sum. If you haven't tried it, I urge you to do so. If you are a dumpling veteran, just take note of my restaurant recommendations and look forward to a great meal.

In many Chinese restaurants, dim sum is served from late morning until around 2pm, but not later. In fact, if you arrive much past 1pm, as I did during Chinese New Year last February, you run the risk of the kitchen losing interest in providing much of anything to eat, while the waitstaff tucks into their lunch and ignores you completely. So plan to arrive around 11am. Dim sum generally enters on carts wheeled about the room by waitresses. (Otherwise, you order from a menu.) Ask for a table near the kitchen in order to get first crack at whatever's on its way around the room. The ladies with their carts will stop by your table and show you what they have. If it looks appealing to you, nod or say yes and the waitress will smack down a dish of perhaps three dumplings and mark your check (the marks add up, but in general, dim sum is remarkably inexpensive). If the dumpling looks like jellied chicken feet and you're not up to it, just say no, thanks. It's okay to order slowly — finishing one plate, sipping tea, then ordering something else. Despite the many parties waiting for tables, you don't have to hurry. By the way, if you run out of tea, open the teapot lid.

Here's a rundown of dim sum that first-timers will definitely enjoy:

- Har Gau: shrimp dumplings encased in a translucent wrapper and steamed
- Sui mai: rectangles of pork and shrimp in a sheer noodle wrapper
- Gau choi gau: chives, alone or with shrimp or scallop
- Jun jui kau: rice pearl balls with seasoned ground pork and rice
- Law mai gai: sticky rice with bits of meat and mushrooms wrapped in a lotus leaf
- Char siu bau: steamed pork buns — bits of barbecued meat in a doughy roll
- Guk char siu ban: baked pork buns — bits of barbecued meat in a glazed roll
- Chun guen: spring rolls — smaller, less crowded versions of egg roll
- Gau ji: potstickers — a thick, crescent-shaped dough filled with ground pork

(continued)

(continued)

Where to go

Yank Sing, in the Financial District at 427 Battery Street (☎ 415-362-1640), is considered by those in the know to be one of the premier dim sum houses in town. A bit more expensive than most (but still a good bargain), Yank Sing specializes in this fare, so novices will be starting at the top. Highly recommended. In Chinatown, **Gold Mountain**, 644 Broadway (near Stockton St. ☎ 415-296-7733), is typical of the cavernous dim sum parlors that serve hundreds of families on the weekends. Get a number from the hostess when you walk in; otherwise, you'll be waiting for a table forever. Way out in the Richmond District at 6255 Geary at 27th Boulevard is one of my favorites, **The Mayflower** ☎ 415-387-8338. Dim sum is served every day, and the pleasant room caters to a mostly Chinese clientele, so you won't have to queue up behind a throng of impatient yuppies. This would be a convenient place to stop and graze before a trip to the **Palace of the Legion of Honor** (see Chapter 17).

Chapter 15

On the Lighter Side: Top Picks for Snacks and Meals on the Go

*W*ith the exception of Fisherman's Wharf, where people attempt to walk holding bread bowls filled with questionable clam chowder, street food is practically nonexistent in San Francisco. (Although, in a very weak moment, and only for research purposes, I once did buy a hot dog from a cart on Pier 39.) Instead, there are sandwich counters, Asian bakeries, Italian delis, coffeehouses, and pastry shops providing a grand variety of delicious foodstuffs quickly and for reasonable to downright cheap prices.

Whether you're feeling a bit peckish or positively peaked, you'll find something tempting to tide yourself over until the next big meal.

Dining on Foot

Just two long blocks west of the Ferry Building on the Embarcadero, next to Pier 5, is a bench-lined, refurbished wooden wharf with fine views that practically begs for an impromptu picnic lunch. But there are plenty of other spots around the city to unpack a brown bag, too.

Serving up sandwiches on-the-go

You can happily fill it at **Panelli Bros.**, a second-generation family-run Italian delicatessen with a fantastic assortment of cheeses, good, inexpensive Italian wines, and friendly people who make excellent sandwiches to go. It's located at 1419 Stockton St. near Vallejo Street in North Beach. Open daily. Also in North Beach, on the corner of Columbus and Kearny, is a cafe owned by the director Francis Ford Coppola. Surprisingly, **Café Niebaum-Coppola** — part wine bar, part kitchen store — serves the most delicious muffalatta (comprised of olive salad, mortadella, and provolone) outside of New Orleans, a sandwich that once made my husband so ecstatic that he squirreled away half to eat the following day. The cafe is open daily until 11pm. Three blocks from the Embarcadero on Mission and Main is **Palio Paninoteca,** where $7 gets you a panino large enough for two. Fillings range from grilled vegetables or meats to smoked prosciutto with gorgonzola, mascarpone, and arugula. Closed weekends. Closer to Union Square, with another two locations in the Financial District, is **Specialty's Café & Bakery,** 1 Post St. at Market. This spot is popular for a vast array of fresh sandwiches served on made-from-scratch breads. Also open only on weekdays.

Down on the farm — farmer's market, that is

Saturday mornings at the Ferry Plaza Farmers' Market at Green Street and Embarcadero (open from 8am to 1pm) is a jumble of basket- and canvas sack-wielding couples picking over the heirloom tomatoes and grabbing the last of the wild arugula while juggling coffee and a cell phone. The beauty of the organic vegetables and flowers makes a walk around the market an enormous pleasure, despite the crowd. The **Hayes Street Grill** and **Rose Pistola** restaurants cook gourmet breakfasts from their booths, and other vendors sell items such as bottles of olive oil, jars of local honey, and exotic orchid plants. This is also a great place to gather picnic food — fresh bread, artisan cheeses, fruit — for later in the day. The F-Market streetcar makes a stop on Green Street.

Snacking at the Wharf

Let's be frank. **Pier 39/Fisherman's Wharf** is the most touristy part of town. The restaurants that crowd Jefferson Street exist for the people who are here today and gone tomorrow. I have learned to accept this, if not to embrace it, and I'm not going to sneer at anybody who spends part of a day here on the way to Alcatraz or simply to see what all the fuss is about. But let's say that this person is hungry. Let's say that this person has heard about all the crab vendors and the delicious sourdough bread, and thinks to himself, "That sounds like fun." This is what I'd suggest: Buy a bottle of beer, buy a little round of sourdough bread, and ask one of the guys at a crab stand (try **Fisherman's Grotto No. 9**) to cook, clean, and crack a live crab for you. Then take these goodies and lots of napkins through the doors marked "Passageway to the Boats," walk down this relatively quiet area, sit on the dock, and have a good time. Remember, the local Dungeness crab season is from November through May. In the summer, the crabs are flown in from Alaska or parts east.

Unless you purchase a freshly cracked crab, rest assured that the $4.25 crab cocktail you ordered is made of canned crab or even imitation crab!

Bakery Finds

You can have a swell time hunting and gathering among the bakeries in North Beach. For starters, drop by **Liguria Bakery** on the corner of Stockton and Filbert Streets for a sheet of plain focaccia, or maybe one topped with green onions or tomato. They are all delicious and wrapped for portability. Liguria is open every day by 8am and closes when the last piece of focaccia is sold, usually by 2pm. I also love **Victoria Bakery,** 1362 Stockton St. at Vallejo, which sells a large selection of Italian sweets (the chewy almond cookies are good enough to give as a gift) and slices of its justly popular cakes.

Alfred Schilling, on Market and Valencia Streets in Hayes Valley, is a chocolatier/bakery/restaurant with a nice selection of homemade desserts, cookies, and truffles to take with you or enjoy with coffee at one of the inside tables. It's near **Bellochio** (see Chapter 19) and **Flax,** so you can get a little shopping in while visiting the neighborhood.

Chinese Bakeries

Chinese bakeries, which sell savory as well as sweet items, abound in Chinatown, in the Sunset District on Irving Street, and in the Richmond District on Clement Street. For snacking on the premises or on the go, delicious baked or steamed porkbuns (baked buns are golden brown and steamed buns are white) are ideal and a big hit with kids. If you want something on the sweet side, custard tarts and sesame seed–covered balls of rice surrounding a bit of sweet bean paste are standard issue. Look also for *bo lo bow,* slightly puffy and sweet bread with a crust that resembles the outside of a pineapple, or *chung yow bow,* green onion bread. You may have to point to whatever looks appetizing, since, especially in Chinatown, the folks behind the counter don't always speak English.

Coffee and Tea, If You Please

Places to sit and sip are as prevalent as pigeons in this caffeine-crazed piece of paradise. Coffeehouses, and I'm not even including the mega-chains, nestle in every neighborhood, seemingly on every block. I don't think drinking coffee as a lifestyle was invented in North Beach, but based on sheer numbers, it could have been. Regulars, of course, have their favorite blends and favorite tables, but no one will argue against hanging out at **Mario's Bohemian Cigar Store** on the corner of Columbus and Union Street. Along with excellent coffee (Graffeo), you can graze on a mouth-watering chicken parmigiana on focaccia. **Caffé Trieste,** on Vallejo and Grant Streets, is a mob scene on Saturday afternoons, when the owners and friends take a turn at the microphone to sing. Coffee is served daily with or without opera.

While that Seattle-based coffee Goliath continues to snap up real estate in a quest to make everyone drink frappacinos, we have our own local chain to kick around. Actually, **Peet's Coffee and Tea** is worshipped by caffeine aficionados, and if you love really strong coffee, it's worth dropping by one of their many stores. The one closest to Union Square is in the Financial District at 22 Battery St. (at Bush). You can also try the shop on Chestnut Street between Steiner and Pierce Streets in the Marina. They're both open daily.

The peaceful **Imperial Tea Court,** 1411 Powell St., near Broadway, is a must-stop in which to rest your feet and take stock of your life — or maybe just the last half hour — over a pot of exotic leaves and blossoms that would make Celestial Seasonings hesitate to package one more teabag. This is the place to sample the highest quality teas as they were meant to be brewed — and the staff will be happy to show you how it's done. Open daily.

Breakfast of Champions

Touring is hard work. You need a good breakfast. Around Union Square you can find lots of restaurants serving in the morning, including **The Grand Café** (see Chapter 14), **Sears Fine Food** on Powell across from Union Square, and my favorite, **Dottie's True Blue Café,** 522 Jones St. between Geary Boulevard and O'Farrell Street. Open Wednesday through Sunday only, this tiny diner offers daily specials as well as the basics — eggs, pancakes, sausage — all prepared with great flair. The baked goods are so delicious, you may want to purchase some to go.

Doige's Kitchen, in the Marina/Cow Hollow neighborhood at 2217 Union St. (near Fillmore; ☎ 415-921-2149), serves a substantial breakfast until 2pm daily, although you can also drop by for lunch (forget the salads) every day and dinner Wednesday through Saturday. There's always a line here on the weekends, but reservations are accepted and the service is sweet and friendly.

Around the Embarcadero on Battery Street, **Il Fornaio** (see Chapter 14) opens early and offers an excellent small breakfast menu with egg dishes, oatmeal, and an array of house-made baked goods to enjoy. Right on the Embarcadero at Battery is **Pier 23 Café.** This is as much a bar/club as it is a fun place for lunch and dinner with live music weekend evenings, but brunch is served on the outdoor patio (weather permitting) on Saturdays and Sundays. The eggs Benedict are quite lovely.

Pizza and Other Cheap Eats

While I am known to criticize fast food, I consider pizza an exception. Good pizza is as close as one gets to a perfectly satisfying, easygoing, low-rent dish. And while San Francisco doesn't have the reputation of either New York or Chicago in the pizza department, you won't have any difficulty finding a ready slice in any neighborhood.

He doesn't deliver, but **Uncle Vito's Pizzadelli,** on the corner of Bush and Powell Streets, serves credible pie with a big selection of toppings, good salads, and enough pasta dishes to carbo-load for the next day's adventures. Uncle Vito's is inexpensive and convenient to Nob Hill and Union Square, so you'll see lots of foreign tourists here, attempting to put together just the right combination of pizza and beer. **Vicolo Pizzeria** is in Civic Center, at 150 Ivy, an alley off Gough Street between Hayes and Grove Streets; it's perfect for a quick bite before the symphony or other cultural pursuits. Vicolo's makes a cornmeal-crusted pizza that is truly memorable, as well as inviting salads that are freshly made.

Mo's Grill is south of Market at Folsom and 4th Streets, the eastern-most side of Yerba Buena Gardens. Mo's serves hamburgers of all kinds, shakes, and fries — you know, those things we aren't supposed to eat. But if burger cravings start to haunt you, you'll know where to get a great one. You can also find a branch in North Beach on Grant Street, between Vallejo and Green.

North Beach also shelters at least two little eateries specializing in roasted chicken, the oldest being **Il Pollaio,** 555 Columbus Ave., between Union and Green Streets. A very casual place to sit down for savory chicken and other meats and salads, this is where you go when the kids start rolling their eyes if you mention dim sum or sea bass. It's also a good choice when you're tired of spending too much money on dinner.

Part V
Exploring San Francisco

The 5th Wave   By Rich Tennant

©RICHTENNANT

Well this is just a whole lot more than I expected from a tour of the Golden Gate Bridge.

In this part . . .

*N*ow we get to the meat and potatoes. This part tells you about the landmarks and neighborhoods that define San Francisco to the world. And you know what? Most of them are worthy of their star billing.

How do you take everything in? That depends on how much time you have, of course. If you only have a day or two to spare, a guided tour may be the best way of at least seeing, if not savoring, the sites. Or you can pick and choose from a list of a few places to see, spend some quality time on each of those sites, and plan on coming back to the city another time to catch the rest. If you have three or more days to wander, take a look at my suggested itineraries at the end of this part for an idea of how to absorb as much of the city as possible.

Don't forget the shopping opportunities while the pleasure of browsing in one-of-a-kind stores is still possible. An entire shopping chapter awaits and it's filled with suggestions of where to find interesting clothes, gifts, and comestibles you won't find in your local shopping mall. Leave room in your suitcase — it's going to be heavier on the trip home.

Chapter 16

San Francisco's Top Sights

- -

In This Chapter

▶ Touring the great museums and gardens, and riding the famous cable cars

▶ Getting information on the top attractions' complete hours of operation and admission prices

▶ Finding out about the famous neighborhoods of the city and which top sights are where

- -

Something is bringing you to San Francisco. It could be

✔ Visions of the Golden Gate Bridge spanning the icy waters of the bay

✔ Recollections of old Rice-A-Roni commercials ("the San Francisco treat"), whose jingle became synonymous with cable cars

✔ Views out your window are a bit too flat, and the thrill-seeker in you is ready for the action our hills provide to drivers and passengers alike

You might be curious to understand firsthand why this city is different from any other urban center and why its residents are so fiercely passionate about where they live. The following index gives you a quick reference of the features that make San Francisco, well, San Francisco.

Index of Attractions by Neighborhood

Chinatown

Chinese Culture Center
Chinese Historical Society of America
Golden Gate Fortune Cookies Company
Portsmouth Square
Tin Hou Temple

Fisherman's Wharf

Alcatraz Island
Cable Cars
The Cannery
Ghirardelli Square
Hyde Street Pier
Maritime National Historical Park
Pier 39
USS Pampinito

North Beach/Telegraph Hill

Coit Tower
Lombard Street

Marina/Cow Hollow

The Exploratorium/Palace of Fine Arts
Golden Gate Bridge

The Richmond District

Golden Gate Park
Asian Art Museum
California Academy of Sciences
Japanese Tea Garden
M. H. de Young Memorial Museum
Strybing Arboretum and Botanical
Gardens

SoMa

Museum of Modern Art
Metreon
Yerba Buena Gardens
Zeum

The Top Attractions from A to Z

Alcatraz Island

Fisherman's Wharf

Located in **San Francisco Bay, "The Rock" — Alcatraz Island —** has been transformed from a run-down prison remnant to a must-see attraction, thanks to Hollywood's exciting depiction of the maximum-security prison. Visitors can choose from taking either a self-guided tour or a tour guided by a National Park ranger, who is chock-full of interesting anecdotes of **Alcatraz's** infamous residents. The self-guided tour runs approximately 2½ hours and includes an orientation video. Because the prison is out in the **Bay,** remember to bring a jacket due to windy conditions, as well as comfortable shoes for the steep walk up to the **Cell House.** Another path up to the prison is now wheelchair accessible.

To get the full effect of what it might have been like to be an inmate, try the **"Alcatraz After Hours" tour.** The prison becomes especially sinister when the sun goes down, so use discretion when deciding to bring youngsters along. The tour is offered Thursday through Sunday only; the ferry departs at 6:15pm and 7pm (4:20pm during the winter).

From maximum prison to maximum attraction

Alcatraz Island was first discovered in 1775. Due to its strategic location in San Francisco Bay, the U.S. Army took notice and began building a military fortress atop "The Rock." From 1850 to 1933, it served as a military post and army prison, housing Civil War, Spanish-American War, and, then, civilian prisoners. In 1934, it was converted into a maximum security prison. The prison was home for famous gangsters like Al Capone; Robert Stroud, the so-called Birdman of Alcatraz (because he was an expert on ornithological diseases — he never kept birds on Alcatraz); and "Machine Gun" Kelly. Twenty-nine prisoners tried to escape from Alcatraz — two made it ashore, only to be captured almost immediately, and five drowned, presumably, although their bodies were never recovered. All 29 attempts are said to have failed. The prison closed in 1963, due to deterioration of the buildings and it being prohibitively expensive to maintain. Alcatraz became part of the Golden Gate National Recreation Area in 1972.

*Pier 41, at **Fisherman's Wharf**. ☎ 415-773-1188, for information only. Internet:* www. blueandgoldfleet.com. *Open: winter daily, 9:30am–2:15pm; summer daily, 9:15am–4:15pm. Ferries run approximately every half hour. Arrive at least 20 minutes before sailing time. Cable car: **The Powell-Mason line** ends a few blocks from **Fisherman's Wharf**. Muni: The 30-Stockton bus from **Union Square** stops one block south of the wharf. The F-Market streetcar stops at **Fisherman's Wharf**. Admission (includes ferry and audio tour): $12.25 adults, $7 children 5–11, $10.50 seniors 62 and older.*

You must order tickets far in advance for the ferry ride to the island. Call ☎ **415-705-5555** to purchase tickets over the phone. You'll be charged a $2-per-ticket service charge.

Cable Cars

Union Square/Financial District

San Francisco's most notable icon is probably the **cable car.** These cherished wooden cars creak and squeal up and around hills while passengers lean out into the wind, running the risk of getting their heads removed by passing buses. San Francisco's three existing lines comprise the world's only surviving system of cable cars, and they are a delight to ride. The sheer joy of whizzing down a hill with the bay glistening in the foreground will linger in your memory. Besides that, these legendary icons are not only fun, they're a useful means of transportation. The **Powell-Mason line** conveniently wends its way from the corner of Powell and Market Streets through North Beach and ends near **Fisherman's Wharf.** The **Powell-Hyde line,** which starts at the same intersection, ends up near the **Maritime Museum** and **Ghirardelli Square.** The less-thrilling **California line** begins at the foot of Market Street and travels straight up California Street over **Nob Hill** to Van Ness Avenue.

San Francisco's Top Sights

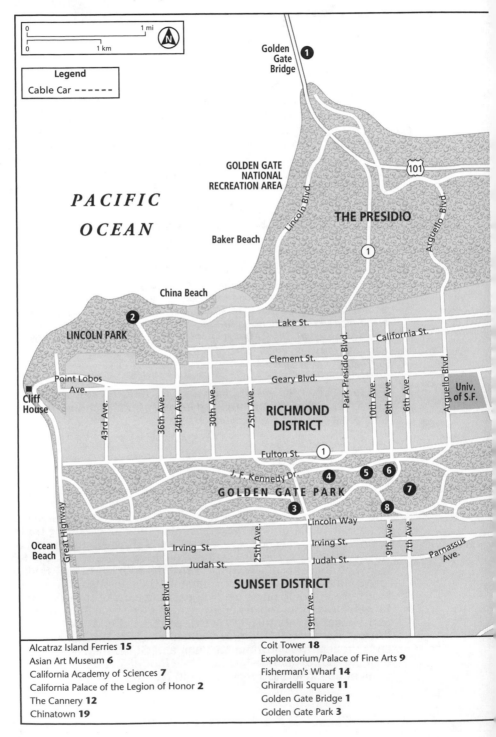

Alcatraz Island Ferries **15**	Coit Tower **18**
Asian Art Museum **6**	Exploratorium/Palace of Fine Arts **9**
California Academy of Sciences **7**	Fisherman's Wharf **14**
California Palace of the Legion of Honor **2**	Ghirardelli Square **11**
The Cannery **12**	Golden Gate Bridge **1**
Chinatown **19**	Golden Gate Park **3**

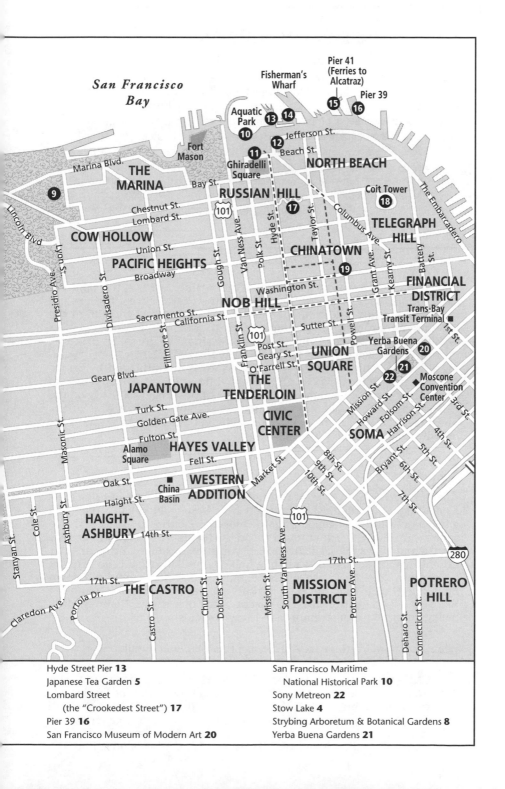

San Francisco Bay

Pier 41 (Ferries to Alcatraz)

Fisherman's Wharf

Pier 39

Aquatic Park ⑬ ⑭

⑮ ⑯

⑩

Jefferson St.

⑫

Fort Mason

Beach St.

⑪

Ghiradelli Square

Bay St.

THE MARINA

RUSSIAN HILL

⑰

NORTH BEACH

Coit Tower

⑱

TELEGRAPH HILL

⑨

Marina Blvd.

Chestnut St.

Lombard St.

101

COW HOLLOW

Union St.

PACIFIC HEIGHTS

Broadway

CHINATOWN

⑲

FINANCIAL DISTRICT

Sacramento St.

California St.

NOB HILL

Washington St.

Trans-Bay Transit Terminal ■

Post St.

Geary St.

O'Farrell St.

Sutter St.

UNION SQUARE

Yerba Buena Gardens ⑳

101

Geary Blvd.

JAPANTOWN

THE TENDERLOIN

⑳

⑤

Moscone Convention Center

Turk St.

Golden Gate Ave.

Fulton St.

CIVIC CENTER

SOMA

Alamo Square

HAYES VALLEY

Fell St.

Oak St.

China Basin

WESTERN ADDITION

Market St.

HAIGHT-ASHBURY

Haight St.

14th St.

101

17th St.

280

17th St.

THE CASTRO

MISSION DISTRICT

POTRERO HILL

The steel wheels tour

The famous cable cars you see going up and down the hills of downtown San Francisco were invented in 1869 by Andrew Hallidie. Hallidie saw the need for a new mode of transportation when he witnessed a horse-drawn streetcar slide backward down one of the many steep slopes that make up San Francisco's unique topography. Here's how the cable car system works: A steel cable is housed just under the street in a rail, kind of like an inside-out train rail (it's the cable that makes that clickity-clanking sound). Powered by electricity, this cable constantly moves, or runs, through the rail. Each cable car has a lever which when pulled back, closes a pincer-like "grip" on the cable. The person who pulls the lever is called a gripper — some would call this person a driver, but he doesn't drive, he "grips" the cable. The cable car is then "attached" to the cable that runs through the rail under the pavement, and the car begins to move at a constant 9 miles per hour — the speed at which the cable is set to travel.

I thought I had a foolproof method of avoiding the crowds at the cable car turnarounds by waiting two blocks from the Powell Street turnaround (which is literally where the cars are turned around at the end of the line), but after forcing my visiting brother to wait watching one car after another pass us by ("and you do this professionally?" he said, unkindly), my only other suggestion is to get up early to ride. You can also try walking a few more blocks to the next stop. (Stops are indicated by brown signs with a white cable car on them.) While at first it will appear that there's no room for you among the zillions of passengers already on the car, by magic a foothold may open up. Cars run from 6:30am to 12:30am. The fare is $2 per person one-way, payable on board; Muni Passports are accepted. See Chapter 11 for more details.

Chinatown

Take your time as you walk through this enclave — it's easy to miss something. The **Dragon Gate** arch at Grant Avenue and Bush Street (just a few blocks north of Union Square) marks the entry to **Chinatown.** To get a more authentic experience, avoid the tourists and explore the side streets and alleys off Grant Avenue. If you stay for lunch or dinner, your **Chinatown** adventure takes about a half day. Walking from Union Square is the more sensible way to get there, but you can also reach **Chinatown** by taking the 30-Stockton bus; parking is nearly impossible, although there is a lot on Kearny Street at Portsmouth Square. (See Chapter 14 for dining suggestions and Chapter 19 for where to shop.)

While you're in **Chinatown,** don't miss the following highlights:

The Chinese Historical Society of America, 964 Clay St. (☎ 415-391-1188), is a good place to begin your **Chinatown** tour. The fascinating history of the Chinese in California is well documented here through photographs and artifacts, and you can browse through a gallery and a gift shop. The museum is open Tuesday 1 to 4pm, and Monday and Wednesday through Friday from 10:30am to 4pm. Admission is free.

Tin Hou Temple, 15 Waverly Pl. (an alley off Clay Street between Stockton and Grant), is one of the oldest Chinese temples in the United States. The temple is open to the public, but please remember to enter it respectfully, as you would any house of worship. Be prepared to climb a narrow staircase, and make an offering or buy some incense on your way out.

Golden Gate Fortune Cookies Company, 956 Ross Alley, between Jackson and Washington Streets near Grant Avenue, is a working factory where you can buy bags of inexpensive and fresh fortune cookies. And don't forget the delicious almond cookies as well! You may find it somewhat claustrophobic, but you can enter the factory and watch rounds of dough transform into cookies. Open daily from 10am to 7pm.

Portsmouth Square, a park above the **Portsmouth Square** parking garage on Kearny Street between Washington and Clay Streets, is the site of the first California public school, which opened in 1848, and marks the spot where San Francisco was originally settled. A compact but complete playground attracts all the neighborhood preschoolers, and in the morning, elderly Chinese practice their tai chi exercises. The landscape includes comfortable benches, attractive lampposts, and young trees. The distinctly San Francisco view includes the **Transamerica Pyramid** looming above the skyline. The garage below is a good place to know about if you're driving. Interestingly, the garage's fourth floor is most likely to have empty spaces, because in Cantonese, the number four sounds like the word for death, so superstitious Chinese won't park on that floor.

The pedestrian bridge over Kearny Street leads directly into the third floor of the Chinatown Holiday Inn, where the **Chinese Culture Center** is located. A gift shop leads to the sole gallery, where changing exhibits may feature, for example, photographs from pre-earthquake Chinatown, Chinese brush painting, or exquisitely embroidered antique clothing and household items. The center is open from 10am to 4pm Monday through Saturday. Admission is free.

Coit Tower

Telegraph Hill (Near North Beach)

Erected in 1933 with funds bequeathed to the city by Lillie Hitchcock Coit, this 210-foot concrete landmark is visible from much of the city. But everyone needs to take a closer look to see the beauty of the tower. The decor inside features walls with dramatic murals inspired by and commissioned during the Great Depression. Take an elevator to the top for panoramic views of the city and the bay. This diversion will probably take about 30 minutes from start to finish.

Atop Telegraph Hill. ☎ 415-362-0808. Bus: Take the 39-Coit bus or walk from Lombard St. where it meets Telegraph Hill Blvd. (two blocks east of Stockton St.). Parking: The drive up and the parking lot are always a mass of cars. Open: daily, 10am–6pm. Admission to top of tower: $3.75 adults, $2.50 seniors, $1.50 kids 6–12.

Chinatown

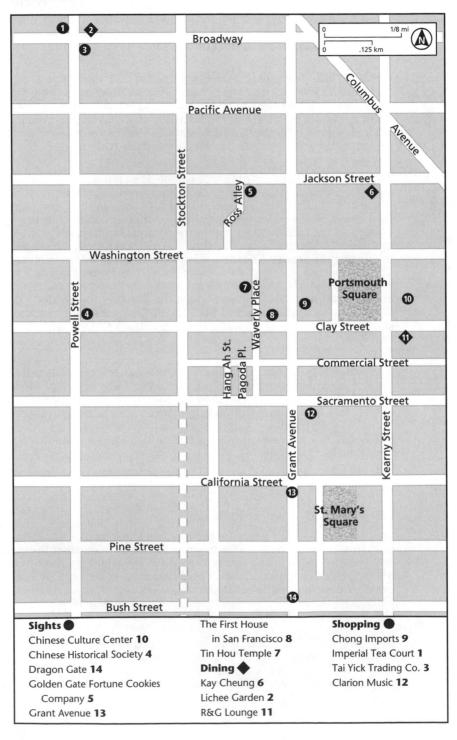

Broadway

Columbus Avenue

Pacific Avenue

Stockton Street

Jackson Street

Ross Alley

Washington Street

Powell Street

Waverly Place

Portsmouth Square

Clay Street

Hang Ah St.
Pagoda Pl.

Commercial Street

Sacramento Street

Grant Avenue

Kearny Street

California Street

St. Mary's Square

Pine Street

Bush Street

Sights ●
Chinese Culture Center **10**
Chinese Historical Society **4**
Dragon Gate **14**
Golden Gate Fortune Cookies
Company **5**
Grant Avenue **13**

The First House
in San Francisco **8**
Tin Hou Temple **7**
Dining ◆
Kay Cheung **6**
Lichee Garden **2**
R&G Lounge **11**

Shopping ●
Chong Imports **9**
Imperial Tea Court **1**
Tai Yick Trading Co. **3**
Clarion Music **12**

Exploratorium/Palace of Fine Arts

Marina District

Scientific American magazine rates the Exploratorium as "the best science museum in the world," and it's certainly an intriguing space that appeals to all ages. The exhibits explore many different topics, such as technology, human perception, and natural phenomena. Well-written text accompanies the exhibits to further enhance the learning experience. Don't worry about feeling like a science dunce if you're visiting with children; a well-informed volunteer staff is ready to answer any questions you may have. Expect to spend about two hours exploring the museum, especially if you're traveling with kids. A walk around the grounds of the **Palace of Fine Arts** is a great way to unwind after exploring the museum. Better yet, if the weather's balmy, bring a picnic and stay awhile.

3601 Lyon St. at Marina Blvd. ☎ *415-561-0360. Internet:* www.exploratorium.edu. *Bus: 30-Stockton to Marina stop. Parking: free and easy. Open: Tues–Sun from 10am–5pm, daily in the summer. Admission: $9 adults, $7 seniors, $5 kids 6–17, $2.50 kids 3–5. Free first Wed of the month.*

 ### Fisherman's Wharf

When you arrive at **Fisherman's Wharf,** you may notice lots of people wandering around, none of whom fish for a living. This was once a working set of piers, but today it is an outdoor shopping mall masquerading as a bona fide tourist destination. Some people really enjoy examining the refrigerator magnets and cable car bookends stocked in one olde shoppe after another, and for this the merchants are grateful. Other visitors, perhaps confused by the surrounding jungle of kitsch, hastily plan their escape. But almost everybody comes down here at some point. Here's a rundown of what you'll find:

 Pier 39. No matter the weather, tourists crowd this multi-level, Disneyesque shopper's dream (or nightmare). Video arcade halls, lined with deafening video games, anchor the pier on each end. You also find T-shirt and sweatshirt shops and plenty of fried food here. Join the mob if you want to see the golden views of **Alcatraz** visible from the end of the pier, or to watch the huge sea lions that loaf around on the west side of the pier (follow the barking). Catch the ferry to **Alcatraz** or bay cruises here as well. If you're hungry, stop by the only authentic place to eat, the **Eagle Cafe** (☎ 415-433-3689), open daily from 7:30am to 3pm on the second floor. This inexpensive breakfast and lunch joint opened in 1920. If you're arriving by car, park on adjacent streets or on the wharf between Taylor and Jones Streets. But be advised, the parking garage charges $5.50 per hour! Do your best to avoid these price-gougers and don't bring a car here. Besides, it's much more fun to take the F-Market down the **Embarcadero** (see Chapter 11).

Underwater World, Pier 39 at Fisherman's Wharf (☎ 415-623-5300) is a $38 million aquarium. I'm frankly unimpressed with the place. You view the undersides of fishes from a moving walkway — a crowd-control device that makes me feel rather unwelcome. At $12.95 for adults, $9.95 for seniors 65

and over, and $6.50 for kids, maybe you ought to go to the **California Academy of Sciences** instead. Be sure to call first in any event because the aquarium filed for bankruptcy protection in early 2000.

The San Francisco Maritime National Historical Park is a small two-story museum overlooking the bay and **Alcatraz.** It takes only 15 minutes or so to examine the model schooners, figureheads, and photographs illustrating the city's maritime heritage, although children may lose interest after the first 5 minutes. Still, it's very sweet and admission is free.

 If you have small children along (or anyone interested in history), you won't want to miss touring the **USS Pampanito** on **Pier 45** (☎ 415-775-1943). This submarine saw active duty during WWII and helped save 73 British and Australian prisoners-of-war. The $27 family pass (for two adults and up to four children) also gets you into the **Hyde Street Pier** (see following). Otherwise, submarine-only admission, which includes a 20-minute audio tour, is $6 for adults, and $4 for seniors, students, and children 6 to 12. Kids under 6 are free. Open daily from 9am to 6pm in winter, and until 8pm in summer.

 The Hyde Street Pier, two blocks east of the **Maritime Museum,** is where a number of historic, refurbished ships, on which you can roam around, are located. Of particular note is the 112-year-old **Balclutha,** a square-rigger with an interesting past. During the year, activities that take place on the **Balclutha** include concerts, sea chantey sing-alongs, and children's events. Call ☎ 415-556-3002 for a schedule. It takes at least an hour or so to tour the vessels. The pier is open daily 9:30am to 5pm. Admission is $4 adults, $2 kids 12–17, free for kids 11 and under during the summer. Winter admission is half price.

Ghirardelli Square, which is the site of the original Ghirardelli chocolate factory, across the street from the **Maritime park,** offers one of the more pleasant shopping mall experiences in the area. Granted landmark status in 1982, the series of brick buildings is home to a roster of special events, including an annual chocolate-tasting benefit in September. Street performers entertain regularly in the **West Plaza.** Open daily 10am to 6pm in winter, to 9pm in summer.

 Go one block east of **Ghirardelli Square** and you find what was once a peach canning facility, **The Cannery.** It now features shops, jugglers, musicians, and food. Visitors especially enjoy **Lark in the Morning** (☎ 415-922-HARP), a music haven with an array of early music and modern instruments. Gift shoppers of a practical bent and people with newly formed blisters will also love **Sox, Sox, Sox** (☎ 415-563-7327), which, as the name implies, sells foot coverings in both silly and conventional patterns. On the second floor, look for **San Franciscow** (☎ 415-440-7042), a silk-screen T-shirt and kids' clothing store. The owners started as sidewalk vendors outside on Beach Street. If the kids get wiggly (or if the weather is ugly and you need something to keep them occupied), head to the **Basic Brown Bear Factory** (☎ 415-931-6670), which is located on the second floor of the South Building. Customers stuff and help sew teddy bears to take home. Or you could paint pottery plates, cups, and other useful items at **Handmade Ceramic Studio** (☎ 415-440-2898), which is happy to ship your work home once it has been fired.

*At the foot of Polk St., on the western edge of the **Embarcadero.** ☎ 415-556-3002.*
Cable car: Take the Powell-Hyde line to the last stop. Muni: F-Market streetcar; 19-
Polk, 30-Stockton, 42-Downtown Loop, or 47-Van Ness bus. Parking: pricey lots and
garages. Street parking is difficult. Open: daily, 10am–5pm. Admission: free.

Golden Gate Bridge

The quintessential San Francisco landmark spans 1.7 miles and soars hundreds of feet above the water. Bundle up against the windy conditions, then set out from the **Roundhouse** on the San Francisco side of the bridge lot (see Chapter 17 for information on walking to the bridge). It can get pretty noisy, but the views can't be beat. Remember that the only way to return from the other side is on foot, so know your limits before crossing the whole bridge and finding out you're too tired to make it back. Afterward, take some time to climb below the bridge to see the five-acre garden there. The bridge is open to pedestrians from 5am to 9pm daily. The 28-19th Ave. or the 29-Sunset bus deposits you across from the viewing area, right by a parking lot. If you're driving, take 19th Avenue or Lombard Street and pay attention to the sign that indicates when to exit for the parking lot. Otherwise, enjoy your drive across the bridge. There's a $3 toll upon your return to the city. The bridge has no phone.

Golden Gate Park

The park features 1,017 acres of greenery and cultural attractions that have something in store for everyone. People can be found doing just about everything at the park from playing soccer to sailing model yachts to running. On Sundays, when John F. Kennedy Drive is closed to street traffic, bicyclists ride with impunity and in-line skaters converge for dance parties. On Sundays, from April through the middle of October, the **Golden Gate Park Band** plays from 1 to 3pm in the **Music Concourse,** between the **de Young Museum** and the **California Academy of Sciences.** Enter the massive **Children's Playground** and a beautifully restored carousel through the grand new park entrance on Stanyan Street (off Waller Street). Your kids will have fun for hours on the imaginative structures and swings. The remodeled entrance cut down on the rather large number of street people who hung out there (a lot of homeless and runaways populate the **Haight**), but you never know if that will change. In any case, don't let that keep you from enjoying the park. Another entrance at 9th Avenue on Lincoln Way brings you to the **Strybing Arboretum,** the **Japanese Tea Garden,** the **Academy of Sciences,** and the **de Young** and **Asian Art museums.**

Joggers and parents pushing baby strollers make regular use of the path around man-made **Stow Lake.** It's the perfect place to take advantage of a sunny day by renting a paddleboat and having a picnic. The **boat house** (☎ 415-752-0347) also rents bikes and in-line skates by the hour, half day, and full day. If you aren't driving, it's a bit of a walk to the **boat house,** which is west of the **Japanese Tea Garden** on Martin Luther King Drive. It's open daily from 9am to 4pm.

*The **N-Judah Muni Metro streetcar** drops you off on 9th Ave. and Judah St.; from*
there it is a three-block walk to the park. Numerous bus lines drive close to or into
the park, including the 44-O'Shaughnessy, which you can catch on 9th Ave.; the
21-Hayes; and the 5-Fulton.

Fisherman's Wharf & Vicinity

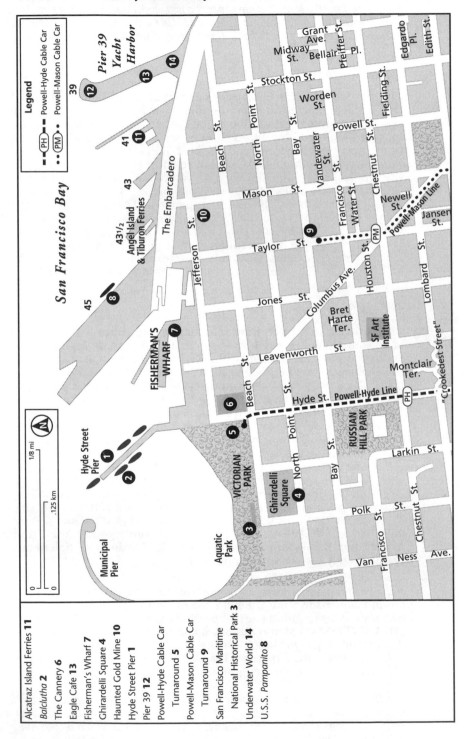

Legend

- (PH) —— Powell-Hyde Cable Car
- (PM) •••• Powell-Mason Cable Car

California Academy of Sciences

Golden Gate Park

The Academy features traveling exhibits on everything from dinosaurs to spiders that complement the informative permanent natural history exhibits that put to shame the dusty moose dioramas you may remember from grammar school field trips. You know you're in Southern California when you visit the Earth and Space exhibit, which includes a popular earthquake simulation — it's as close as you want to get to the real thing. Check out the **Morrison Planetarium** and the **Steinhart Aquarium,** too. Planetarium sky shows are scheduled frequently; call ☎ 415-750-7141 for show schedules. At the Steinhart Aquarium, kids love the hands-on tide pool, where they get to touch starfish and sea urchins. The seals and dolphins at the Steinhart Aquarium are fed every two hours, beginning at 10:30am; the penguins are fed at 11:30am and 4pm. You can find rest and relaxation in the cafeteria in the basement and enjoy strategically located gift shops for creative shopping. Plan on spending an hour or two here, longer if you attend a planetarium show.

*On the **Music Concourse.** ☎ 415-750-7145. Internet:* www.calacademy.org. *Open: Memorial Day–Labor Day 9am-6pm; Labor Day–Memorial Day 10am-5pm. Admission: $8.50 adults, $5.50 seniors and students 12–17, $2 children 4–11, free for children 3 and under. Free admission the first Wed of every month. Planetarium show, $2.50 adults, $1.25 seniors and children under 18.*

M. H. de Young Memorial Museum and the Asian Art Museum

Golden Gate Park

Just hop across the **Music Concourse** from the **Academy of Sciences** to explore these two museums, which are in the same building. You're at the right building when you see steel beams set up to help reinforce the structure in case of an earthquake. The **Memorial Museum** exhibits beautiful examples of American art and textiles, while the **Asian Art Museum** displays 6,000 years of Asian history. However, traveling exhibits no longer stop here due to the lack of a retrofit (they now go to the **Palace of the Legion of Honor**). Free docent tours are available. The excellent **Cafe de Young** serves salads and sandwiches to keep you going. Count on spending an hour to an hour and a half to tour the exhibits of both museums.

*75 Teagarden Dr., to the west of the **Music Concourse.** M. H. de Young Memorial Museum. ☎ 415-863-3330. Internet:* www.deyoungmuseum.org. *Asian Art Museum. ☎ 415-379-8801. Internet:* www.asianart.org. *Open: Tues–Sun 9:30am–5pm, until 8:45pm first Wed. of the month. Admission: $7 adults, $5 seniors, $4 for children 12–17, free for children under 12. Free first Wed of the month. The de Young Museum is going to close at the end of 2000 for almost five years for rebuilding. The Asian Art Museum is going to be open until the fall of 2001; it will be relocated to the Civic Center.*

Golden Gate Park

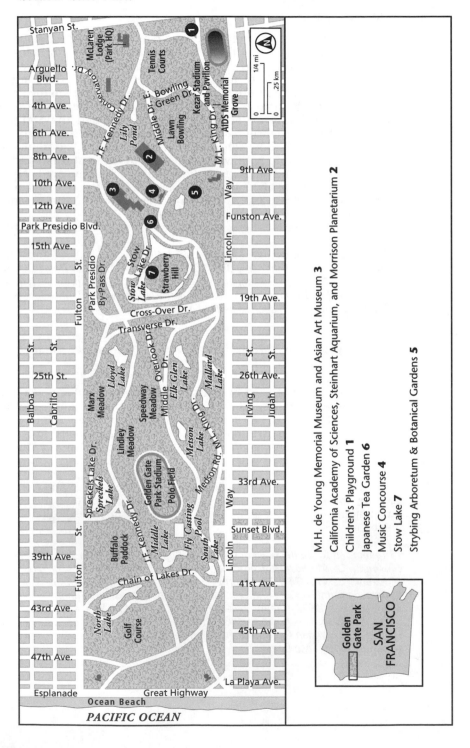

M.H. de Young Memorial Museum and Asian Art Museum **3**

California Academy of Sciences, Steinhart Aquarium, and Morrison Planetarium **2**

Children's Playground **1**

Japanese Tea Garden **6**

Music Concourse **4**

Stow Lake **7**

Strybing Arboretum & Botanical Gardens **5**

Golden Gate Park

SAN FRANCISCO

The Strybing Arboretum and Botanical Gardens

Golden Gate Park

With over 6,000 species of well-tended plants, flowering trees, and theme gardens, you'll find this to be a splendid oasis. It is exceptionally lovely in late winter when the rhododendrons blossom and wild iris poke up in corners, and there is no more peaceful a place when the skies are drizzling. You can catch a free docent tour offered daily at 1:30pm; I recommend it for those, like myself, who are arboreally and botanically challenged when trying to identify any but the most basic of flowers and trees. Plan to spend at least a half hour here just wandering around.

*9th Ave. at Lincoln Way, left of the tour bus parking lot by the **Music Concourse**. ☎ 415-661-1316, ext. 314 for docent tour info). Internet:* www.strybing.org. *Open: Mon–Fri, 8am–4:30pm, Sat–Sun, 10am–5pm. Admission: free.*

Japanese Tea Garden

Golden Gate Park

Enjoying this tranquil spot, with colorful pagodas, koi ponds, bridges, and a giant bronze Buddha, you feel that you're in the Orient. Young children find this part of the park particularly memorable — they can climb over a steeply arched, wooden bridge here, just as I did when I was much younger and more limber than I am today. The **Tea Garden's** beauty is slightly marred by its gift shop, full of miniature license plates and other junk. Tourists overrun this major touring destination some parts of the day. Try to get to this attraction before 10am or after 4pm during the summer to avoid the onslaught of tourists. You can partake in Japanese tea and snacks in the teahouse for $2.95 per person. While the garden is arguably worth the small admission fee, you won't be missing anything if you pass on the tea and crackers.

The garden entrance is to the left of the de Young Museum. ☎ *415-752-4227. Open: Oct–Feb, 8:30am–dusk, Mar–Sept, 8:30am–6:30pm. Admission: $3.50 adults, $1.25 seniors and children 6–12.*

Lombard Street

Russian Hill (Near North Beach)

Lombard Street, or to be exact, the part of Lombard with the moniker "crookedest street in the world," begins at Hyde Street below **Russian Hill.** This whimsical, flower-lined block attracts thousands of visitors each year. You should try driving down the red-brick street (it's one-way, downhill; take the curves slowly), as do many tourists. If you do, try it early in the morning before everyone else does. Or, if you want to take time to enjoy it, walk down the stairs to fully admire the flowers, the interesting houses with their colorful exteriors, and the stellar view. This portion of Lombard is between Hyde and Leavenworth Streets. Lombard Street is most convenient to the **Powell-Hyde cable car line.**

San Francisco Museum of Modern Art (MOMA)

SoMa

The handsome **Museum of Modern Art** houses an impressive collection of twenth-century paintings, sculptures, and photographs. The beautiful interior exudes a warmth that makes viewing the exhibits even more enjoyable. Among the Diebenkorns and Rauschenbergs, you may be surprised to see Jeff Koons' gold and white sculpture of Michael Jackson and his chimp pal Bubbles (an acquisition I think better suited to a Las Vegas hotel lobby, but perhaps the curators know something I don't?). The exhibits, excellent museum cafe, and the artfully stocked museum store keep you there for a good half-day.

151 Third St. (two blocks south of Market near Howard St.). ☎ 415-357-4000. Internet: www.sfmoma.org. *Muni: Take any Muni streetcar to the Montgomery St. Station or the 15-Third, 30-Stockton, or 45-Union/Stockton bus. Open: Thurs 11am–9pm, Fri–Tues, 11am–6pm. Closed Wed and major holidays. Opens at 10am during the summer. Admission: $8 adults, $5 seniors, and $4 students with ID. Half price Thurs 6–9pm. Free for children under 12. Free first Tues of the month.*

Yerba Buena Gardens and Center for the Arts

SoMa

An ice-skating rink/bowling alley, a children's garden and carousel, and an arts/technology studio for older kids joins this collection of galleries, gardens, a dance space, and a theater. An entertainment behemoth in a separate building across the street, accessible by way of a pedestrian bridge, houses restaurants, retail shops, and a multiplex movie screen. The 22-acre complex is now a micro-destination where there used to be only parking lots and derelicts. You can easily spend all day and evening here if you take advantage of all that **Yerba Buena Center** has to offer. Use public transportation or walk if at all possible because parking is difficult and/or expensive.

East of the carousel you can find the enclosed, but light-filled, **Yerba Buena Ice-Skating Rink** and the tidy 12-lane **Bowling Center** (☎ 415-777-3727). Public skating session times vary from day to day, so you want to phone before strapping on your figure skates and taking to the ice. Admission is adults $6, seniors and children 12 and under $4.50. Skate rental $2. The **Bowling Center** is open Sunday to Thursday 9am to 10pm, until midnight Friday and Saturday. Admission for adults is $3.50/game or $18/hour; seniors and children 12 and under $2/game or $12/hour.

Zeum (☎ 415-777-2800) is a rare and wonderful art/technology center in that the hands-on labs give visitors the opportunity to create animated video shorts with clay figures; learn about graphics, sound, and video production in the second floor studio; and interact with the changing gallery exhibits. The center is rare in that it's probably the only city attraction specifically designed for older kids and teens that doesn't rely on video games. Nevertheless, any bored adolescent would find it difficult not to succumb to a **Zeum** offering.

Yerba Buena Gardens

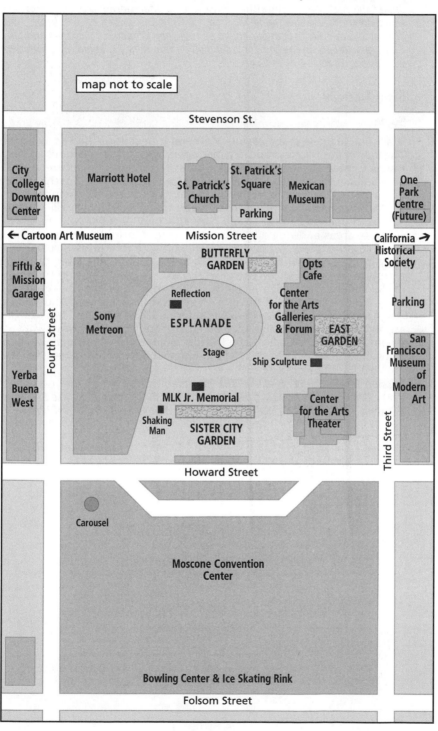

map not to scale

Stevenson St.

City College Downtown Center

Marriott Hotel

St. Patrick's Church

St. Patrick's Square

Parking

Mexican Museum

One Park Centre (Future)

← Cartoon Art Museum   Mission Street   California →

Fifth & Mission Garage

BUTTERFLY GARDEN

Opts Cafe

California Historical Society

Sony Metreon

Reflection

ESPLANADE

Stage

Center for the Arts Galleries & Forum

EAST GARDEN

Parking

Fourth Street

Ship Sculpture

San Francisco Museum of Modern Art

Yerba Buena West

MLK Jr. Memorial

Shaking Man

SISTER CITY GARDEN

Center for the Arts Theater

Third Street

Howard Street

Carousel

Moscone Convention Center

Bowling Center & Ice Skating Rink

Folsom Street

701 Mission St., between 3rd and 4th Streets. ☎ 415-978-2700 or 415-978-ARTS (box office). Internet: www.YerbaBuenaArts.org. Muni: streetcars to the Powell or Montgomery St. stations or 14-Mission, 15-Third bus among others. Open: Hours are Sat to Sun 11am to 5pm during the school year; Wed to Fri 12 to 6pm and Sat to Sun 11am to 5pm in the summer. Admission is adults $7, seniors and students $6, kids 5 to 18 $5.

Sony Metreon

SoMa

Noisy and lit like a Vegas casino, **Metreon** is best described as awesome. The four stories of glass and brushed metal anchoring one block of **Yerba Buena Center** are quite the sight. Some are calling it the future of entertainment centers, and, at the moment at least, there isn't anything like it on the planet. Of course, eating and spending are the big themes here — the Metreon has many places to fill one's tummy and empty one's wallet. Microsoft opened its first — and currently only — retail store here, with separate areas showing off the latest in games, productivity tools, hardware, colorful accessories, and music software (featuring a remarkable baby grand piano with a built-in LED screen). Sony has a big presence, naturally — a great showcase in which to ogle what's new in the way of digital cameras and other gadgets. On the third floor are 15 — count 'em 15 — movie screens and the city's very first Imax theater. And you can also find what Sony refers to as family-friendly attractions, two of which are cleverly based on popular children's books, *The Way Things Work* and *Where the Wild Things Are.* The third is an interactive game arena, likely to swallow up a generation of video-enhanced teens and young adults.

Mission at 4th St. ☎ 1-800-METREON. Internet: www.metreon.com. Open: daily, 10am–10pm. Admission: The prices for all three attractions are $17 adults, $13 seniors and kids 3–12. Individual attraction prices range from $7–$10.

Chapter 17

More Cool Things to See and Do

● ●

In This Chapter

▶ Keeping the kids content

▶ Indulging fans of history, art, and architecture

▶ Taking to the great outdoors

▶ Finding a spiritual spot

● ●

*J*ust because you've visited the top sights, doesn't mean you've seen San Francisco. You've only just had a taste of what makes San Francisco one of everybody's favorite cities.

This chapter gives ideas on how to entertain your younger children and keep your teenagers interested, how to get a taste of San Francisco history and more than a taste of art, where to take your hiking shoes and where to grab a bike, and much more. Read the listings to get an overview of the city, or just take a look at the categories that interest you most. Regardless, your tour of San Francisco is not over yet. In fact, we've only just begun.

Especially for Kids

The **San Francisco Zoo,** Sloat Boulevard and 45th Avenue (☎ 415-753-7080) is known as one of the nation's best animal parks. You'll find an innovative and noteworthy primate center, a carousel, a children's zoo, and — this is the clincher — a sizable children's playground near the front entrance. Stroll the more than 65 acres to see the animals, then park your tired body on a bench within yelling distance and let the under-10 members of the family climb to their heart's content. The L-Taraval Muni streetcar deposits riders in front of the zoo — this is the easiest way to get there from downtown. Admission is $9 adults, $6 seniors and kids 12 to 15, $3 kids 3 to 11, free for babes 2 and under. Take note of the Carousel hot dog parlor across Sloat Boulevard

The Zoo & Lake Merced Area

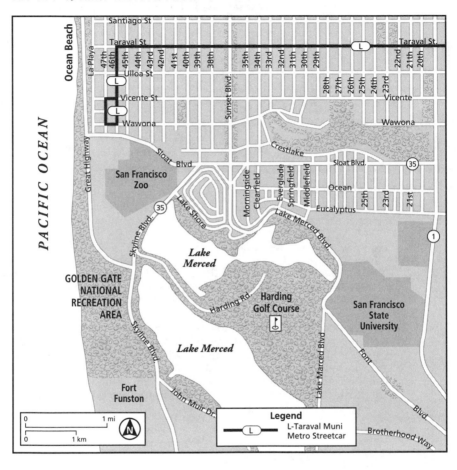

marked by a fiberglass, chef-hatted dachshund. Formerly one of many Doggie Diners in town, this puppy has been the center of heated controversy between those who want to grant it landmark status and those who want it moved so the site can be turned into a parking lot.

Another kid-pleaser is the **Museé Mecanique** (below the Cliff House, 1090 Point Lobos Rd., at the Great Highway; ☎ **415-386-1170**), which contains beautifully restored and maintained mechanical marvels that are the grandfathers of pinball machines. Get a roll of quarters to bring along (and boycott the obnoxious video games in a room at the back). The 38-Geary Bus takes you here. Otherwise, drive down Geary Street to Point Lobos Road. Park in the lot across the street from Louie's Diner. The museum is open daily from 10am to 8pm. Admission is free.

China Beach has picnic facilities and awe-inspiring views of the Golden Gate Bridge. It's also one of the few safe swimming beaches in town, but the water is chilly. The 29-Sunset bus stops at 25th Avenue and El Camino del Mar. From there it's a walk of about six blocks north to the beach.

Especially for Teens

The **Cartoon Art Museum,** 814 Mission St., at 4th Street (☎ **415-227-8666**), located near Yerba Buena Gardens, presents exhibits on all kinds of cartoon art and often showcases local cartoonists, such as the late Charles Schultz and Bill Griffith (creator of Zippy the Pinhead). The museum is open Wednesday through Friday from 11am to 5pm, Saturday from 10am to 5pm, and Sunday from 1 to 5pm. Admission is $5 adults, $3 seniors, $2 for children 6 to 12. The first Wednesday of each month is free.

San Francisco Centre, on the corner of Market and 5th Streets, is a nine-story mall containing many familiar names beloved by teenaged girls, including a huge **Nordstrom** department store. It doesn't have any shops unique to San Francisco, but it is convenient to downtown. Your young shopper may be just as happy exploring the stores around Union Square (see Chapter 6), and at least there you'll get a little fresh air on your way in and out of the revolving doors.

Teenagers adore **Metreon** (see Chapter 16) because the technology stores contain all the latest widgets, some of which they can audition. When they tire of gawking at stuff, the video games in the Airtight Garage can occupy as many minutes as you'll allow or that they can pay for. And once you've had enough, you can coax them to follow you with promises of food at one of the many cafes.

Zeum (see Chapter 16) was designed for 8 to 18-year-olds and is staffed by teens. Even recalcitrant 15-year-olds can find something engaging to do here, whether or not they admit it.

I saved the best for last. Take your teen to Haight Street for some shopping (and shock) therapy. The N-Judah streetcar deposits you a few blocks south of Haight, and it beats parking. One of the best music stores in town is here, **Amoeba Records,** and both the used and new clothing stores — in particular stop by Villians, 1672 Haight St. (☎ **415-626-5939**) — stock the coolest stuff around. I don't mean to make too much of the street scene, but youthful runaways do congregate in this neighborhood and it can feel equally attractive, poignant, and scary to adolescents. At the very least, you'll have something interesting to talk about on the ride back to your hotel.

Especially for History Buffs

To find out about San Francisco's gold rush history, take the free "Gold Rush City" walking tour offered by City Guides Sundays at 2pm and Wednesdays at noon. Meet by the flower stand at Clay and Montgomery Streets. The walk encompasses **Jackson Square** (Jackson and Montgomery Streets), a National Historic Register Landmark admired for its many restored Gold Rush–era brick warehouses. Call ☎ 415-557-4266 for details.

Levi Strauss and Co., whose namesake dressed the original 49ers, opens its historic Valencia Street plant (250 Valencia St., near 16th Street; ☎ 415-565-9159) to the public for tours every Tuesday and Wednesday at 9am, 11am, and 1:30pm. Reservations are necessary, but the tour is free. A company store is also available on the first floor of the factory.

The **Wells Fargo History Museum,** 420 Montgomery St., at California Street, ☎ 415-396-2619, displays mining equipment, antique stage-coaches, and gold nuggets in its collection. The museum is open weekdays from 9am to 5pm. Admission is free.

Especially for Art Lovers

You don't want to miss **Friends of Photography/Ansel Adams Center for Photography** if you're a photography fan. The new location is at 655 Mission St., ☎ 415-495-7000, around the corner from the Museum of Modern Art. Here you can see five galleries — one is devoted to Adams — and a bookstore. Admission is $5 adults, $3 students, $2 seniors and children 12 to 17. The easiest way to reach the center is to take Muni to the Montgomery Street. Station and walk one block east to Mission Street. It's open daily from 11am to 5pm.

The inspiring **California Palace of the Legion of Honor,** (in Lincoln Park between Clement Street and 34th Avenue in the outer Richmond District, ☎ 415-750-3600), exhibits an impressive collection of paintings, drawings, decorative arts, and one of the world's finest collections of Rodin sculptures, including an original cast of *The Thinker.* The grounds around the Palace are a draw as well. You can take the 38-Geary bus to 33rd Avenue, then transfer to the 18-46th Avenue bus for a ride to the museum entrance. Open Tuesday through Sunday from 9:30am to 5pm. Admission, which also includes same-day entry into the Asian and de Young art museums in Golden Gate Park (see Chapter 16), is $7 adults, $5 seniors over 65, $4 children 12 to 17, and free for children under 12 free. Admission is free on the second Wednesday of the month.

Some people like gallery hopping, and if that's your thing, direct yourself to **Union Square,** where you find art galleries in every nook and cranny. The area from Grant Avenue to Mason Street and Geary to Post Street is home to a number of fine-arts dealers where you can treat your eye to works from both contemporary and not-so-contemporary artists.

Of note are the **Stephen Wirtz Gallery** (☎ 415-433-6879) and **Toomey Tourell** (☎ 415-989-6444), both located in the canvas-rich building at 49 Geary St. at Grant, the **John Berggruen Gallery** at 228 Grant St. between Sutter and Post, ☎ 415-781-4629. The galleries are closed on Mondays. Serious art lovers can book an art gallery expedition through **Artline** (☎ 650-494-1368; Internet: www.e-artline.com). Lead by professional art consultant Danielle Wohl, the three-hour tours are offered the first Tuesday and Thursday of the month, or by appointment.

Architectural Highlights

When you visit the **Alamo Square Historic District,** you may feel a touch of déjà vu. That's because this is where the famous picture of the Victorian row houses was photographed. The "Painted Ladies," which front the San Francisco skyline, is still being sought by photographers, probably on a daily basis. You'll find this historic block between Steiner, Scott, Hayes, and Grove Streets, west of the Civic Center. The 21-Hayes bus takes you right there from Market and Hayes Streets.

The **Haas-Lilienthal House** (☎ 415-441-3004) is a Victorian open to the public. You can take one-hour tours of this 1886 Queen Anne, featuring many original furnishings, on Wednesdays from noon to 3pm and Sundays from 11am to 4pm. It's located at 2007 Franklin, at Jackson Street. To get there by bus, take the 12-Folsom, the 27-Bryant, the 42-Downtown Loop, the 47-Van Ness, the 49-Van Ness/Mission, or the 83-Pacific. Admission is $5 adults, $3 seniors 65 and older and children under 12.

You may also want to check out the **New Main Library,** 100 Larkin St. between Grove and Fulton Streets. Natural light streams in from a 5-story atrium skylight and windows that encircle the stacks. This is a library committed to the future, as you can see from the modern finish and feel; although critics say it's rather difficult to get to the books (and they are right). If you have kids along, definitely seek the children's section. The library even has — gasp — a gift shop. Take any Muni streetcar to the Civic Center station and walk a block west on Grove Street.

While you're in the Civic Center neighborhood, drop by the refurbished **City Hall** on Van Ness Avenue. between McAllister and Grove Streets. The building originally debuted in 1915, but it's never looked better. Not only did the building get a seismic retrofitting (*de riguer* in this town) and a good cleaning, but also the dome and ornamental balcony railings were regilded, creating an impressive landmark and adding golden highlights to the view.

For architectural wonders, see Chapter 18 to read about walking tours.

Golden Gate National Recreation Area

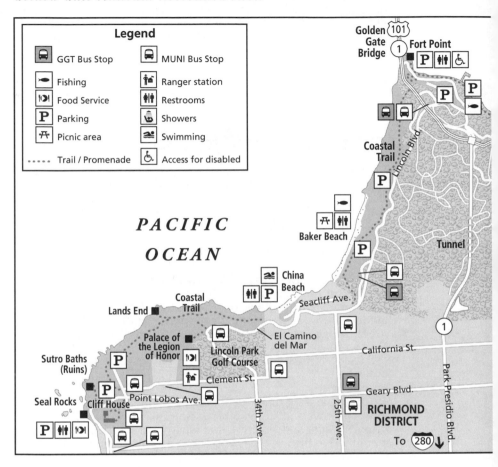

Especially for Bicyclists

Enjoy San Francisco from the seat of a bicycle. You can rent bikes and helmets from quite a few locations around town. For a ride in beautiful Golden Gate Park, run by one of the nearby bike stores, such as **Park Cyclery,** 1749 Waller St., ☎ **415-751-7368.** For real convenience, **Holiday Adventures,** 1937 Lombard St., ☎ **415-567-1192,** will pick you up at your hotel and drive you to its store in the Marina, which is convenient for rides over the Golden Gate Bridge or around the Presidio. Both shops charge $5 per hour; per day rates are $25 and $19 respectively for bikes and helmets. **Adventure Bicycle Company,** 968 Columbus Ave. near Chestnut Street (take the Powell/Mason cable car), ☎ **415-771-8735,** has rental packages that include ferry tickets at $25 for a full day and $20 for a half day. Finally, the not-for-profit Bike Hut at South Beach (on the Embarcadero at Pier 40) is the place to show up for high quality bikes to pedal along the waterfront. It's open Friday through Sunday from 10am to 5pm. Rentals are $5 per hour or $20 per day.

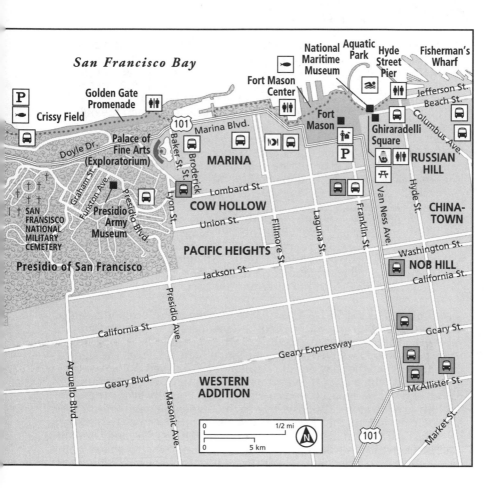

Another bike escape is to pedal across the Golden Gate Bridge into Sausalito, have something to eat, do a little sightseeing in this arty, touristy town, then return by ferry. The boats to San Francisco, **Blue and Gold** (☎ 415-773-1188) and **Golden Gate Ferry** (☎ 415-923-2000), depart the Sausalito ferry dock at least half a dozen times a day. Call for a schedule. One-way Blue and Gold Fleet fares are $6 adult and $3 children 5 to 11; one-way Golden Gate Ferry fares are $4.80 adults; $3.60 children 3–12; $2.40 seniors. The nine-mile ride to Sausalito is challenging mainly because of the wind that blows on the bridge and the other bicyclists you're competing with for space. If you prefer to have an escort on this ride, **Bay Bicycle Tours in the Cannery,** ☎ 415-923-6434, offers a 3½-hour, $45 tour that includes the bike, accessories, and ferry-boat fare.

Especially for Hikers

Angel Island, a federal and state wildlife refuge that is the largest of San Francisco Bay's three islets, is located eight miles from San Francisco and accessible only by ferry (a 20-minute journey) or private boat. Plan to spend the entire day on the island, hiking or biking, if you decide to go during the week (because of the limited ferry schedule). The ferry departs San Francisco sometime after 10am, and the only return trip departs sometime after 3pm. (The schedule changes seasonally.) On the weekends, you have the choice of four return trips. In any case, it's fun to bring a picnic with you, as opposed to using the small store and cafe that operate near the dock. Check out the beautiful 12 miles of hiking trails, and climb up Mt. Livermore for yet another spectacular view of the Golden Gate Bridge. Mountain bike rentals are also available on Angel Island, but for an exorbitant $10 an hour, which can really add up, especially for more than one person. Because of the cost, it's a good idea to rent a bike in San Francisco and bring it on the ferry. Call **Blue and Gold Ferry** (☎ **415-773-1188**) for a current ferry schedule. Round-trip fares are $11 adult, $10 kids 12 to 18, $6 children 5 to 11. For recorded information about the island, call ☎ **415-435-1915.** Ferries leave from Pier 41 in Fisherman's Wharf.

Fort Point (☎ **415-556-1373**), which dates from 1857, lies underneath the Golden Gate Bridge at the tip of the peninsula. Along with Civil War–era cannons, you can see surfers who appear to be risking their lives more than the soldiers once stationed here did. From the Hyde Street Pier, take the easy 3½-mile stroll along the paved Golden Gate Promenade, which hugs the coast as it passes through the Marina Green and the Presidio. Or, you can get to Fort Point by taking the 28-19th Avenue or the 29-Sunset bus to the Golden Gate Bridge and climbing down from the viewing area to a short trail leading to the Fort. You can take a self-guided audio tour of the fort if you like, and afterward backtrack to the Hyde Street cable car turnaround, where you can hop on a cable car to Union Square. Fort Point is open Wednesday through Sunday from 10am to 5pm. You can begin the Coastal Trail here as well, if you're up to a rigorous hike.

If you're new to hiking, the **Coastal Trail** to the Cliff House isn't a hike for you. It's rigorous! The trailhead, a bit east of Fort Point, is well marked. Heading south, the trail parallels the Pacific Ocean through the Presidio.

You can see small beaches below the trail on this hike, but if you're tempted to feel sand beneath your toes, please follow the marked paths to get there. Don't climb over any rocky cliffs; the land here isn't stable enough to guarantee your safe return.

When you reach Baker Beach, about 1½ miles from Fort Point, be prepared to see nude sun-worshippers. As you continue on the trail, you'll pass the Lobos Creek Water Treatment Plant. From there it's a short way to El Camino Del Mar, a street leading through Sea Cliff, a fancy residential neighborhood. At the end of El Camino Del Mar you'll pick up the trail near the Lincoln Golf Course. Continue apace, with the land and the views rewarding your every step. Eventually you'll arrive at the Cliff House, which has been serving refreshments to visitors since 1863. If you can resist having a well-deserved drink here, keep walking down the Great Highway until you reach the **Beach Chalet** restaurant and brewery (☎ 415-386-8439). After lunch you can return toward the Cliff House and catch the 38-Geary bus at La Playa and Balboa Street, or keep walking to Judah Street and take an N-Judah streetcar downtown.

Named in honor of Sierra Club founder and conservationist John Muir, 553-acre **Muir Woods** is what's left locally of the redwood forests that once dominated the coast of Northern California. While not as sizable as Redwood National Forest further north, these old growth redwoods are beautiful, and a range of trails here benefits hikers of all levels. From the Golden Gate Bridge, take the Stinson Beach/Highway 1 exit west and follow the signs. Parking is limited, so try setting out early in the day on weekends or go during the week. Muir Woods Park is open from 8am until sunset. For additional information call ☎ 415-388-2595.

Especially for Sports Fans

The San Francisco Giants major league baseball team opened the fabulous, 40,000-seat **Pacific Bell Park** stadium on the bay on opening day in April 2000. Season ticket holders have already bought up all the best seats, but buying bleacher seats to any but the most sought after games (all Giants versus Dodgers contests, for example) shouldn't be impossible, because they are sold only on game days. However, to purchase regular tickets or tickets from season ticket holders who are unable to make it to a particular game, plug onto their Web site (www.sfgiants.com) before you arrive. Transportation to the ballpark is easy — take Muni to the Embarcadero Station and transfer to the King Street extension.

The San Francisco 49ers play at **3Com Park.** Home games have been sold out for the last 12 years or so, but should you feel like trying your luck, the ticket office number is ☎ 415-656-4900. Scalpers sell tickets outside the park, but these are often counterfeit. The best method of transport to the park is by Muni bus. The 9X-San Bruno Express bus leaves from Sutter Street near Union Square; the 28X-19th Avenue bus runs along 19th Avenue; and the 47X-Van Ness cruises Van Ness Avenue.

Some Spiritual Pursuits

Arrive a good ½ hour early to claim a seat at the 9am Sunday services (an hour early for the 11am) at **Glide Memorial United Methodist Church,** 330 Ellis St., ☎ 415-771-6300. The Reverend Cecil Williams, a local celebrity and genuinely great man, lets the multi-ethnic gospel choir do most of the sermonizing, and they're wildly effective. A cross section of friendly San Franciscans packs the pews, clapping, singing, and celebrating. It's church, it's theater, and it's amazing.

Grace Cathedral, the magnificent Episcopal Church at the top of Nob Hill, 1100 California St. between Taylor and Jones Streets, ☎ 415-749-6300, has an outdoor stone terrazzo labyrinth that might promote a meditative moment. It's open to visitors daily, anytime. You can rent a labyrinth audio tour, complete with walking music provided by the Grace Choir, at the gift shop.

Old First Presbyterian Church, 1751 Sacramento St. at Van Ness Avenue, ☎ 415-474-1608, sponsors a concert series leaning heavily toward the classical that's low-cost and high quality. You can call for a list of upcoming events or check the Web site, www.oldfirstconcerts. org. It's a snap to get from downtown to the church on the California Street cable car line.

Mission Dolores at Dolores and 16th Streets, is a fine example of Mission architecture and the oldest building in the city. This is one of the 21 missions founded under the auspices of Franciscan Missionary Junipero Serra and built by Native Americans. Services were first held on the site a few days before the Declaration of Independence was signed. It's open daily from 9am to 4pm. A self-guided audio tour takes 40 minutes. Admission is by donation; the audio tour costs $1. The J-Church Muni streetcar stops one block east.

Garden and Park Respites

San Franciscans cherish the city's open spaces. If you know where to look, you will find little parks and secret gardens in some unlikely places. For example, at the end of Market Street in the Embarcadero, two simple gardens grace the seventh floor of One Market Plaza. Elevators to the gardens are situated in the Spear and Steuart Street lobbies. Upon exiting, walk toward the bay; you'll find two patios surrounded by well-tended circular expanses of lawn bordered by pansies and primroses overlooking a classic bay view.

Not far afield at **Rincon Center** (corner of Mission and Steuart Streets) is a courtyard garden replete with aqua-colored iron benches sitting among a generous array of ornamental hedges, potted azaleas, and seasonal plantings. You can get a snack inside and enjoy it in the garden, which is quiet until the office workers are released for lunch. A few blocks away at 100 1st St. you'll find the award-winning second-floor garden in the Delta Tower, which is a lush respite from the madness of the Transbay Terminal and Mission Street. The black granite and green glass fountain sculpture provide a soothing counterpoint to the street traffic. **Yerba Buena Gardens** (see Chapter 16) features willow trees, a sweep of bright green lawn, and blossoms that put the commercial aspects of the development into perspective. Behind the garden's 22-foot waterfall is a memorial to Martin Luther King Jr., featuring a series of glass panels etched with quotations from Dr. King's speeches and writings.

Levi's Plaza, located between the Embarcadero and Sansome Streets, consists of the company's multiple buildings and two plazas separated by Battery Street. The centerpiece of the *hard* plaza is a fountain you can walk through on paving stones — a big favorite with kids. The *soft* plaza across the street is really a park with fir trees and grass; jeans-clad workers relax here on balmy days.

 Cross the plaza to Sansome Street and look for the bottom of the Filbert Steps, a steep staircase that rises to Montgomery and Filbert Streets. Around the midpoint of the stairway you'll find a sight so profoundly San Francisco that you'll immediately understand what all the fuss is about. This is the Grace Marchand Garden; its roses and ferns adding a wild elegance to the hillside. The residents don't like the tourists who clog the steps, especially on weekends, but that's the price they have to pay for living next to a minor landmark. In any case, this is a garden to admire from outside the wooden fence only.

Chapter 18

And on Your Left, Golden Gate Park: Seeing San Francisco by Guided Tour

. . . .

In This Chapter

▶ Deciding whether guided tours are right for you

▶ Taking in the sights by bus, on foot, or by boat

▶ Touring on your own

▶ Thinking up unusual ways to see the city

. . . .

Don't feel self-conscious about taking a guided tour of the city. Actually, guided tours are a sensible way to get your bearings in a new place and see a great deal in a relatively short period of time. Yet many travelers, myself included, hate the idea of being herded on and off large buses like cattle. But don't count out guided tours just yet. I can think of several valid reasons for taking a guided tour. You may not have much time to explore on your own and just want to catch the major sights in one day. Or perhaps you have difficulty getting around, or you don't want to drive. Or you need an overview to find out what interests you in a specific city, or you're traveling alone and want some company.

You can find as many varieties of guided tours as there are varieties of people in San Francisco. Not all tours have you peering out a dirty bus window at some national landmark while straining to hear the muffled guide's voice on the microphone. If you decide a tour is for you, call the companies or individual guides for their brochures or ask your hotel to send you information. Most tours require advanced reservations.

 Hotels generally recommend "preferred providers" for guided bus tours. But, since often the concierge is getting a small kickback for every tour recommendation, the providers are sometimes less than the best companies. If you favor one tour company over another, book it yourself or request that tour specifically when you speak to the concierge. Don't leave the decision up to the hotel.

The Bus Stops Here — Touring by Bus

If you want to say that you at least "saw" San Francisco's major attractions, then orientation tours that skim the surface of the city may be just the ticket. Some tour operators spiff up the tours with motorized cable cars or double-decker buses, whereas other companies use lower profile minibuses that appeal to tourists who don't want to stand out in a crowd.

Be advised that not all trips are narrated by the bus driver; some just have recorded commentary. I do not recommend these audio tours. The sound quality is miserable and some of the information is outdated, such as the part about the prices of homes you see on the tour. As a matter of fact, I think prices went up another 10 percent while you were reading this book.

Gray Line Tours (☎ 415-558-9400; Internet: www. graylinesanfrancisco. com), the big kahuna of the tour industry, schedules a number of orientation tours around the city and beyond in red double-decker buses, motorized cable cars, and smaller vans. The deluxe 3½-hour city tour ($31 for adults; $15.50 for children 5 to 11) hits the highlights — Twin Peaks, Mission Dolores, the Cliff House, Golden Gate Park, the Golden Gate Bridge — and you can option for tacking on a trip to Alcatraz.

Tower Tours (☎ 415-434-8687; Internet: www.bayareacitysearch. com/E/V/SFOCA/0001/04/02/1.html) is popular with many people because the company uses sleek, low-profile minibuses that carry only about two dozen people. Tower's city tour stops at the same sites as Gray Line's buses. The cost is $29 for adults and $14 for children 5 to 11.

Save Money on Muni and Tour-It-Yourself

Stopping at every other corner and having a driver that doesn't give much, if any, commentary may not seem like the ideal tour situation. But, touring by Muni public buses isn't as silly as it sounds, especially considering that the tour will only cost you $1 or $2. These "orientation" tours are not for the impatient traveler or for anyone who requires a great deal of comfort — city buses are, after all, creaky and well-worn. But they're cheap and they let you come and go at your leisure — if you decide 25 minutes at Golden Gate Park isn't enough, who cares if the bus leaves? There's always another one coming!

Ask for a free transfer when you board the bus. With the transfer, you can get off the bus whenever you like and catch another bus or a Muni streetcar at no additional charge (within 90 minutes). Transfers are not valid on cable cars, however.

Muni tour #1 — the 42-Downtown Loop bus

The 42-Downtown Loop bus, as its name implies, makes a big loop around downtown. The route starts at the CalTrain Depot at 4th and Townsend Streets and, depending on which direction you go, travels past Civic Center on Van Ness Avenue, then continues along Van Ness Avenue to Fisherman's Wharf, then travels along Northpoint Street over to the Embarcadero, and then goes down the Embarcadero back to 4th Street (or vice versa).

Muni tour #2 — traveling on the West side

Another do-it-yourself tour takes you around the western perimeter of the city using a combination of buses and a streetcar. From any downtown Muni station (Powell Street is closest to Union Square), catch the L-Taraval or N-Judah streetcar, both of which travel through some well-kept residential neighborhoods. Get off at Sunset Boulevard in the outer Sunset District. On Sunset Boulevard, at Taraval Street or Judah Street, depending on which streetcar you rode, pick up a 29-Sunset bus going to the Presidio (*not* to California and 25th Avenue, which travels over to 25th Avenue and enters the former military base). The spectacular views on this part of the ride include the Pacific Ocean and the Golden Gate Bridge. In fact, the bus stops right by a viewing area where you can get off the bus and walk across the bridge and back. The ride also includes a look at a pet cemetery inside the Presidio.

The 29-Sunset terminates at Letterman Hospital in the Presidio, but you can then catch the 43-Masonic bus from the same bus shelter, which takes you down Lombard Street and over to Chestnut Street in the Marina district. From there, the 30-Stockton meanders along Chestnut over to Van Ness Avenue, and then travels down Van Ness to Northpoint Street, close to Aquatic Park and Ghirardelli Square. The route then goes through North Beach, Chinatown (where the bus fills up with hordes of old Chinese ladies carrying grocery bags), and back to Union Square. Alternatively, you can walk to Pier 39 and catch the F-Market streetcar for a ride down the Embarcadero and up Market Street. Allow three hours without breaks.

One If by Sea — Touring by Boat

Boat cruises provide a view of the city from an unusual vantage point and are the only way to experience the bay in all of its glory. There are quite a few options for riding the waves of the bay. One of which is the ferries. Ferries pick up passengers from Fisherman's Wharf (Pier 41) and the Ferry Building.

The Blue and Gold Fleet (☎ 415-773-1188) operates ferries to and from Marin County. This is also the only company that will take you to Alcatraz Island (see Chapter 16). Blue and Gold's one-hour bay cruise ($17 for adults, $13 for seniors and kids 12 to 18, $9 for kids 5 to 11) sails under the Golden Gate Bridge; past Sausalito, Angel Island, and Alcatraz; then back to Fisherman's Wharf. This tour will be a satisfying, if brief, encounter with the bay, as long as you have no particular interest in landing on these shores.

You want something a little more exciting than a ferry? Try cruising on *The Ruby* (☎ 415-861-2165). This 60-foot steel sloop, which holds about 30 passengers, skims the white caps in the bay daily with a lunch cruise from 12:30 to 3pm and an early evening sail with hors d'oeuvres from 6 to 8:30pm. The cost is $35 per person (includes the food); beer and wine are available but at an additional cost. Reservations are necessary. The Ruby is docked by The Ramp, which is at the foot of Mariposa Street at 3rd. The 22-Fillmore or 15-Kearny bus drops you off a block away.

You could also voyage from Sausalito on the *Hawaiian Chieftain* (☎ 415-331-3214). This is a 103-foot steel-hulled, square-rigged topsail ketch, designed to resemble a late-18th-century European trading vessel. It glides into the sunset April through October only, from 6 to 9pm Wednesday through Friday. The cost is $35 on Wednesday and Thursday, $40 on Friday (hors d'oeuvres and drinks included). You can also choose a three-hour Sunday brunch sail with live music for $50 per person, and a four-hour Saturday adventure sail for $45 per person, including lunch.

Hornblower Dining Yachts (☎ 415-788-8866) let you fine-dine as you sail, offering lunch, dinner, and brunch cruises around the bay. Cruises last from 1½ hours for lunch to 3 hours for the nightly dinner/dance. The food isn't the finest, but this is a wonderful way to dine — surrounded by superb views. Dinner rates per person are $69 Sunday through Friday, $81 Saturday. Lunch is $35; Saturday brunch, $43; and Sunday brunch, $47. Kids are half price. Reservations required.

Take a Walk on the Wild Side — Walking Tours

Friends of the Library sponsor **City Guides walking tours** (☎ 415-557-4266; www.hooked.net/users/jhum). There are 26 different paths to choose from, all for free — that's right, no charge! And it's simple; all you have to do is pick the tour that interests you and show up at the proper corner on time. You can get an insider's view of Chinatown; admire the "Painted Ladies," San Francisco's collection of beautifully restored Victorian homes on the Landmark Victorians of Alamo Square tour; or explore the haunts of the original 49ers on the Gold Rush City tour. Tours run about two hours on average. Highly recommended!

The Victorian Home Walk (☎ 415-252-9485; Internet: www. victorianwalk. com) combines a trolley car excursion with a walking tour through a number of celebrated neighborhoods. During the 2½-hour tour, you see an array of houses in areas where tour vans are prohibited from entering; and the guide promises the walk isn't strenuous. The cost is $20. Tours leave daily at 11am from the lobby of the Westin St. Francis, 335 Powell St. (between Geary and Post Streets) in the Union Square neighborhood.

San Francisco Architectural Heritage conducts a Pacific Heights walk (☎ 415-441-3000 for reservations) on Sundays at 12:30pm beginning at the Haas-Lilienthal house (see Chapter 17). The two-hour tour through this swanky neighborhood costs just $5 for adults and $3 for seniors and children.

Eating Your Way through San Francisco

Shirley Fong-Torres, a local writer and personality, has been operating Chinatown food tours for 15 years. The 3½-hour walk manages to demystify the exotic rather irreverently. It includes running commentary about the history of this fascinating neighborhood and stops at an artist studio, a one-room temple, a market, an herbal shop, and a tea company, where you're treated to a tasting. Shirley's company, **Wok Wiz Chinatown Walking Tours & Cooking Center,** 654 Commercial St., between Kearny and Montgomery Streets, ☎ 800-281-9255 or 415-981-8989, schedules the tours daily. They cost $37 for adults, $35 for seniors, and $28 for kids under 12 (dim sum lunch included).

The popular North Beach neighborhood reaches new heights of giddiness on Saturdays when food writer GraceAnn Walden leads **Mangia!** North Beach, a 4½-hour, $45 walking, eating, shopping, and history tour. GraceAnn and her followers traipse in and out of a deli, an Irish pub (stout is actually rather bracing in the morning), a truffle factory, a bakery, a pottery store, and two lovely churches, before ending with a multi-course family-style lunch at one of her favorite restaurants. Lots of samples, lots of tidbits about the Italians, and lots of fun. Call ☎ 415-397-8530 to make reservations.

Special Interest Tours

Get a great introduction to gay and lesbian history from the Gold Rush to the present with the delightful Trevor Hailey, a 27-year Castro resident, on her four-hour **Cruisin' the Castro** walking tour (☎ 415-550-8110). Brunch is included in the $40 price. Tours depart from the Harvey Milk Plaza, which is atop the Castro Street Muni Station at the corner of Castro and Market Streets. Reservations are required.

Caffeine-addicts and coffee connoisseurs alike will enjoy this walking tour devoted entirely to the tasting of java. With Elaine Sosa, guide of **Javawalk** (☎ **415-673-WALK;** Internet: www.javawalk.com), you spend two hours sipping java in the North Beach cafes, learning how to take coffee breaks with finesse. Tours run Tuesdays through Saturdays, beginning at 10am. The cost is $20 for adults and $10 for kids.

The **Precita Eyes Mural Arts Center,** 348 Precita Ave. (☎ **415-285-2287**), a not-for-profit arts center, shows you more than 50 murals on one of its Mission District walking tours that it sponsors. The eight-block walk departs Saturdays at 11am near the 24th Street BART station or at the center itself at 1:30pm. The cost is just $5 for adults, $4 for seniors, and $1 for children under 18. You can also experience a Mexican Bus Mural Tour, also sponsored by the Center, which includes public wall art outside the Mission. This two-hour tour runs only on the third Sunday of the month. The charge is $16 adults, $12 children 18 and under.

An easy way to explore the redwood groves of Muir Woods (see Chapter 17) is with Sierra Club guide Tom Martell, of **Tom's Scenic Walking Tours** (☎ **800-909-9255** or 415/381-5106). He'll pick you up (and drop you off) at your hotel, provide a picnic lunch, and drive up to six adventurers to the lovely redwoods just beyond the Golden Gate Bridge for a two- to four-mile hike. Cost for the 3½-hour walk with lunch is $49.95.

Chapter 19

A Shop-'Til-You-Drop Guide to San Francisco

In This Chapter

▶ Locating San Francisco's big name shops and specialty boutiques

▶ Discovering the main shopping neighborhoods

▶ Shopping for bargains

▶ Finding the right store for the merchandise you're looking for

*A*lthough most people might associate Union Square as the hub of San Francisco shopping, downtown shopping has plenty of competition. Nearly every San Francisco neighborhood boasts a thriving "main street" of locally owned boutiques, cafes, and bookstores. You can find shops with unique arts and crafts, clothing stores that eschew chain-mentality fashion, even houseware havens that reflect the style of the local clientele. Shopping in San Francisco is never mundane. Depending on where you head, you can try on a different attitude as easily as a different outfit.

The Shopping Scene

If you know where to look, there's some very interesting shopping you can do around here. Oh, plenty of people complain about the city being Starbucked and Gapped to death, but they aren't looking beyond the obvious retail centers. Not all the entrepreneurs in San Francisco are going into dot.com businesses (believe it or not) — some are actually opening boutiques with a personal stamp. In particular, check out Valencia Street for post-modern street wear and decor, Sacramento Street for contemporary clothing and accessories, and Hayes Street for design trends.

You'll find that stores are generally open Monday through Saturday from 10am to 6pm and on Sunday from noon to 5pm, even on many holidays. Shops around Fisherman's Wharf tend to stay open later, as do most department stores.

San Francisco Shopping

African Outlet **11**
Belden Place **27**
Bell'occhio **15**
Biordi Art Imports **20**
Books, Inc. **1**
Britex Fabrics **33**
Burton's Pharmacy **2**
Carol Doda's Champagne and Lace **6**
Chong Imports **25**
City Art **17**
City Lights Bookstore **23**
Clarion Music Center **26**
Dandelion **39**
Encantanda Gallery **17**
Espirit Factory Outlet **40**
Fillamento **9**
Forrest Jones **42**
Gazoontite **5**
Golden Gate Fortune Cookies Company **24**
Goodbyes **41**
Gump's **31**
Home Remedies **17**
House of Magic **3**
Imperial Tea Court **6**
Insolent **19**
Isda & Co. **37**
Joesph Schmidt Confections **16**
Macy's **33**
Maiden Lane **32**
Mrs. Dewson's Hats **10**
Mudpie **7**
Neiman Marcus **34**
Nest **8**
Nuts About You **14**
Original Levi's Store **29**
Paxton Gate **17**
Richard Hilkert, Bookseller **13**
Rolo **35**
Rolo Garage **38**
Saks Fifth Avenue **28**
San Francisco Centre **36**
Star Classics **12**
Wilkes Bashford **30**
Tai Yick Trading Company **22**
Virginia Breier **43**
XOX Truffles **18**

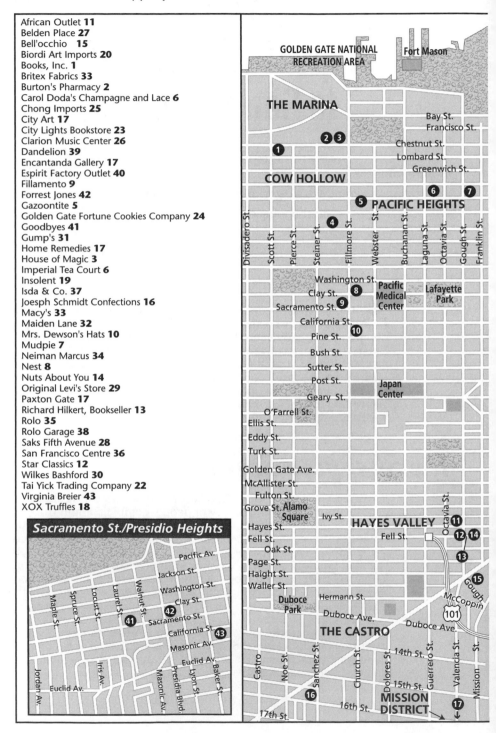

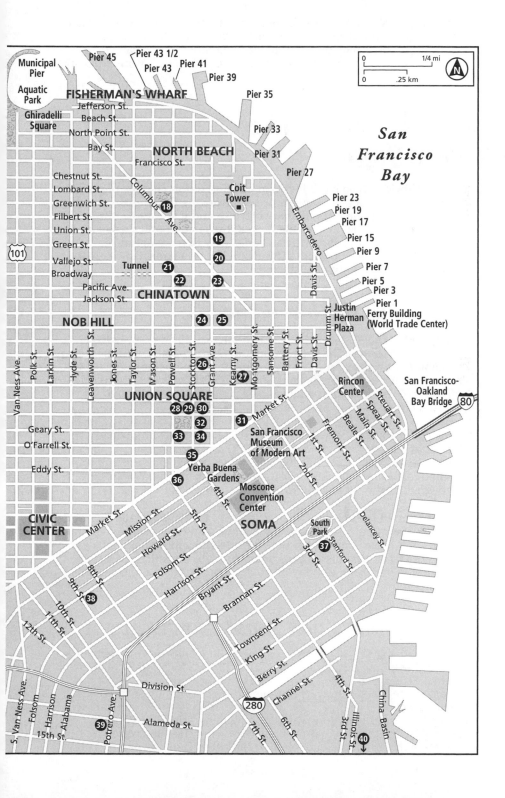

Municipal
Pier

Aquatic
Park

Ghiradelli
Square

FISHERMAN'S WHARF

Pier 45

Pier 43 1/2

Pier 43

Pier 41

Pier 39

Pier 35

Pier 33

Pier 31

Pier 27

Jefferson St.

Beach St.

North Point St.

Bay St.

NORTH BEACH

Francisco St.

Chestnut St.

Lombard St.

Greenwich St.

Filbert St.

Union St.

Green St.

Vallejo St.

Broadway

Pacific Ave.

Jackson St.

CHINATOWN

Tunnel

NOB HILL

Coit
Tower

Columbus Ave.

Embarcadero

Pier 23

Pier 19

Pier 17

Pier 15

Pier 9

Pier 7

Pier 5

Pier 3

Pier 1

Justin
Herman
Plaza

Ferry Building
(World Trade Center)

Davis St.

Drumm St.

**San
Francisco
Bay**

101

Van Ness Ave.

Polk St.

Larkin St.

Hyde St.

Leavenworth St.

Jones St.

Taylor St.

Mason St.

Powell St.

Stockton St.

Grant Ave.

Kearny St.

Montgomery St.

Sansome St.

Battery St.

Front St.

Davis St.

UNION SQUARE

Geary St.

O'Farrell St.

Eddy St.

San Francisco
Museum
of Modern Art

Yerba Buena
Gardens

Moscone
Convention
Center

Market St.

Rincon
Center

Steuart St.

Spear St.

Main St.

Beale St.

Fremont St.

1st St.

2nd St.

San Francisco–
Oakland
Bay Bridge

80

**CIVIC
CENTER**

Market St.

Mission St.

Howard St.

Folsom St.

Harrison St.

4th St.

5th St.

SOMA

South
Park

3rd St.

Stanford St.

Delancey St.

Bryant St.

Brannan St.

8th St.

9th St.

10th St.

11th St.

12th St.

Townsend St.

King St.

Berry St.

Channel St.

4th St.

3rd St.

Illinois St.

China Basin

S. Van Ness Ave.

Folsom

Harrison

Alabama

15th St.

Division St.

Alameda St.

7th St.

6th St.

280

18 19 20 21 22 23 24 25 26 27 28 29 30 31 32 33 34 35 36 37 38 39 40

0   1/4 mi

0   .25 km

N

Sales tax in San Francisco is 8.5 percent, and the salesperson will add it at the register for all goods. You don't have to pay the sales tax if the store ships something out of state for you, but shipping can cost as much or more than the tax, unless you're purchasing a very expensive item.

Finding the Stores That Suit Your Style

The worldwide chain store invasion has not, unfortunately, passed San Francisco by. In fact, we accept the blame for the Gap frenzy — the headquarters are near the Embarcadero — and if you see a Pottery Barn or a Gymboree in your midst, well, those companies originated in the Bay Area, as well. But you can find plenty of truly unique emporiums that will make shopping a joy again. Here's a short list of great places to get your shopping started:

Shopping the big names

Gump's (☎415-982-1616), in Union Square at 135 Post St., between Kearny Street and Grant Avenue, is famous for its Asian antiques, silver, and china, as well as for longevity — has been in business since 1861. Anyone who receives a gift from Gump's will shower impressive thanks on the giver because of the name itself. Open Monday through Saturday from 10am to 6pm, until 7pm Thursday.

Looking for the perfect place for one-stop-shopping? Then head over to the remodeled **Macy's** (☎ 415-397-3333) on Union Square, at Stockton and O'Farrell Streets. At 700,000 square feet, this eight-story, glass-fronted fashion legend is bigger than some towns! Open Monday through Saturday 10am to 8pm, Sunday from 11am to 7pm.

The Original Levi's Store, 345 Stockton St., ☎ 415-501-0100, is a showcase for more than 501s — you'll see some wild designs stitched onto jackets and jeans. One corner of this three-story monument to denim is dedicated to alterations, in case your shrink-to-fits still need a tuck here and there. Open Monday through Saturday 10am to 8pm, Sunday 11am to 6pm.

Other places you should know about

Bell'occhio (☎415-864-4048) has long been a favorite among decorators and wedding planners. But, with its hidden location in an alley off Market Street near Civic Center, it was widely unknown even among locals. Once Martha Stewart discovered this bewitching little place, things started to change. Stewart features it on her television show every now and then. Along with cunning decorations and French ribbons, you can buy interesting items the owner has discovered on her travels, such as a bit of chocolate or imported face powder. The shop is at 8 and 10 Brady Alley, off Market Street between 12th and Gough Streets. Take the F-Market streetcar to Civic Center. Open Tuesday through Saturday from 11am to 5pm.

Dandelion, 55 Potrero Ave., at Alameda, ☎ **415-436-9500,** isn't a place you can find by accident. You have to have heard about this place from a devoted customer, with its out-of-the-way location, close to the Design Center south of Market Street. The owners seem to be magnets for beautiful objects. Their prices are very fair; their taste impeccable. The 9-San Bruno bus from Market and 9th Streets can take you right here. Open Monday through Saturday 10am to 6pm, Sunday noon to 5pm.

Famed *San Francisco Chronicle* journalist Herb Caen's favorite clothing store, **Wilkes Bashford,** 375 Sutter St., between Stockton Street and Grant Avenue, near Union Square, ☎ **415-986-4380,** was often mentioned in his columns. San Francisco's natty mayor, famous for his wardrobe, purchases his Brioni suits here. Open Monday through Saturday 10am to 6pm, Thursday to 8pm.

Candy connoisseurs will no doubt recognize the name **Joseph Schmidt,** an artist whose medium is chocolate. Surprisingly, there are no known permanent collections of his edible work. His gallery — er, confectionery shop — is in the Castro at 3489 16th St., at Sanchez Street, ☎ **415-861-8682.** Take the J-Church Muni Metro streetcar to 16th Street and walk one block west. Open Monday through Saturday from 10am to 6:30pm.

For CDs, vinyl (remember that?), and an in-depth selection of preplayed music, the cognoscenti shop at **Amoeba Records,** 1855 Haight St., ☎ **415-831-1200,** in the musically famous neighborhood of the same name, is open Monday through Saturday from 10am to 10pm, Sunday 11am to 9pm.

When those cognoscenti stroll down Haight Street, they often wear really cool clothes from **Rolo,** a locally grown retailer with four stores around town. The flagship store, which carries streetwear for both men and women, is on Union Square at 21 Stockton St., between Ellis and O'Farrell Streets, ☎ **415-989-7656.** Open Monday through Saturday from 10am to 8pm and Sunday 11am to 7pm.

Great Shopping Neighborhoods

Looking for that perfect little doodad for Aunt Jane back home? Or do you just like to browse and see what catches your fancy? Below is a rundown of the city's best shopping areas, with a few highlights in each. Happy hunting!

Union Square

You're never far from a department store here. From one spot in the middle of Union Square you can see **Neiman Marcus** on Stockton and Geary Streets, **Saks Fifth Avenue** on the corner of Powell and Post

Streets, Levi's on Post and Stockton, and Macy's everywhere else. Ah — Shopping! A half-block north of Neiman's on Stockton Street is Maiden Lane, which is lined with designer shops. You can also find an entrance here to **Britex Fabrics,** probably the most well-stocked notions and fabric store in the country. Walk another block east and two blocks north and watch for tiny **Belden Place** between Bush and Pine Streets (see Chapter 13). A covey of delicious little restaurants lines the alley, and any one of them makes a satisfying place to stop for a meal. At lunchtime on fair days, Belden, which is blocked off to car traffic, is filled with cafe tables, giving the street a partylike atmosphere.

An unfortunate development along with the tourist trade is the multitude of shady salespeople that operate questionable electronics/camera, luggage, and gift shops on certain blocks of Mason, Powell, and Market Streets around Union Square. Out-of-town customers have been known to discover inflated charges on their credit cards after shopping at these places, so buyer beware.

Chinatown

Chinatown is known for its cheap trinkets and clothing. The items in the tiny shops that line Grant Avenue are not the must-haves you come to San Francisco seeking. If you venture off Grant Avenue, however, shop to your heart's content in Chinese herbal shops with strange remedies and unique jewelry stores full of jade of varying quality. The merchants in the less touristy stores don't always speak English, and they may seem less than friendly, but don't let that stop you from looking around.

The "going-out-of-business" signs you see taped to the windows of perhaps several Chinatown antique and souvenir stores are nearly as old as the grandmothers you see on the street with babies tied to their backs. These stores have been going out of business for years. Don't expect any bargains.

If you prefer to stay on Grant Avenue, the best place to find inexpensive (or expensive) gifts and housewares is **Chong Imports,** 838 Grant Ave., in the Empress of China building between Clay and Washington Streets, ☎ **415-982-1432.** This basement-level treasure house stocks a little of everything. Open daily from 10am to 9pm.

At the **Clarion Music Center,** 816 Sacramento St., near Grant Avenue, ☎ **415-391-1317,** www.clarionmusic.com, check out the amazing instruments, including traditional Chinese musical instruments like moon-shaped guitars, plus Chinese lion dance masks. Open Monday through Friday from 11am to 6pm, Saturday from 9am to 5pm. Call for a Friday night world concert series schedule.

Tai Yick Trading Company, 1400 Powell St., at Broadway (☎ **415-986-0961**), sells teapots, dishes, lamps, porcelain and pottery vases, and statues at reasonable prices. The owners are helpful and friendly, and native San Franciscans assure us that this is the best store of its kind in town. Open daily from 9:30am to 6:30pm.

The Imperial Tea Court, 1411 Powell St. near Broadway (☎ **415-788-6080**), already noted as a tranquil place to rejuvenate oneself, sells everything you need to brew a proper cup of Chinese tea. Open daily from 11am to 6:30pm.

Legend has it that fortune cookies were invented at the Japanese Tea Garden in Golden Gate Park. But if you want to watch these tasty cookies being made, head over to the Golden Gate Fortune Cookies Company in Chinatown (see Chapter 16). The fresh cookies make wonderful gifts to take back home. The working factory is located at 956 Ross Alley, between Jackson and Washington Streets near Grant Avenue. It's open daily from 10am to 7pm.

North Beach

North Beach is more than just a food and drink mecca — you can find all sorts of curiosities and clothing off Columbus Street. The section of Grant Avenue (completely different from the street of the same name in Chinatown) from Green to Greenwich Streets has a more Parisian accent, with stylish boutiques for clothes and accessories. If you're in the market for women's French designer shoes, be sure to walk into **Insolent,** 1418 Grant, ☎ **415-788-3334,** open Monday through Saturday 11am to 7pm, Sunday 11am to 6pm.

There's no need to fly to Italy, when you can shop at **Biordi Art Imports,** 412 Columbus Ave., at Vallejo Street, ☎ **415-392-8096.** Peruse the most beautiful hand-painted Majolica dishes and serving pieces from Italy. You may find them just too pretty to eat off. Open Monday through Saturday from 9:30am to 6pm.

City Lights Bookstore, 261 Columbus Ave., ☎ **415-362-8193,** is famous for its Beat Generation roots, but it's also a book-fiend's paradise. The first all-paperback bookstore in San Francisco, this city institution dates to 1953, when it was opened by Beat poet Lawrence Ferlinghetti. Most people at the time thought hardcover books were superior to paperbacks in terms of both the quality of the content as well as the quality of the paper. Ferlinghetti challenged this attitude and made great literature available to everyone by stocking his bookstore with less costly paperback editions. Open daily from 10am to midnight.

Admirers of chocolate can wedge themselves into **XOX Truffles,** 754 Columbus Ave., ☎ **415-421-4814,** a tiny store devoted to nickel-sized truffles in a huge assortment of flavors. These bites of bliss are all handmade by a young French chef, who removed himself from the rigors of the restaurant world to bring pleasure to us chocoholics.

Union and Chestnut Streets

According to a 1995 survey, one out of four visitors to San Francisco plans on visiting Union Street between Fillmore Street and Van Ness Avenue in the Marina district. Folks who love wandering in and out of specialty shops will think they've hit pay dirt. Muni buses 22-Fillmore,

41-Union, 42-Downtown Loop, and 45-Union/Stockton all run on Union Street.

Carol Doda, who shaped a career out of her chest long before implants were considered accessories, runs a lingerie shop, **Carol Doda's Champagne and Lace** at 1850 Union St., ☎ **415-776-6900.** She carries bras in regular and hard-to-find sizes, plus lots of other fun things. Open daily from 12:30 to 7pm (to 6pm on Sunday).

If you find yourself sneezing and sniffling on a regular basis, or if you surround yourself with people who do, help now comes in the form of **Gazoontite**. Located at 2157 Union St. (☎ **415-931-2230**), useful products for your favorite asthmatic or allergy-prone relative are attractively displayed. Open Monday to Thursday 10am to 7pm, Friday to Saturday until 8pm, Sunday 11am to 6pm.

Mudpie, 1694 Union St. (☎ **415-771-9262**) sells incredibly expensive children's clothes and gifts. Sticker shock is slightly lessened in the downstairs sale room, where everything is half price. Open Monday to Saturday 10am to 6pm, Sunday 11am to 5pm.

Another highly attractive, healthy shopping area is Chestnut Street in Cow Hollow, patronized by highly attractive and healthy locals with plenty of discretionary cash. Neither Chestnut nor Union Street, a few blocks south, have been able to fight off the invasion by some of the more ambitious chain stores, but local neighborhood and merchant groups are vigilant enough to keep them at a minimum. Muni bus 30-Stockton and 43-Masonic will get you to Chestnut Street.

Among the Banana Republic, Pottery Barn, and Williams-Sonoma stores lining the area is an anomaly, **Burton's Pharmacy,** 2016 Chestnut St. (☎ **415-567-1166**), one of the few remaining independent drug stores left. Open weekdays 9am to 6:30pm, Saturday 9:30am to 6pm, and Sunday 11am to 4pm.

On the other end of Chestnut is another independent, **Books, Inc.,** 2251 Chestnut (☎ **415-931-3633**), which has a broad inventory of fine reading material for the entire family. Open Sunday through Thursday from 9am to 10pm and Friday and Saturday 9am to midnight.

Wow your friends and family with some cool magic tricks from the **House Of Magic,** at 2025 Chestnut St. (☎ **415-346-2218**). Plenty of spellbinding tricks and gag gifts are on hand, along with a vast array of masks and wigs. Kids love this place, too. Open Monday through Saturday from 10am to 7pm, Sunday from 11am to 4pm.

Pacific Heights

The tony neighborhood of Pacific Heights offers shoppers Fillmore Street, which is chock full of hip clothing boutiques and other cool places to shop. Between Jackson and Sutter Streets, you won't be able to put your credit card away.

Fillamento, 2185 Fillmore St., at Sacramento Street (☎ 415-931-2224), participates in the houseware-as-art movement, with three floors of well-chosen home accessories. Open Monday through Saturday from 10am to 6pm, Sunday from noon to 5pm.

Nest, 2300 Fillmore St., at Clay Street (☎ 415-292-6199), is yet another home store, but one that carries many old French decorative items, including quilts and linens. Open Monday through Saturday from 10:30am to 6:30pm, Sunday from noon to 6pm.

You don't see many hat shops left in the world, so a visit to **Mrs. Dewson's Hats,** 2050 Fillmore St. (☎ 415-346-1600), is a must if your chapeau is a little tattered. This place is home to the "Willie Brim," a snappy fedora named after Mayor Willie Brown. Open Tuesday through Saturday from 10am to 6pm and Sunday noon to 4pm.

Hayes Valley

Destination: Hayes Street. The stretch of Hayes Street that runs between Octavia and Gough Streets is rapidly becoming a prime clothing shopping area. It won't take you long to see all the stores in the area, but I'll talk about some of the non-apparel ones, just so you don't overlook them.

Nuts About You, 325 Hayes St., between Franklin and Gough Streets (☎ 415-864-6887), has a varied selection of candy, nuts, chocolate, and tea. People with a sweet tooth can revel in front of the glass cases of treats. Open Monday through Saturday from 10am to 7:45pm.

If you believe one-man independent bookshops are a thing of the past, **Richard Hilkert, Bookseller,** 333 Hayes St., between Franklin and Gough Streets (☎ 415-863-3339), will dissuade you of that notion. Always friendly and helpful, the shop is open Monday through Friday from 9am to 5:30pm, Saturday and most Sundays from 11am to 5pm.

Painless Henna tattoos (they're painted on your skin and fade away), may be the most talked-about memento of your trip to San Francisco. If you want to shock your children — or just feel daring — make an appointment at the **African Outlet,** 524 Octavia St., near Hayes Street (☎ 415-864-3576). You can also find artwork, jewelry, and fashions exclusively from Africa here. Open Monday through Friday from 10am to 7pm, Saturday and Sunday from 10am to 8pm.

Classical music lovers and devotees of musical theater will find happiness at **Star Classics,** 425 Hayes St. at Gough Street ☎ (415-552-1110), which stocks CDs you'll never find in your run-of-the-mill record store. Open Tuesday to Saturday 11am to 7:30pm, Sunday noon to 6pm, Monday 11am to 6pm.

Sacramento Street

Some exclusive shops and also some of the best secondhand stores in town can be found in the section of Sacramento Street between Spruce and Divisadero Streets in Presidio Heights. The 1-California bus takes you within one block of Sacramento Street.

Virginia Breier, 3091 Sacramento St., near Baker Street (☎ 415-929-7173) shows the work of local craftspeople and artists. You'll be surprised at what you'll find — paintings, jewelry, glass, furniture, or crafts — whatever it is, it will be one-of-a-kind, high quality, and expensive. Open Monday through Saturday from 11am to 6pm.

Before housewares were considered a lifestyle choice, **Forrest Jones,** 3274 Sacramento St. (☎ 415-567-2483), was stocking an array of kitchen tools, linens, lovely porcelain lamp bases and vases, cookbooks, glassware, and other necessities. The variety of goods crowded about makes the store very appealing.

If you want to see what the swells have cleaned out of their closets (the locals are going to hate me for this), head to **GoodByes,** 3464 Sacramento St., between Walnut and Laurel Streets (☎ 415-346-6388). This is the place for gently worn men's and women's clothing. Open Monday through Saturday from 10am to 6pm (Thursday until 8pm), Sunday from 11am to 5pm, Thursday until 8pm. A second store for women only is across the street (☎ 415-674-0151).

Valencia Street

In the last two years, Valencia Street in the Mission District has been developing into an up-and-coming shopping district. The blocks from 19th to 23rd Streets still hold plenty of storefront churches and used appliance dens, but the cafes and restaurants that ventured here in the first wave of gentrification have been joined by sellers of youthful fashions, local art, and goods for the home. Of note is **Paxton Gate** (824 Valencia St., ☎ 415-824-1872), part entomological display, part garden store, but neither description does this place justice. Almost next door is **City Art** (☎ 415-970-9900), a co-op gallery featuring San Francisco artists and photographers. For whimsical linens, festive candles, original art, or perhaps a new sofa, drop into **Home Remedies** at 1026 Valencia, ☎ 415-826-2026. And don't pass by **Encantada Gallery of Fine Arts,** 904 Valencia St., ☎ 415-642-3939, which has a wonderful collection of Mexican art, pottery, and a changing exhibit of paintings and mixed media. From downtown, use BART, exit at the 24th Street Station, and walk one block west. Some of the Valencia Street shops are closed on Mondays.

What a Steal! Bargain Hunting in San Francisco

The discount manufacturers based south of Market (SoMa) have made bargain shopping in San Francisco a popular pursuit. While outlets can be found around SoMa and beyond, the area between Townsend and Bryant Streets and 2nd and 4th Streets is especially great for bargains.

Attention serious factory outlet and discount store shoppers: You'll want to get your hands on a copy of Sally Socolich's *Bargain Hunting in the Bay Area.* It's available in every local bookstore for the bargain price of $6.95.

Take advantage of the **Esprit Factory Outlet,** 499 Illinois St., at 16th Street (☎ 415-957-2550), for shoes, discounted clothing, and accessories for women and children. Many visitors rank a shopping trip here as important as a visit to Lombard Street. Take Muni bus 15-Third to 16th Street and walk east one block. Open daily from 10am to 7pm, Sunday from 11am to 5pm.

The hip retailer Rolo has an outlet for sale merchandise called **Rolo Garage,** 1301 Howard St. at 9th Street (☎ 415-861-1999). It's open every day from 11am to 7pm.

If you wear ladies clothes in the vicinity of a size 6 or 8, drop by the **Isda & Co.** outlet (☎ 415-512-0313) at 29 South Park to see what's in. Isda manufactures contemporary, but not stuffy, separates for women. Open Monday to Saturday 10am to 5pm.

Index of stores by merchandise

Arts and Crafts
City Art
Encantada Gallery of Fine Arts
Virginia Breier

Books
Books, Inc.
City Lights
Richard Hilkert Bookseller

Chocolate
Joseph Schmidt
Nuts About You
XOX Truffles

Clothing, Children's
Esprit Outlet
Macy's
Mudpie
Neiman Marcus

Clothing, Menswear
Goodbyes
Macy's
Neiman Marcus
Original Levi's Store
Rolo
Rolo Garage
Saks Fifth Avenue
Wilkes Bashford

Clothing, Womenswear

African Outlet
Esprit Outlet
Goodbyes
Isda & Co.
Macy's
Neiman Marcus
Original Levi's Store
Rolo
Rolo Garage
Saks Fifth Avenue
Wilkes Bashford

Comestibles

Golden Gate Fortune Cookies Company
Imperial Tea Court

Fabric

Britex

Gifts

Biordi Art Imports
Burton's Pharmacy
Chong Imports
Dandelion
Gazoontite
Gump's
House of Magic

Hats

Mrs. Dewson's Hats

Home Decor & Housewares

Bell'occhio
Fillamento
Forrest Jones

Home Remedies

Nest
Paxton Gate
Tai Yick Trading Company

Lingerie

Carol Doda's Champagne and Lace

Music

Amoeba Records
Clarion Music Center
Star Classics

Shoes

Insolent
Macy's
Neiman Marcus
Saks Fifth Avenue

Chapter 20

Four Great Itineraries to Make Your Day

● ●

In This Chapter

▶ Making the most out of three to five days

▶ Showing the kids a good time

▶ Taking a food lover's spree

● ●

*T*ourists naturally want to pack as much as possible into a sightseeing trip, fearing that they won't have a chance to return. Having been in that position myself, I've come to the conclusion that travel isn't pleasurable if all you do is run around like mad checking off sights as if you're grocery shopping. My idea of a good time is visiting one or two important sights in a day (or sometimes just walking past the front portal and waving) and then finding somewhere to sit and watch the world pass by. (But I must admit that I felt really foolish for missing the Eiffel Tower on my first visit to Paris — and I was in the neighborhood.) You may prefer a compromise between these two approaches, in which case I suggest you make an advance decision about what you absolutely must see, based on how much time and energy you have.

On that note, the following suggested itineraries are intended for first-time visitors who want to catch as much as possible without completely exhausting themselves or their companions. I've packed a lot in, but you can pick and choose (or completely ignore) pieces of each.

San Francisco in Three Days

Three days is barely enough to "get" San Francisco, so I'm going to keep you within the city limits for the entire time. The following list takes you step-by-step through the city.

✔ **Day 1:** Find Market Street and catch one of the historic F-Market **streetcars** (see Chapter 11) heading toward Pier 39 and Fisherman's Wharf. If you haven't eaten breakfast, try the **Eagle Café** on the 2nd floor of the pier. If it happens to be a Saturday, stop at Green Street on the Embarcadero and breakfast at the

Ferry Plaza Farmers' Market. Once you reach **Pier 39,** greet the sea lions (follow the barking) and continue to the end of the pier for a dead-on view of Alcatraz Island. Walk to **Aquatic Park** to complete a tour of **Fisherman's Wharf** (see Chapter 16). You'll pass the Hyde Street Pier and the Maritime National Museum — pop in if you like ships — as well as Ghirardelli Square. On Bay Street, catch a 30-Stockton bus to Chestnut Street. If it's not too soon to shop or eat, **Café Marimba** (see Chapter 14) is a great choice for Mexican food. The bus ends up at Beach Street, and your task is to walk from the **Palace of Fine Arts,** through the **Presidio** to the **Golden Gate Bridge.** Follow the joggers along the bay; there's a path. The 29-Sunset bus will also take you there and back. End the afternoon around **Union Square,** window shopping along Stockton and Sutter. Change your clothes, then go to the **Top of the Mark** (see Chapter 14) for an aperitif and a grand view. For dinner, see what's cooking on **Belden Place** (see Chapter 13) and if you still have a bit of steam left, drop by **Biscuits and Blues** (see Chapter 22) for a musical nightcap.

✔ **Day 2:** This day starts with another transportation highlight. Fling yourself on a Powell-Hyde **cable car** (see Chapter 11) for the brief ride to Lombard Street. Walk down via the staircases on either side and, heading north, find the **San Francisco Art Institute** at 800 Chestnut St. Inside the campus, follow the signs to the café for breakfast or a snack. This is a funky place with unobstructed views of the bay and a menu of sandwiches, bagels, and vegetarian entrees priced for starving artists. Follow Filbert Street to **Washington Square Park** in North Beach, a modest pocket of green with plentiful benches on the perimeter and the twin spires of Saints Peter and Paul's Church solidly cutting into sky to the north. Park yourself on a bench, maybe with a latté in hand from **Mario's Bohemian Cigar** on the corner. Then, stroll around North Beach if you like or walk up Grant Avenue past Union Street and follow the signs to **Coit Tower** (see Chapter 16). From there, return to North Beach for a leisurely lunch at **Moose's** (see Chapter 14), which is on the east side of the park, or pick up a sandwich at one of the delis and have a picnic of sorts in Portsmouth Square, a short walk away. Spend the afternoon exploring **Chinatown** (see Chapter 16). If you're in the mood for Chinese cuisine for dinner, see Chapter 14 for suggestions. Then back to North Beach for a performance of **Beach Blanket Babylon** (see Chapter 21).

✔ **Day 3:** Enjoy a walk in the park, **Golden Gate Park** (see Chapter 16), where you can get in some culture at the **De Young** and **Asian** Art Museums and some fresh air in the **Strybing Arboretum.** Find lunch over on 9th Avenue and then stroll down **Irving Street,** a typical neighborhood shopping block. In the afternoon, a trip to the **Museum of Modern Art** (see Chapter 16) finishes the artistic portion of your vacation. Take a rest stop in **Yerba Buena Gardens** (see Chapter 16) across the street. Then dine around **Union Square** if you're ambitious enough to see an 8pm show at ACT or another theater. Otherwise, hail a cab and head to a Mission District restaurant such as **Delfina** (see Chapter 14), and pretend you're a local. Night owls can finish the evening at a salsa dance club such as **Rockapolco.**

San Francisco in Five Days

✔ **Day 4:** By now, you've already covered a fair portion of the city; it's probably time to hug a tree (well, you are in Northern California after all). Rent a car (see Chapter 9) or take a guided tour (see Chapter 18) and cross the Golden Gate Bridge into **Marin.** Hike **Muir Woods** in the morning (take the Stinson Beach exit) and have lunch by Muir Beach at the English Tudor–style **Pelican Inn** (located at the end of Muir Wood Road at Hwy 1 (☎ **415-383-6000;** Internet: www.pelicaninn.com). The inn is a short walk from the beach, which lies below a hikable hill. Stop in **Sausalito** on your way back to the city for an ice cream or just a walk along the bayfront — the San Francisco skyline is quite the sight, but Sausalito itself, while postcard pretty, is quite touristy. This evening, eat dinner in Japantown at either **Mifune** in the Japan Center for noodles or **Isuzu** for sushi or tempura (see Chapter 13).

✔ **Day 5:** This may be the morning to get in your trip to **Alcatraz Island** (see Chapter 16) or to trek to the beautiful **Palace of the Legion of Honor** (see Chapter 17) for another dose of culture. For lunch try the **Tadich Grill** (see Chapter 14), the oldest restaurant in California (although it's been in its current location since 1967). The menu of old favorites, such as lobster thermidor, is accompanied with a side of local history and an active bar. Then, spend the afternoon catching up on shopping, or stroll to the **Ferry Building** down on Pier 5 (just to the east of Broadway), where you can hang out on benches and watch skateboarders or just admire the view. In the evening, splurge with an upscale dinner around Nob Hill — **Charles** is romantic (see Chapter 14) — followed by a show at the **Plush Room** (see Chapter 22).

San Francisco with Kids

How to keep the kids engaged and happy (for example, not asking what time it is and what are we doing tomorrow and when are we eating) depends on their ages and interests, of course.

✔ **For families with little kids:** A day around **Golden Gate Park** is ideal. The **Academy of Sciences** was developed with children in mind, and youngsters with energy to spare will gravitate toward the big, imaginatively designed playground. When lunch beckons, you can feed the family reasonably at **Park Chow** on 9th Avenue, just a block from the park entrance. The **zoo** (see Chapter 17) is a logical alternative for a morning's activity as well. In the afternoon, consider a **ferry boat ride** to Sausalito and back.

✔ **For families with slightly older progeny:** Spend a delightful day taking the cable car to **Fisherman's Wharf** (see Chapter 16), where Pier 39 holds sway, with its many shops and video games. You can avoid the scene, if you prefer, with strategically timed tickets to

Alcatraz (see Chapter 16); think about bringing along sandwiches or snacks because the food around the pier is overpriced and underwhelming. If you can stave off starvation until your return from solitary confinement, hustle everyone over to **North Beach** on the Mason/Powell cable car and eat at **Il Pollaio** (see Chapter 15). **Chinatown** is convenient to North Beach and kids generally love browsing in the shops. For dinner, **Lichee Gardens** (see Chapter 14) is a good family-style Chinese restaurant, or you can eat at one of the North Beach big food eateries, such as **La Felce,** 1570 Stockton St. at Union, ☎ **415-392-8321,** where platters of antipasti, pasta, and roast meats satisfy diverse tastes.

✔ **For families with kids of varied ages: Yerba Buena Gardens** (see Chapter 16) is a godsend. Teens are usually more than happy to hang out in **Metreon's Airtight Garage** and at **Zeum,** while younger siblings can ride the merry-go-round and then run around the Metreon attraction "Where the Wild Things Are." Skating or bowling works for everyone, and there is plenty of food to be had within walking distance. For a step above the center's offerings, **Pazzia** (see Chapter 14) is an excellent choice for dinner, as is **Buca di Beppo** (see Chapter 14), especially if your family is sizable. In the evening, play around at **The Great Entertainer,** 975 Bryant Street between 7th and 8th Streets (☎ **415-861-8833**), a family-friendly billiards hall serving food and drink along with pool, video games, and even table tennis.

San Francisco for Foodies

You could come here and spend a week honing your talents in the kitchen at **Tante Marie's cooking school** (☎ **415-788-6699;** Internet: www.tantemarie.com) and that would certainly qualify you as a foodie. Or, you could imitate my friend Bev, who flies up from Los Angeles on a regular basis to raid **North Beach** for supplies and then orders huge meals at the restaurant of the moment. Since the cooking classes run until 4pm, let's make like Bev for a day instead.

Wake up and smell the cappuccino and a raisin roll at a local favorite, **Caffè Greco,** 423 Columbus Ave. in North Beach, ☎ **415-397-6261.** While you sip, make a mental note of how much room you have in your suitcase for imported Italian delicacies, then walk a block to **Molinari's** delicatessen on the corner of Columbus and Vallejo Street, ☎ **415-421-2337.** If you have some way of refrigerating fresh sausages and cheese, you can take better advantage of the selection here — otherwise, consider ordering a sandwich to go for later. Drop by **Liguria** (see Chapter 15) for a sheet of pizza focaccia, which will make you the envy of your fellow airplane passengers on the ride home. If you need a new pizza stone, go to **A. Cavalli & Co.,** 1441 Stockton St., which also sells Italian cards and maps, as well as cooking utensils.

Don't miss immersing yourself in San Francisco's many cultures by eating dim sum and discovering the wealth of ingredients available in its ethnic enclaves. The **Mayflower** in the Richmond District (see Chapter 14) makes great dumplings and won't be mobbed like the dim sum places in Chinatown (few tourists venture this far out on Geary Boulevard). After lunch, walk or take a bus north down Clement Street, one block west of Geary, and stop by **Green Apple Books,** 506 Clement St., to peruse a sizable selection of used cookbooks. You can find many produce, fish, and meat markets along Clement, as well as houseware stores; **May Wah** at 547 Clement St. is worth a look, as is **Kamei** at 606 Clement. Those who are serious about eating are ready for a snack by this time. **Pancho Villa** (see Chapter 13) creates a steak and prawn quesadilla that is unparalleled for quality and price. Since you'll find it in the Mission District, you'll also want to visit **La Palma,** 2884 24th St. at Florida, ☎ **415-647-1500,** for fresh tortillas, dried chilies, and other essentials for cooking Mexican food. Then head South of Market to the **Wine House** at 535 Bryant St. (between 3rd and 4th Streets), where the staff is very knowledgeable. For dinner, consider a leading neighborhood destination such as **Delfina** (see Chapter 14) or a high-end experience such as **Gary Danko** (see Chapter 14). If you're ready for more, see Chapter 23, "Checking Out Berkeley."

Part VI
Living It Up After the Sun Goes Down: San Francisco Nightlife

The 5th Wave   By Rich Tennant

"For tonight's modern reinterpretation of Carmen, those in the front row are kindly requested to wear raincoats."

In this part . . .

Because San Francisco appeals to such a diverse populace to begin with, no single form of entertainment has come to be associated with the city in the same way that music is associated with New Orleans or theater with New York, for example. Instead, San Francisco offers an eclectic mix of dance, music, performance art, theater, and opera, with plenty to choose from on any given night. For those who shun anything requiring a trip to a box office, you can choose from plenty of bars and clubs to keep you off the streets until the wee hours.

Even travelers with kids don't have to limit after-hours activities to dinner and a movie. A few clubs offer shows for patrons of all ages featuring local alternative or blues bands. (Your kid will think you're very cool.) A night at the theater is also a great family alternative; you can usually find something playing with intergenerational appeal.

Chapter 21

San Francisco Really Puts On a Performance

In This Chapter

▶ Finding out what's going on in town when you're here

▶ Getting tickets to concerts, theater, and other events

▶ Enjoying the major opera, ballet, theater, and classical music scenes

▶ Broadening your horizons with experimental theater and dance

▶ Dining before or after the show

*L*overs of the performing arts can find plenty of interesting offerings. As for drama, there's a bit of the tried and true when Broadway road companies drop into town, and our own **American Conservatory Theatre (ACT)** regularly produces works that are visually inspired and well acted. Opera is just as vibrant. Although the great Enrico Caruso never returned to San Francisco after the shock of the 1906 earthquake, plenty of other stars have aria'd their way through town, raising the local opera company to world-class heights. The **SF Symphony** is in a similar league, and while I'm bragging, I'd better mention the ballet. It, too, is as fine a company as you'll see anywhere. But don't let the big brands sway you from trying smaller stages outside the Civic Center. Experimental theater abounds and often creates one of those "only in San Francisco" moments that make a vacation.

Getting the Scoop on Seeing the Arts

Three or four weeks before you arrive, order the *San Francisco Chronicle/Examiner* **Sunday paper** or a copy of *San Francisco magazine;* or, if you have access to the Internet, look up a local Web site (see Chapter 9). The Internet is the most efficient way to discover what's playing in town, but the Pink Pages in the Sunday paper are easier to scan quickly.

Whether a particular performance sounds like something you'd enjoy is a trickier matter. On the Web you can search sites such as www.bayareacitysearch.com and the *San Francisco Chronicle and Examiner* **Web site,** www.sfgate.com, for reviews and synopses; otherwise, take your chances. You may stumble onto something wonderful.

Buying tickets

For tickets to any theater, dance, symphony, or concert performance, you can call the appropriate box office directly and order them with a credit card (charges are non-refundable if, for some reason, you don't show up). **City Box Office,** 153 Kearny St., Suite 402 (☎ **415-392-4400**), also sells tickets to most events. If you didn't order tickets before you arrived in town, visit **TIX Bay Area** (☎ **415-433-7827**) for half-price tickets for same-day performances (a $1 to $3 service charge is tacked on). **TIX,** which is also a **BASS TicketMaster outlet,** is located on the Stockton Street side of Union Square between Post and Geary Streets. It's open Tuesday through Thursday from 11am to 6pm, Friday and Saturday until 7pm.

Don't buy tickets from anyone outside TIX or a box office claiming to have discount or scalper tickets, especially to sporting events. Folks get duped all the time, forking over real cash for counterfeit tickets. Another common scalper scam is to sell tickets to an event that has already taken place.

The concierge at your hotel can be another source for hard-to-get tickets. The larger the hotel, the more likely it is that the concierge will be successful; but in any case, it's worth asking. If he or she does manage to come through, a $5 to $10 tip is appropriate thanks.

If you are really flexible about your plans for the evening and don't mind possibly wasting your time, go to the box office of the theater you want to attend and stand in line for last-minute cancellations by season-ticket holders or the release of tickets held for media or VIPs. With luck, you can score seats in the orchestra. Without luck, you'll have wasted an hour or so.

The inside edge

Don't be late to the theater, symphony, or opera. Curtains usually rise on time, and if you're late, you won't be seated until there's a break in the action. Anyway, do you really want to crawl in the dark over people to get to your seat?

As for seats, buy the best ones available. Shows are much more enjoyable when you can see the stage and not just the top of the performers' heads. And avoid the boxes on either side of the **Geary Theater.** They are positioned to obscure half the stage, generally the half where the action takes place.

As for what to wear, you'll see a little of everything from tailored evening clothes to jeans. People seem to dress up a bit more Friday and Saturday nights, especially in the orchestra seats, but your Sunday best isn't necessary.

Comings and goings

Cable cars will get you to Union Square theaters if you're coming from North Beach; from the Marina or Union Street, take a 30-Stockton or 45-Union/Stockton bus. If you prefer to take a cab to your lodgings afterward, walk to a big hotel to catch one. You can find a number of parking garages near Union Square with fees beginning at $10 for the evening.

The Civic Center, where the opera, ballet, and symphony are located, is reachable by any Muni Metro streetcar or any bus along Van Ness Avenue. I wouldn't walk around this area unescorted after dark to get back to the Muni station, and taxis aren't always immediately available. If you feel stuck, walk to one of the many nearby restaurants and ask the host to call a taxi for you. Relax, and prepare to wait a while at the bar. Drivers should note that a parking garage is located on Grove Street between Franklin and Gough Streets.

South of Market and Mission neighborhood venues (see "Broadway West: The Theater Scene" later in this chapter for venue listings) have troubles similar to **Civic Center.** You can usually get to the performance by public transportation, but returning late at night by bus is less interesting (or perhaps more interesting, depending on your perspective). Again, if you're attending a show in this area, don't expect to automatically hail a cab afterwards. Instead, walk to a nearby restaurant or bar and call. These numbers for local cab companies can help:

- ✔ Yellow Cab ☎ 415-626-2345
- ✔ Veteran's Cab ☎ 415-552-1300
- ✔ Desoto Cab ☎ 415-673-1414
- ✔ Luxor Cabs ☎ 415-282-4141
- ✔ Pacific ☎ 415-986-7220

San Francisco Performing Arts

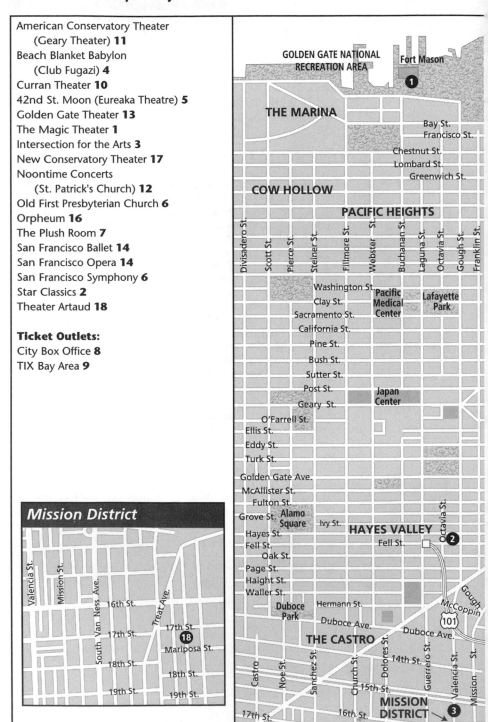

American Conservatory Theater
  (Geary Theater) **11**
Beach Blanket Babylon
  (Club Fugazi) **4**
Curran Theater **10**
42nd St. Moon (Eureaka Theatre) **5**
Golden Gate Theater **13**
The Magic Theater **1**
Intersection for the Arts **3**
New Conservatory Theater **17**
Noontime Concerts
  (St. Patrick's Church) **12**
Old First Presbyterian Church **6**
Orpheum **16**
The Plush Room **7**
San Francisco Ballet **14**
San Francisco Opera **14**
San Francisco Symphony **6**
Star Classics **2**
Theater Artaud **18**

Ticket Outlets:
City Box Office **8**
TIX Bay Area **9**

Municipal Pier

Pier 45

Pier 43 1/2

Pier 43

Pier 41

Pier 39

Aquatic Park

Pier 35

FISHERMAN'S WHARF

Jefferson St.

Beach St.

Ghiradelli Square

Pier 33

North Point St.

Bay St.

NORTH BEACH

Pier 31

Francisco St.

Pier 27

Chestnut St.

Lombard St.

Greenwich St.

Filbert St.

Union St.

Green St.

Coit Tower

Pier 23

Pier 19

Pier 17

Pier 15

Pier 9

Pier 7

Columbus Ave.

101

Vallejo St.

Broadway

Tunnel

Pacific Ave.

Jackson St.

CHINATOWN

Pier 5

Pier 3

Pier 1

NOB HILL

Justin Herman Plaza

Ferry Building (World Trade Center)

Van Ness Ave.

Polk St.

Larkin St.

Hyde St.

Leavenworth St.

Jones St.

Taylor St.

Mason St.

Powell St.

Stockton St.

Grant Ave.

Kearny St.

Montgomery St.

Sansome St.

Battery St.

Front St.

Davis St.

Drumm St.

Rincon Center

San Francisco–Oakland Bay Bridge

80

Market St.

Steuart St.

Spear St.

Main St.

Beale St.

Geary St.

O'Farrell St.

Union Square

San Francisco Museum of Modern Art

1st St.

Fremont St.

2nd St.

Eddy St.

Yerba Buena Gardens

Moscone Convention Center

SOMA

South Park

Delancey St.

CIVIC CENTER

Market St.

Mission St.

5th St.

4th St.

3rd St.

Howard St.

8th St.

Folsom St.

Harrison St.

Bryant St.

Brannan St.

9th St.

10th St.

11th St.

12th St.

Townsend St.

King St.

Berry St.

Channel St.

4th St.

3rd St.

Illinois St.

China Basin

Division St.

280

Alameda St.

S. Van Ness Ave.

Folsom

Harrison

Alabama

15th St.

Potrero Ave.

6th St.

7th St.

San Francisco Bay

0 — 1/4 mi

0 — .25 km

N

The Civic Center

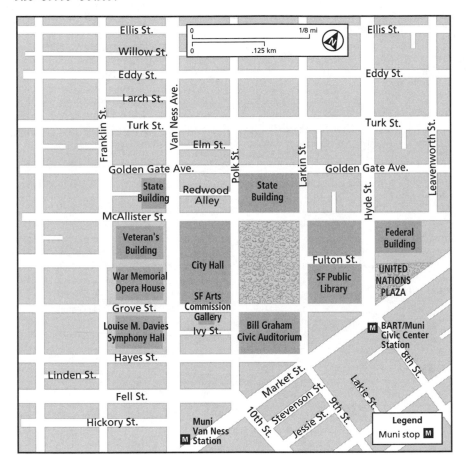

Broadway West: The Theater Scene

Yes, I am exaggerating, and no, I would never seriously compare our little theater district to the Great White Way in New York, but there are a fair number of professional stages in town. At least ten in varying sizes are housed around **Union Square,** and experimental theaters are scattered about the **South of Market** and **Mission** districts in converted warehouses and gallery spaces. Productions may include a musical or two, distinguished classics, and world-premiere comedies and dramas.

The American Conservatory Theater (ACT) is the pre-eminent company in town and produces a wide variety of things during its season, which runs October to June. The acting is first-rate, and the costumes and sets are universally brilliant. The choice of material ranges from new works by playwrights such as Tom Stoppard, can't-lose American chestnuts, and Shakespeare, all the way to not-quite-ready-for-prime-time works that receive a careful rendering. The lovely **Geary Theater** is where you can see the productions, at 415 Geary St., at Mason Street, ☎ **415-749-2228.** Ticket prices range from $11 to $55, and the box office is open every day from 10am.

Broadway hits and road shows appear down the block at the **Curran Theater,** 445 Geary St., between Mason and Taylor Streets, ☎ **415-551-2000,** the **Golden Gate Theater,** 1 Golden Gate Ave., at Market Street, and the **Orpheum,** 1192 Market St., at 8th Street. The phone number above is shared by all three venues, and the recorded message explains what's playing, where to buy tickets, and how to get to the theaters.

You may like your theater a lot less expensive and a little more cutting edge. If so, check out **The Magic Theater** at Fort Mason Center, Bldg. A, ☎ **415-441-8822,** where Sam Shephard's Pulitzer Prize–winning play *Buried Child* premiered. Tickets range from $18 to $23. Or try **Intersection for the Arts,** a 72-seat theater in the Mission District at 446 Valencia St., between 15th and 16th Streets, ☎ **415-626-2787.** Ticket prices run between $9 and $15.

Close to Civic Center in an impressive former Masonic Temple built in 1911 is the **New Conservatory Theater (NCT)** complex at 25 Van Ness Ave., a half block off Market Street, box office ☎ **415-861-8972.** NCT, which consists of three small theaters, presents a variety of productions throughout the year. From September through July is **"Pride Season,"** during which a series of six plays with gay themes are presented. The summer **Women's Festival** features plays by women writers. **NTC** also produces children's theater programming all year long.

Admirers of musical theater should keep an eye out for productions by **42nd Street Moon.** This company presents long-forgotten American musicals in concert format and gives audiences an opportunity to hear delightfully clever tunes that somehow "disappeared." Check the Web site www.capybara.com/42ndStMoon for shows and dates. Productions take place at the **Eureka Theatre,** 215 Jackson St. (at Battery in the Financial District), ☎ **415-243-9895.**

Classical Music and Opera

You can find many venues for listening to classical music in San Francisco. Local papers and Web sites are your best source for event listings. You can see major groups such as the **San Francisco Symphony,** which performs in the **Louise M. Davies Symphony Hall,** 201 Van Ness Ave., at Grove Street, ☎ **415-864-6000,** in the **Civic Center.** The season runs from September through July, and tickets run $15 to $78. Also at **Civic Center** is the **Herbst Theater,** 410 Van Ness Ave. ☎ **415-621-6600,** home to the **Women's Philharmonic, SF Performances,** and other professional groups.

You can also enjoy piano and violin duos, chamber music ensembles, and singers at **Old First Presbyterian Church,** 1751 Sacramento St., at Van Ness Avenue, ☎ 415-474-1608. These less formal concerts are scheduled afternoons and evenings, and tickets are a mere $9. The California Street cable car takes you to within 2 blocks of the church. If you are around **Yerba Buena Gardens** at lunchtime on a Wednesday, head to **St. Patrick's Church,** 756 Mission St., which is the site for one-half hour concerts produced by **Noontime Concerts** (☎ 415-777-3211). These tidbits may be solo or full orchestral performances. Admission is $5. **Noontime Concerts** also uses the **A.P. Giannini Auditorium** at the Bank of America headquarters, 555 California St., in the Financial District. Concerts are currently held there on the 2nd and 4th Tuesday of the month, but call for an updated schedule. You can also hear live classical music for free at **Star Classics,** the record store located at 425 Hayes St. (near Gough Street), ☎ 415-552-1110. The store sponsors concerts every Friday at noon, and presents amateur local talent performing jazz, Broadway, and classical music on Sundays at 5pm.

The San Francisco Opera opens its season with a gala in September and ends quietly in early January. Performances are produced in the **War Memorial Opera House,** 301 Van Ness Ave., at Grove Street, ☎ 415-864-3330, in the **Civic Center.** Tickets run from $10 to $140. **Pocket Opera** (☎ 415-575-1100) delivers opera to the masses in stripped-down, English-language versions that are quite entertaining and highly professional. The season begins in February and ends in June; productions are held at different locations, so you'll need to phone for a schedule or check the Web site www.pocketopera.com.

Ballet and Beyond

You can find plenty of classical and modern dance in San Francisco, the **San Francisco Ballet** being the most well known. Their season runs from February to June and performs in the War Memorial Opera House, 301 Van Ness Ave., at Grove Street. Call ☎ 415-865-2000 for tickets. Prices run from $7 for standing room to $100 for orchestra seats.

You can find an adventurous season of modern dance, performance art, and theater at the **Theater Artaud,** 450 Florida St., at 17th Street, ☎ 415-621-7797, in the Mission District. Ticket prices are $20 or less depending on day and type of show.

A San Francisco Institution: Beach Blanket Babylon!

You may not want to miss **Beach Blanket Babylon,** a San Francisco institution. The musical revue is known for wildly imaginative hats and incredible costumes that seem to live lives of their own. The spectacle is so popular that even after celebrating 25 years of poking fun at stars, politicians, and San Francisco itself, seats for the constantly updated shows are always sold out. Purchase tickets ($18 to $45) through TIX or by mail at least 3 weeks in advance (especially if you want to attend a weekend performance). Children are only admitted for Sunday matinees — no liquor is sold on Sundays. You can see this great show in North Beach at Club Fugazi, 678 Green St., between Powell Street and Columbus Avenue, ☎ 415-421-4222. You've got to see it to believe it.

Asia SF, at 201 9th St. at Howard, ☎ 415-255-2742, is a newish restaurant/club featuring "gender illusionists." The deal here is the "waitresses" are in drag, and once an hour a few of them make their way onto the bar and lip sync or sashay about. Patrons seem to enjoy themselves, in part because the food is pretty good. It's open Wednesday to Sunday from 5pm to 2am (the kitchen closes at 10pm). The dance club downstairs is a changing scene in itself.

The Kinsey Sicks, a local fave, bill themselves as Everybody's Favorite Dragapella Group, and it probably isn't necessary to mention that they are, in all likelihood, America's sole dragapella group. In any case, these are four guys with big hair, great taste in clothes, and lots of attitude who harmonize sans accompaniment. They perform at the New Conservatory Theatre twice a year for two-month runs. For their schedule call the theater at ☎ 415-861-8972.

Pre- and Post-Theater Dining

It's possible to eat before attending any 8pm performance. If you are dining near the concert hall or theater, allow 90 minutes if you need to park or are arriving via public transportation. After the show, your dining choices are somewhat more limited. On Union Square, a branch of **The Cheesecake Factory** has arrived on the 8th floor of Macy's. It's open until 11pm. **The Grand Cafe** (see Chapter 14) also serves until 11pm from a bar menu. If you are attending an event around Civic Center and want to eat before the show, be sure to make reservations. **The Hayes Street Grill** (see Chapter 14) originally opened to accommodate the culture crowd, and this restaurant has been joined by a great many more on and around Hayes Street.

Chapter 22

Seeking the Nightlife

● ●

In This Chapter

▶ Checking out the coolest clubs and bars for live music

▶ Twisting at the hoppin'est dance clubs

▶ Seeking out atmosphere

▶ Getting a good laugh

▶ Broadening your horizons at some unique establishments

● ●

*W*hat I love about this city is there's no end to the good times. You can have a night at the theater, followed by a night shimmying through a few bars and clubs, followed by a night at the opera. There are so many places for drinking and dancing and socializing, and for enjoying some culture.

Livin' It Up with Live Music

Bars, all of which by law must close from 2am to 6am, are self-explanatory. **Clubs** are a different story altogether. South of Market, dance clubs that have different styles and names may share the same space. For example, a particular club may feature 1970s-revisited disco catering to the Velvet Elvis crowd on Friday, and then have Gothic industrial "music" on Monday. Take a careful look at the listings in the *SF Weekly* or *Bay Guardian* so you'll have a clue to what you're getting into in case pierced tongues make you cringe but '80s-style dance clubs make you smile. Since most clubs don't get going until after 10pm, plan to take cabs anywhere not within walking distance of your hotel.

Finding some cool jazz

Jazz at Pearl's, 256 Columbus Ave., at Broadway, ☎ **415-291-8255,** showcases a Monday Big Band Night and local jazz musicians Tuesday through Saturday. Pearl's also serves a menu of burgers, ribs, pizza, and other popular items. There's no cover charge, but there's a two-drink minimum. A bit outside the tourist neighborhoods is **Storyville,** 1751 Fulton St., at Masonic Avenue (close to the upper Haight—take a cab), ☎ **415-441-1751.** This jazz supper club features mostly local groups, but now and then books obscure musicians known only to serious jazzophiles. A New Orleans-inspired dinner menu, served Tuesday through Saturday nights, is sincere if not exceptional. Cover varies, but starts at $4. Closed Sundays and Mondays. The **Elbo Room,** 647 Valencia St., near 17th Street, ☎ **415-552-7788,** blasts acid jazz for a youthful crowd. Cover starts at $3.

Feelin' blue — blues bars

John Lee Hooker's **Boom Boom Room,** 1601 Fillmore St., at Geary Street, ☎ **415-673-8000,** is named after the legendary blues musician, who occasionally plays here. It's open every night for dancing, cocktails, and jiving. Lines often form on the weekends, so it doesn't hurt to arrive on the early side and sip your drink slowly. Cover charges vary depending on the night and the act. Check the Web site www.boomboomblues.com for more info.

Just follow the crowds to **The Saloon,** 1232 Grant Ave., at Fresno Street near Vallejo Street, ☎ **415-989-7666,** as your first stop on a walking tour of North Beach blues bars. If you can get close enough to get inside, the cover is usually around $4 to $5. Also in North Beach, check out the **Lost and Found Saloon,** 1353 Grant Ave., between Vallejo and Green Streets, ☎ **415-675-5996.** You will easily find this place, but it is difficult to get into on weekend nights. **Grant & Green,** 1371 Grant Ave., ☎ **415-693-9565,** is the third in the North Beach blues triumvirate. The **Blue Bar,** downstairs from the Black Cat restaurant at the corner of Kearny and Broadway (☎ **415-981-2233**), has comfortable furniture and serves from the upstairs menu, meaning you can munch while you listen to the band. There's no room for dancing, though.

Jammin' with the locals

During the day, **Pier 23,** The Embarcadero, at Front Street, ☎ **415-362-5125,** serves lunch to fashionable business executives on the patio. At night, hot local blues and funk musicians play for fans ages 21 to 70. **Mick's Lounge,** 2513 Van Ness Ave., at Union Street, ☎ **415-928-0404,** may be a small venue, but when the rock and roll cooks, you can feel it in your bones. Mick's sometimes features way-cool musicians such as Kermit Ruffins, whose shows sell out well in advance, so check to see who's playing before dropping by. Another hot spot that features local bands on the move, the **Paradise Lounge,** 1501 Folsom St., at 11th Street south of Market, ☎ **415-861-6906,** has three different rooms people move around and socialize in, making it easy to lose your friends. Cover starts at $3 — it's more on weekends. Next door is the **Transmission Theater,** 314 11th St., ☎ **415-621-1911,** more for clubbing than relaxing with a drink.

Catching the big-name acts

You'll want to contact the box office directly or purchase tickets from **BASS** at ☎ **415-776-1999** for major acts. Ticket prices vary at the following clubs, depending on the act.

The **Great American Music Hall,** 859 O'Farrell St., near Polk Street (☎ 415- 885-0750), books everything from rhythm and blues acts to Cajun bands to Grammy award-winning acts like Bonnie Raitt. Feel at home in the large room, or step out onto the balcony. Although you'll notice the club isn't in a squeaky-clean neighborhood, safety isn't a problem because so many people are going in and out of the place. If it's available, use the valet parking in front or park in the AMC 1,000 garage up the block. Take a cab home after the show if you aren't driving. You can find the club schedule on the Web at www.musichallsf.com (you can order tickets online).

It won't be the Grateful Dead, but you can find out who's playing **The Fillmore,** 1805 Geary St., at Fillmore Street, by checking out its Web site www.thefillmore.com or by calling the box office at ☎ 415-346-6000. **The Warfield,** 982 Market St., ☎ 415-775-7722, is a huge theater that hosts big-time musicians, mostly rock and roll. **Slim's,** 333 11th St., between Folsom and Harrison Streets, ☎ 415-522-0333, is a smaller club owned by singer Boz Scaggs, who comes to the club to play every now and then. A much bigger room that some grown-ups I know find extra palatable is the **7th Note,** 915 Columbus Ave. (near Lombard), ☎ 415-921-2582. It's booked by the same people that run Slim's and has bar tables and chairs around the dance floor and upstairs.

Also in North Beach is **Bimbo's 365 Club,** 1025 Columbus Ave. at Chestnut Street, ☎ 415-474-0365. It's a roomy, good-looking club where you can dance or listen in comfort to bands with names you may recognize. **Bottom of the Hill,** 1233 17th St. at Texas Street, ☎ 415-621-4455, is a small venue that caters to nationally touring acts that sometimes play under assumed names. This Potrero Hill–based club also serves bar and grill food.

Getting Your Dancing In

The Ramp, 855 China Basin, off 3rd Street at Mariposa Street ☎ 415-621-2378, is an indoor/outdoor bar/restaurant. It isn't open year-round, but between May and October you can dance to live jazz on Fridays from 5:30 to 8pm. Saturdays feature salsa bands, and Sundays bring world music (both days from 4:30 to 7:30pm). The ultra hip but friendly **Cafe du Nord,** 2170 Market St., at Sanchez Street, ☎ 415-861-5016, is a basement-level club and restaurant that features different dance bands or DJs every evening. Cover runs from $3 to $7. The restaurant serves Wednesday through Sunday. Under 21 bohemians are allowed in if accompanied by adults. **DNA Lounge,** 375 11th St., at Harrison Street, ☎ 415-626-1409, holds popular 1970s dance parties on Saturday nights, other styles on other nights. Cover is around $12 on weekends.

Swing and ballroom dancers, and those of us who've never completely let go of our Ginger Rodgers fantasies, will adore the **Metronome Ballroom,** 1830 17th St., ☎ 415-252-9000. You can swoop by at 7:30, take a class, and then stay for a dance party on Friday, Saturday, and Sunday nights, or simply arrive at 9pm to trip the light fantastic. This is strictly a social dancing venue; only snacks and non-alcoholic beverages are available.

San Francisco Clubs & Bars

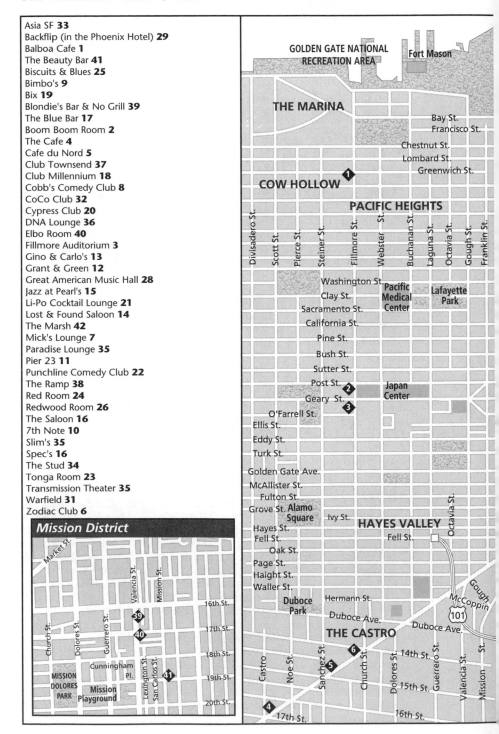

Asia SF **33**
Backflip (in the Phoenix Hotel) **29**
Balboa Cafe **1**
The Beauty Bar **41**
Biscuits & Blues **25**
Bimbo's **9**
Bix **19**
Blondie's Bar & No Grill **39**
The Blue Bar **17**
Boom Boom Room **2**
The Cafe **4**
Cafe du Nord **5**
Club Townsend **37**
Club Millennium **18**
Cobb's Comedy Club **8**
CoCo Club **32**
Cypress Club **20**
DNA Lounge **36**
Elbo Room **40**
Fillmore Auditorium **3**
Gino & Carlo's **13**
Grant & Green **12**
Great American Music Hall **28**
Jazz at Pearl's **15**
Li-Po Cocktail Lounge **21**
Lost & Found Saloon **14**
The Marsh **42**
Mick's Lounge **7**
Paradise Lounge **35**
Pier 23 **11**
Punchline Comedy Club **22**
The Ramp **38**
Red Room **24**
Redwood Room **26**
The Saloon **16**
7th Note **10**
Slim's **35**
Spec's **16**
The Stud **34**
Tonga Room **23**
Transmission Theater **35**
Warfield **31**
Zodiac Club **6**

GOLDEN GATE NATIONAL RECREATION AREA
Fort Mason

THE MARINA

Bay St.
Francisco St.
Chestnut St.
Lombard St.
Greenwich St.

COW HOLLOW

PACIFIC HEIGHTS

Divisadero St.
Scott St.
Pierce St.
Steiner St.
Fillmore St.
Webster St.
Buchanan St.
Laguna St.
Octavia St.
Gough St.
Franklin St.

Washington St.
Clay St.
Sacramento St.
California St.
Pine St.
Bush St.
Sutter St.
Post St.
Geary St.
O'Farrell St.
Ellis St.
Eddy St.
Turk St.
Golden Gate Ave.
McAllister St.
Fulton St.
Grove St.
Hayes St.
Fell St.
Oak St.
Page St.
Haight St.
Waller St.
Hermann St.

Pacific Medical Center
Lafayette Park
Japan Center

Alamo Square
Ivy St.
HAYES VALLEY
Octavia St.
Fell St.

Duboce Park
Duboce Ave.
Duboce Ave.
THE CASTRO
14th St.
15th St.
16th St.
17th St.

Castro
Noe St.
Sanchez St.
Church St.
Dolores St.
Guerrero St.
Valencia St.
Mission

Gough
McCoppin
101

Mission District

Market St.
Valencia St.
Mission St.
16th St.
17th St.
18th St.
19th St.
20th St.
Church St.
Dolores St.
Guerrero St.
Lexington St.
San Carlos St.
San Carlos St.
Cunningham Pl.
MISSION DOLORES PARK
Mission Playground

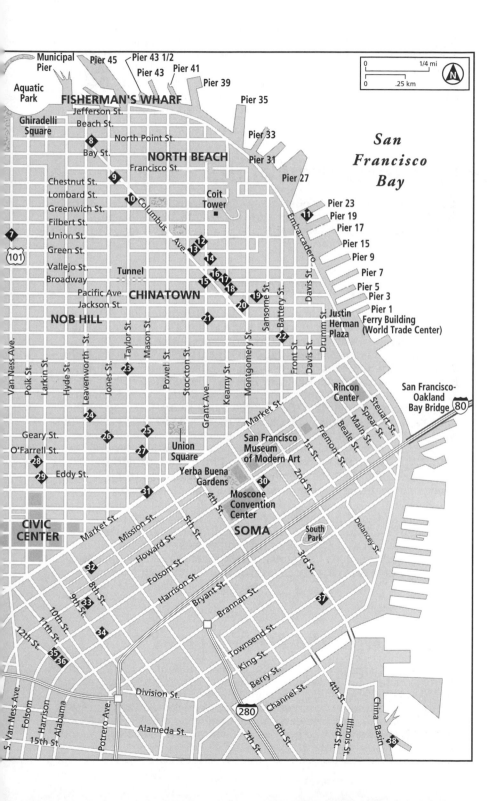

Municipal Pier

Pier 45

Pier 43 1/2

Pier 43

Pier 41

Pier 39

Aquatic Park

FISHERMAN'S WHARF

Jefferson St.

Pier 35

Ghiradelli Square

Beach St.

North Point St.

Pier 33

⑧ Bay St.

NORTH BEACH

Pier 31

Francisco St.

Pier 27

Chestnut St.

⑨

Lombard St.

Coit Tower

⑩ Columbus Ave.

Pier 23

⑪

Greenwich St.

Pier 19

Pier 17

Filbert St.

⑦

Union St.

Pier 15

Green St.

Pier 9

101

⑫

Pier 7

Vallejo St.

⑬

Pier 5

Broadway

Tunnel

⑭

Pier 3

Pacific Ave

⑯ ⑰

Pier 1

Jackson St.

CHINATOWN

⑮ ⑱

Ferry Building (World Trade Center)

NOB HILL

⑲

Justin Herman Plaza

⑳

⑳

㉑

㉒

San Francisco Bay

San Francisco Bay

Embarcadero

Davis St.

Sansome St.

Battery St.

Front St.

Davis St.

Drumm St.

㉓

Taylor St.

Mason St.

Powell St.

Stockton St.

Montgomery St.

Rincon Center

San Francisco-Oakland Bay Bridge **80**

Van Ness Ave.

Polk St.

Larkin St.

Hyde St.

Leavenworth St.

Jones St.

㉔

Grant Ave.

Kearny St.

Steuart St.

Spear St.

Main St.

Beale St.

1st St.

Fremont St.

Geary St.

㉖

㉕

O'Farrell St.

㉗

Union Square

San Francisco Museum of Modern Art

㉘

Yerba Buena Gardens

㉙ Eddy St.

㉛

㉚

2nd St.

Market St.

Moscone Convention Center

CIVIC CENTER

Market St.

Mission St.

SOMA

South Park

Delancey St.

Howard St.

㉜

Folsom St.

3rd St.

㊲

8th St.

㉝

Harrison St.

Bryant St.

9th St.

Brannan St.

㉞

10th St.

11th St.

Townsend St.

4th St.

12th St.

㉟ ㊱

King St.

Berry St.

Division St.

Channel St.

China Basin

S. Van Ness Ave.

Folsom

Harrison

Alabama

280

Alameda St.

7th St.

6th St.

5th St.

4th St.

3rd St.

Illinois St.

15th St.

Potrero Ave.

㊳

There's much more to local nightlife than South of Market dance halls (see "Groovin' it at gay and lesbian bars and clubs" later in this chapter). For a little fiesta in the Mission District, reserve a seat on **El Volado,** the Mexican Bus (www.mexicanbus.com), as it cruises the salsa clubs. The $33 ticket price includes cover charges at three clubs. Call ☎ 415-546-3747 for reservations two or three weeks ahead. **El Volado** rides Friday and Saturday nights and Thursdays as well, if enough people make reservations.

When Atmosphere Counts

San Francisco undeniably offers a special ambiance. From coffee shops and dance clubs, to art galleries and restaurants, there's something that everyone will find memorable. If atmosphere is what you're after, check out these favorites:

Hitting the singles scene

The **Balboa Cafe,** 3199 Fillmore St., between Greenwich and Filbert ☎ 415-921-3944, has withstood the test of time. The bar/restaurant gets lots of repeat customers — they come here after every divorce. In North Beach is **Club Millennium,** 1031 Kearny St., ☎ 415-402-0000, a dance club with lots of young singles wriggling into the wee hours. In and around the Tenderloin, they line up to enter the **Red Room,** 827 Sutter St., between Jones and Leavenworth Streets, next door to the Commodore Hotel, ☎ 415-346-7666. Look sharp. **Backflip,** at the Phoenix Hotel, 601 Eddy St., at Larkin Street, ☎ 415-771-3547, is to blue what the Red Room is to . . . well, you can guess. Good cocktail fare, house music nightly, and the staff wears vinyl. **Blondie's Bar and No Grill,** 540 Valencia St., between 16th and 17th Streets, ☎ 415-864-2419, is on the sizzling Valencia Street corridor in the Mission District. The young and the restless make good use of the free jazz jukebox.

Check out a four-hour, four-club tour, **Three Babes and a Bus,** for a great time on a Saturday night. It's hassle-free without the parking to worry about. Local gals in celebratory moods usually fill the luxury tour bus, and the fun is infectious. The $35-per-person fee includes club cover charges, VIP entry, and transportation to and from Union Square. Call ☎ 415-552-2582 for reservations at least a week in advance.

Mixing with the sophisticates

A cool art deco supper club, **Bix,** 56 Gold St., off Montgomery Street between Pacific and Jackson Streets in the Financial District, ☎ 415-433-6300, will make you want to wear a bias-cut gown and appear very glamorous. Or, you may want to check out the **Cypress Club,** 500 Jackson St., between Columbus Avenue and Montgomery Street, ☎ 415-296-8555, to have a drink and watch the patrons and the decor. Live jazz every night.

The **Redwood Room,** another class act, is located at the Clift Hotel, 495 Geary St., at Jones Street, ☎ **415-775-4700.** You can admire the splendid wood-paneling when you stop in for an after-dinner drink. The **Tonga Room** at the Fairmont Hotel, 950 Mason St., at California Street, ☎ **415-772-5278,** features a happy hour buffet weekdays from 5 to 7pm. For the price of a drink (about $5) you can enjoy hors d'oeuvres and entertainment — a tropical rainstorm hits every half hour. Okay, maybe that isn't so sophisticated, but at least it's fun.

The Plush Room, inside the York Hotel, 940 Sutter St., between Hyde and Leavenworth Streets, ☎ **415-885-2800,** features torch and standards singers of some repute. (More than one songbird has started a career in this intimate room and ended up playing clubs in New York City.) At other times, you may find a musical revue or duo. Cover is around $15, with a two-drink minimum.

Finding places to entertain the kids

Biscuits and Blues, 410 Mason St., at Geary Street, ☎ **415-292-2583,** is near the theater district on Union Square in a basement room. The all-ages venue has food that's inexpensive ($9.95 entrees). The music, played by blues musicians of varied repute, is really good. If you aren't dining here, cover starts at $4. The **Great American Music Hall,** 859 O'Farrell St., near Polk Street in the Tenderloin, ☎ **415-885-0750,** allows children over 6 into some shows; call for an events calendar to see who's playing an early show. (See "Catching the big-name acts," earlier in this chapter.) Because it offers food service, **Jazz at Pearl's,** 256 Columbus Ave., at Broadway, ☎ **415-291-8255,** can also accommodate minors.

Laughing It Up — Comedy Clubs

I probably don't have to remind you that San Francisco is where Robin Williams got his start. While the city is no longer the hotbed of chuckles that it was in the 1970s, the comedy clubs are still packing 'em in. Bring along your monologue — you never know when an open mic may beckon you.

Cobb's Comedy Club, 2801 Leavenworth at The Cannery, ☎ **415-928-4320,** has shows Tuesday through Sunday and a three-hour marathon of comics on Monday nights. A Cajun/Creole restaurant is now part of the mix; inquire about getting into the show free if you eat dinner there. No one under 16 admitted. Next door to Embarcadero 1 is the **Punchline Comedy Club,** 444 Battery St. between Washington and Clay Streets, ☎ **415-397-7573.** Local and nationally known comics play here Tuesday through Sunday at 9pm and 11pm. These shows are only open to folks 18 and over; tickets range from $5 to $15. The Valencia Street corridor in the Mission District is becoming one hot property, but it's the longtime 'hood of **The Marsh,** 1062 Valencia St., ☎ **415-641-0235,** a complex of theaters devoted to developing performances. On Friday and Saturday nights in one of these theaters, you'll find the

Mock Café, with scheduled performers at 8 and 10pm and open mic at 9pm. You won't normally find the polished acts that show up at the other clubs (although Williams himself recently made an appearance), but you'll certainly be closer to the cutting edge of comedy.

Defying Categorization — Unique Bars

A manicure *and* a martini can be yours at **The Beauty Bar,** 2299 Mission St. at 19th Street, ☎ 415-285-0323, where the decor is straight out of a 1959 beauty parlor. (In case you were wondering where all those enormous hair dryers with the hoods ended up, look no further.) Wednesday through Friday happy hour from 6 to 10pm includes a manicurist making the rounds. There's a drag show every other Thursday night. Our local suburbanites join the fun on the weekends, and during the week 'round midnight, hipsters drape themselves over the chrome barstools to exude cool.

If you have stars in your eyes, you might enjoy a gin-and-tonic at the **Zodiac Club,** 718 14th St. around Church and Sanchez Streets, ☎ 415-626-STAR. This is a locals' hangout with Mediterranean-style eats (served until midnight), high-quality booze, and a DJ on Sunday and occasional Thursday nights. **Li-Po Cocktail Lounge,** 916 Grant Ave., at Washington Street, ☎ 415-982-0072, is an authentic, dark, Chinatown dive, complete with dusty Asian furnishings, a huge rice-paper lantern, and a shrine to Buddha behind the bar. If you wish to drink with professionals, head to North Beach and grab a bar stool at **Gino and Carlo's,** 548 Green St., between Columbus and Grant Avenues, ☎ 415-421-0896, which opens early so the regulars can get in a fortifying scotch before lunch. **Spec's,** 12 Saroyan Alley, off Columbus Avenue and Broadway, ☎ 415-421-4112, is another North Beach institution.

Groovin' It at Gay and Lesbian Bars and Clubs

Following, I give you a short list of the many clubs and bars that cater to the gay and lesbian community in the city. Find specific listings in the weekly entertainment guides, *SF Weekly* and *Bay Guardian,* and look for the free *Bay Area Reporter* in bookstores, cafés, and bars, around town.

The Cafe, 2367 Market St. near Castro, ☎ 415-861-3846, is currently *the* place for both sexes to go dancing. It's also *the* place to stand in line on busy weekend nights. **Club Townsend,** 177 Townsend St., between 2nd and 3rd Streets, ☎ 415-974-6020, is another hotspot that offers two "dance nights," two of which are called Pleasuredome and

Universe. For specifics, take a look at the club's Web site at www.
177townsend.com. **The Stud,** 399 9th St., at Harrison Street, ☎ **415-
863-6623,** is a long-time institution in the city. You can even bring your
parents here; it's cool. Cover $2 to $6 on weekends.

CoCo Club, 139 8th St., between Mission and Howard Streets, ☎ **415-
626-2337,** is connected to the Chat House restaurant. Though everyone
is welcome to the cabaret and music shows, on some Friday nights it's
mainly lesbian-only. Cover $4 to $7.

Part VII
Exploring beyond San Francisco: Great Day and Overnight Trips

The 5th Wave   By Rich Tennant

"The problem with wine tastings is you're not supposed to swallow, and Clifford refuses to spit. Fortunately, he studied trumpet with Dizzy Gillespie."

In this part . . .

You'd think it would be enough that San Francisco is a marvel among big cities, but no . . . we toss in a few extra treats for your dining and sightseeing pleasure. Chief among them is the gorgeous Napa and Sonoma valleys, where the sight and scent of grapes and olives act like a restorative. Closer still is Berkeley, a microcosm of Northern California life that revolves around the university and a vibrant dining scene. Finally, nature boys and girls will have a veritable field day hiking or relaxing on the coast in verdant Point Reyes and Inverness.

Chapter 23

Checking Out Berkeley

● ●

In This Chapter

▶ Amusing yourself around town

▶ Shopping opportunities

▶ Satisfying your eating desires

● ●

As you approach Berkeley, a mere 20 minutes over the Bay Bridge, you know you aren't in San Francisco anymore. The weather is an immediate giveaway — while the temperature isn't dramatically different, San Francisco's ever-present summer fog is gone. Berkeley is also smaller than San Francisco, and much of its cultural life revolves around the University of California at Berkeley (UCB) campus. One thing both cities have in common is a devotion to fine dining. In fact, one excellent reason to visit Berkeley is to eat a great meal.

Getting There

You can use BART to reach Berkeley, but your sight-seeing options will be limited. For this day trip, it's really better to take a car. Most people (myself included) drive over the Bay Bridge and follow the signs to Highway 80. The exits include Ashby Avenue, University, and Gilman. If you intend to begin your day on 4th Street (see "Shopping delights"), take the University Avenue exit. If you intend to make the University your first stop, an alternate route is Highway 24, exiting on scenic Claremont Avenue. Claremont intersects College Avenue, which leads directly to the campus while avoiding the less handsome flatlands of Berkeley. I can't tell you a best time to go to Berkeley, although the campus empties out to some extent in the summer. Visiting on a Thursday, however, guarantees free admission to UCB museums and the botanical garden.

Doing Berkeley

To my mind, an ideal day in Berkeley revolves around lunch or dinner at **Chez Panisse** (see "Dining Pleasures"). I have no compelling reason to recommend this restaurant except that the food is as close to perfect as food gets. Those involved in the business of feeding people consider this restaurant a shrine. The question, then, is how do you

keep busy before your reservation? If it's for dinner, you can easily frit-
ter away your time shopping on **4th Street** (see "Shopping delights"),
walking around **Tilden Park,** and seeing what's up at the **University
campus.** If you've made lunch reservations, break up the day by touring UCB in the morning and hiking in Tilden Park or checking out the
merchandise on **Telegraph Avenue** or 4th Street in the afternoon.

Seeing the sights

The **University of California at Berkeley** is the biggest sight in
Berkeley, so to speak, and the attractive, active campus leaves a
positive impression on older kids and teens if you happen to have
any with you. The **Visitor Information Center** is at 101 University
Hall, 220 University Ave. at Oxford Street, ☎ **510-642-5215.** You can
join a free 10am campus tour there Monday through Friday.

Other notable UCB sites include the **Hearst Museum of Anthropology**
(☎ **510-642-3682;** open Wednesday through Sunday; admission $2
adults, $1 seniors, 50¢ children, free on Thursdays), the **University
Art Museum** at 2625 Durant Ave. (☎ **510-642-0808;** open Wednesday
through Sunday; admission $6 adults, $4 seniors and children), and the
307-foot-tall **Sather Tower** (also known as the Campanile) in the center
of campus, in which you can take an elevator to the top for excellent
views of Berkeley and the bay (open daily; admission $2 adults, $1.50
kids 12–17, $1 kids 3–11).

Above the campus in the lush hills is the **UC Berkeley Botanical
Garden** (☎ **510-642-3343**). While Golden Gate Park's Strybing
Arboretum (see Chapter 16) is a pristine example of the gardener's
art, this 34-acre botanical garden is a more natural setting. It features
13,000 plants, including cactus and rose gardens. A good place for an
easy hike. Farther up the road, the kid-friendly **Lawrence Hall of
Science** (☎ **510-642-5132;** open daily; admission $6 adults, $4 seniors
and student, $2 kids 3–6) brings science up close and personal.

The campus is bounded by shops, cafes, and well-stocked bookstores.
To get a sense of Berkeley street life, walk along **Telegraph Avenue**
from Bancroft to Ashby, and get your fill of cappuccino, street vendors,
psychic readers, and the occasional weirdo.

Shopping delights

Close to the University exit off I-80 is **4th Street,** a little Mecca for
shoppers from all over the Bay Area. It started out small, with a few
outlet stores and a popular diner, but over the years developed into a
full-fledged destination for fashion, food, and home decor. Begin by
oohing over the gorgeous accessories for home and garden at **The
Gardener,** 1836 Fourth St. (☎ **510-548-4545;** open daily), and keep
going on down the block. When the stores start to peter out, cross the
street and start over.

Berkeley

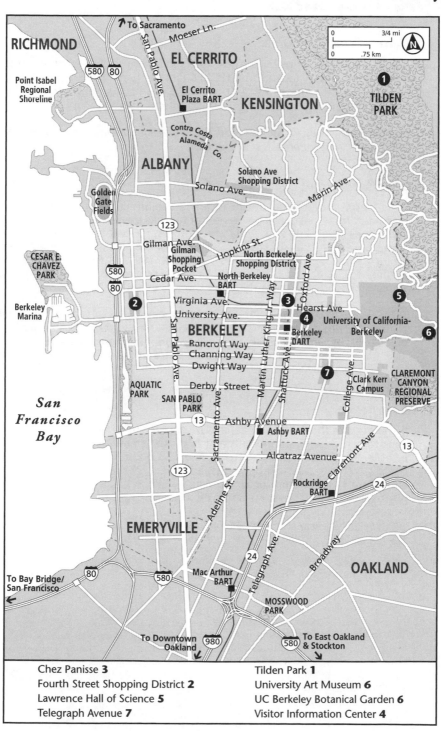

RICHMOND

EL CERRITO

KENSINGTON

TILDEN PARK 1

To Sacramento

Moeser Ln.

San Pablo Ave.

Point Isabel Regional Shoreline

El Cerrito Plaza BART

Contra Costa
Alameda Co.

ALBANY

Solano Ave Shopping District

Solano Ave.

Marin Ave.

Golden Gate Fields

123

Gilman Ave.
Gilman Shopping Pocket
Cedar Ave.

Hopkins St.

North Berkeley Shopping District

Oxford Ave.

CESAR E. CHAVEZ PARK

580
80

North Berkeley BART

Berkeley Marina 2

Virginia Ave.
University Ave.

3
Hearst Ave.

4 University of California-Berkeley

5

6

BERKELEY

Berkeley BART

San Pablo Ave.

Bancroft Way
Channing Way
Dwight Way

Martin Luther King Jr. Way

Shattuck Ave.

College Ave.

7 Clark Kerr Campus

CLAREMONT CANYON REGIONAL PRESERVE

San Francisco Bay

AQUATIC PARK

Derby Street

SAN PABLO PARK

13

Ashby Avenue
Ashby BART

Sacramento Ave.

Alcatraz Avenue

Claremont Ave.

13

123

Rockridge BART

24

Adeline St.

EMERYVILLE

24

Telegraph Ave.

Broadway

OAKLAND

To Bay Bridge/ San Francisco

80

580

Mac Arthur BART

MOSSWOOD PARK

To Downtown Oakland

980

To East Oakland & Stockton

580

0 — 3/4 mi
0 — .75 km
N

Chez Panisse **3**
Fourth Street Shopping District **2**
Lawrence Hall of Science **5**
Telegraph Avenue **7**

Tilden Park **1**
University Art Museum **6**
UC Berkeley Botanical Garden **6**
Visitor Information Center **4**

Dining Pleasures

Bette's Oceanview Diner

You can sit down here for a homey breakfast or lunch featuring tender baked goods, tasty salads, and Bette's famous pancakes. Expect a huge wait on the weekends. Next door, Bette's sells take-out sandwiches, salads, and desserts, to take care of impatient hungry people.

1807 4th St., Berkeley. ☎ *510-644-3230. No reservations. Main courses: $5.95–8.95. MC, V. Open: daily for breakfast and lunch.*

Chez Panisse and Chez Panisse Cafe

Alice Waters, the owner of Chez Panisse, is an icon in the food world, respected for adhering to her vision of food as a gift we give daily to our loved ones (including you) and for serving unbelievably delicious dishes. Eating here in the cafe or restaurant is one of the nicest things you'll ever do for yourself. Dinner downstairs is $39 to $69 prix fixe, depending on the night. The cafe is moderately priced, comparatively speaking, but expect to spend a lot more than you think prudent for lunch. It's worth it.

1517 Shattuck Ave., Berkeley. ☎ *510-548-5525. Advance reservations a must for dinner in the restaurant; same-day reservations accepted for lunch and dinner in the cafe. AE, DC, MC, V. Main courses: $39–$69 prix fixe downstairs; $16–$19 in the cafe. Open: Monday through Saturday for lunch and dinner in the upstairs cafe, dinner only in the downstairs restaurant.*

Cafe Rouge

If you lived in the 4th Street neighborhood, there wouldn't be many reasons to stray. Everything you need is close at hand, including a lovely meal in this French-style bistro opened by a kitchen alumnus of Chez Panisse. Meat eaters will be greatly charmed by the menu (don't fail to admire the butcher counter in the back), while mollusk fans can turn happily to the oysters. Desserts shine as well.

1782 4th St., Berkeley. ☎ *510-525-1440. Reservations advised. Main courses: $13–$24. AE, MC, V. Open: daily for lunch and dinner.*

Chapter 24

Coastal Scenes: Point Reyes and Inverness

....

In This Chapter

▶ Avoiding the crowds

▶ Where the wild things are

▶ Eating and lodging in the choice places

....

A one-hour drive through the small towns of Marin County and Samuel P. Taylor State Park leads you to **Point Reyes National Seashore,** a mix of wild coastline and forest of unequivocal appeal to hikers, nature lovers, and wildlife-watchers. The rocky shore along this part of the coast is a direct result of earthquake activity — you can even get a close-up of the San Andreas fault on a short walk at one of the visitor information centers. In the midst of all this natural beauty, you still aren't far from a few of civilization's pleasures, such as a good meal and a soft pillow. **Point Reyes Station,** the minuscule town nearby, is a bit of a tourist magnet on the weekends, so you can find a selection of excellent restaurants and interesting shops within its four-block radius. **Inverness,** a tiny community on Tomales Bay, a few miles farther north, has a handful of picturesque inns and B&Bs for travelers who don't wish to return too quickly to the big city.

Deciding When to Visit

Because the **Point Reyes Lighthouse** is closed Tuesdays and Wednesdays, try not to go on those days. If you can manage to come later in the week (avoiding the crowded weekends), you'll be treated to relatively empty roads, even during the summer. The best times to view seasonal flora and fauna in **Point Reyes National Seashore** area are as follows:

Point Reyes National Seashore

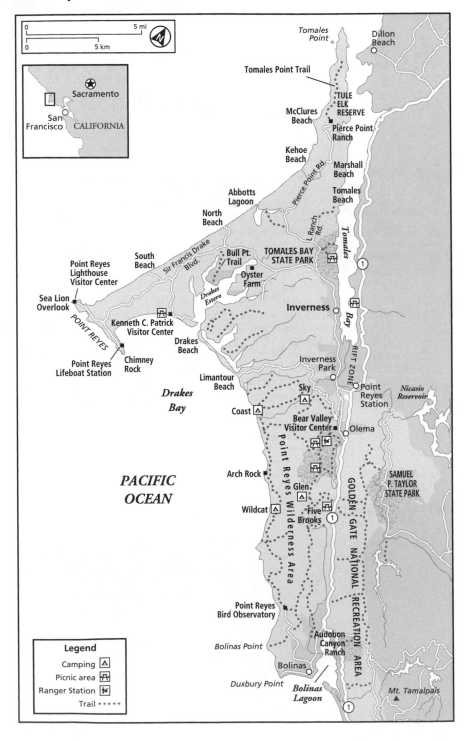

Legend

Camping △

Picnic area ⊞

Ranger Station ⬥

Trail •••••

✔ Wild flowers: February through July

✔ Elephant seals: November through March

✔ Harbor seals: mid-March through mid-June

✔ Gray whales: January through March

 And another word of advice: Bring warm clothes. The weather in Point Reyes mimics San Francisco's. It's often cold and sometimes foggy on this part of the coast in the summer.

Getting to the Point

You can reach Point Reyes in more than one way, but regulars prefer to cross the Golden Gate Bridge and exit on San Anselmo/Sir Francis Drake Boulevard. Then turn left, heading west on Sir Francis Drake, and stay on this road as it passes through the high-priced burgs of San Anselmo, Ross, Woodacre, and Lagunitas. It takes about an hour (with light traffic) to reach the headquarters of **Point Reyes National Seashore.** Admission is free.

We're Here — Now What?

At the junction of Highway 1 and Sir Francis Drake Boulevard in Olema, follow the signs to the **Bear Valley Visitor Center** (☎ 415-663-1092), just about one-minute away. The Center has maps, informative park rangers, a book/gift section, and some interesting exhibits on the ecology of the area. Many trails begin here, including an under-one-mile earth-quake trail along the San Andreas Fault. Another park attraction is **Kule Loklo,** a Coast Miwok Native Indian village replica. If you're visiting during the school year, you may run into groups of school kids.

Hiking is the prime activity in the park, but a drive to **Limantour Beach** is a good alternative or add-on. You get to the beach by turning left on Bear Valley Road and left again on Limantour Road. Although swim-ming is not recommended (and it's usually too cold), you can bird watch and picnic here.

Point Reyes Lighthouse is a big attraction in these parts all year long, but especially from January through March when migrating gray whales pass by. From the Bear Valley Visitor Center, the lighthouse is a 20.5-mile drive along Sir Francis Drake Boulevard through dairy farms and pastures, where you can see many a cow lounging around. At the end of the road is a parking lot. The lighthouse is a half-mile walk away, and down 300 steps. The cliffs all around this area are not stable enough to climb on, and you'll see lots of warnings to that effect. **Sea Lion Overlook** near the lighthouse is the place to watch those crea-tures as well as harbor seals.

From this stop, it's a short drive to **Drake's Beach** (just follow the signs as you drive to or from the lighthouse). Another fine visitor center with friendly park rangers is on the beach parking lot, next to a cafe specializing in fried foods. As is the case at all the area beaches, there is no lifeguard on duty and the undertow can be dangerous, so swimming is not encouraged. At the end of Drake's Beach, past the Point Reyes Lifeboat Station, is **Chimney Rock.** The **Elephant Seal Overlook** nearby is a good vantage point for observing elephant seals in the winter months.

At the northernmost tip of the seashore at **Tomales Point** is the **Tule Elk Reserve,** where over 500 of these once nearly extinct creatures live on 2,600 protected acres. The reserve is a 30-minute drive from Inverness. Stay on Sir Francis Drake Boulevard until you reach Pierce Point Road, which takes you directly into the reserve.

If you happen to be making this trip in August in warmer weather, with or without kids, there are some wonderful swimming beaches along Tomales Bay in Inverness. Look for signs along Sir Francis Drake Boulevard leading to **Chicken Ranch Beach** or **Shell Beach.**

We've Got Tonight . . .

Manka's Inverness Lodge

$$$ Inverness

Inverness consists of a few stores and restaurants, homes tucked into the hills, and some inns. At the high end is Manka's, a handsomely rustic, 80-year-old former hunting and fishing lodge that looks as if it would make Ralph Lauren feel at home. Rooms contain fireplaces, comfy beds, privacy, and that woodsy feeling Red Riding Hood's grandmother must have known and loved. Manka's is also known for its $48 gourmet prix-fixe dinners served Wednesday through Sunday — it's by far the best place in town to eat.

Argyle Rd., Inverness. ☎ 415-669-1034; Internet: www.mankas.com. *Rack rates: $145–$415 double; two night minimum on weekends. Call months ahead for reservations. MC, V. Look for the sign pointing to Argyle Rd., off Sir Francis Drake Blvd.*

Motel Inverness

The recently remodeled rooms, which include a family-sized suite with kitchen, look out onto Tomales Bay, a wildlife refuge populated by many species of birds. The front desk in this low-key and well-kept motel is located in a lodge with views, a television, and a pool table available to guests 24-hours a day.

12718 Sir Francis Drake Blvd. ☎ 800-826-9834 or 415-669-1081; Internet: www.coastaltraveler.com/motelinverness. *Rack rates: $89–$125 double. MC, V.*

Eating at the Point

If you're hungry or want to gather a picnic, continue on Sir Francis Drake Boulevard until it meets Point Reyes-Petaluma Road. Drive across the little bridge and you'll be in Point Reyes Station. The **Pine Cone Diner,** 60 Fourth St., (☎ **415-663-1536**), is open for breakfast, lunch, and dinner. The **Station House,** 111180 State Route 1, (☎ **415-663-1515**), is also immensely popular and moderately priced (and there's live jazz on Friday and Saturday nights). For takeout, **Tomales Bay Foods,** 80 Fourth St. (☎ **415-663-9335**), has a small but fantastic menu of seasonal salads and sandwiches ready to go. It shares a building with a small creamery and a shop featuring lovely hand-woven clothing.

Chapter 25

California Wine Country

*A*bout an hour's drive north of San Francisco are Napa and Sonoma Counties, some of the country's best and best-known wineries. Although Napa and Sonoma are resort-like destinations, many visitors arrive for a day of wine tasting, and then turn around and head back to the city. It's a shame visitors don't take the time to relax awhile during their wine-tasting trip. Unfortunately, visitors to Wine Country cheat themselves of some great reasons for staying: The contrast between the city and the spacious beauty of Wine Country can draw you in and make you want to stop and stay a bit. Also, you don't have to rush around in Wine Country because there aren't any attractions to visit, other than the wineries. So vacationers have a chance to actually relax. Imagine that.

The Taste of a Lifetime: Planning a Visit to Wine Country

This chapter tells you everything you need to know to tour the California wineries and taste their wines like a pro. To get a jump on the intricacies of wine tasting, call **Beaulieu Vineyard** (☎ **707-963-2411**) and request a copy of *From the Grapes to the Glass* by Helene Le Blanc. For $6, the winery will mail you this beginner's guide to wine. Another great guide is *Wine For Dummies* by Ed McCarthy and Mary Ewing-Mulligan, M.W.

Journeying to Wine Country

Earlier in the book I warned you against renting a car during your stay in San Francisco. Well, I've changed my mind — for your Wine Country tour, anyway. Now it's time to call the car rental company and learn to drive through San Francisco traffic, because by car is the best way to tour Napa or Sonoma Valley (see Chapter 9 for car rental information). If you really don't want to drive, you can join an organized tour. But if you are interested in spending a night or two in Sonoma or in one of the charming towns near Napa, or if you want to visit smaller, less commercial wineries than those the tour companies choose, you will need to drive yourself.

The Wine Country

You can take one of two roads to Wine Country. The faster, less scenic route is across the San Francisco–Oakland Bay Bridge (I-80). While the more scenic route crosses the Golden Gate Bridge and meanders up through Marin County on U.S. 101. For the return trip, I highly recommend taking I-80 rather than U.S. 101 over the Golden Gate Bridge, especially if you're traveling on a weekend. But to get back from Sonoma, go the Golden Gate Bridge route.

If you decide to go the Bay Bridge route to Napa, go east over the bridge (I-80) and then north to the Napa/Highway 29 exit near Vallejo. Highway 29 is the main road through the Napa Valley. The trip takes approximately 70 minutes.

If you decide to go over the Golden Gate Bridge, continue on U.S. 101 north to Novato, where you need to pick up Highway 37 east. Then, if you're interested in a pleasant drive and aren't in a big hurry, take Highway 121 (the Sonoma Highway) north toward Sonoma and then east to Napa, if that's your destination, where you'll end up on Highway 29. If Sonoma is your destination, take Highway 12. Make sure to have a map handy. This drive takes about 90 minutes.

You can contact the Napa Valley **Conference & Visitors Bureau,** 1310 Napa Town Center, Napa, CA 94559 (☎ 707-226-7459), Internet: www.napavalley.com, for maps to help get you there.

Picking the best time to visit

The most popular seasons for touring Napa and Sonoma Valleys are summer and fall. The summers are hot in Wine Country, which might be a surprise coming from the city. September and October are extremely busy because of the "crush," or grape harvest, during which time the aroma of must (crushed grapes) fills the air.

You can visit Wine Country any time of year; it's a treat in winter and spring if it doesn't rain. In fact, the comparative lack of traffic on the small roads and smaller crowds at the restaurants is a pleasure that time of year. However, if the forecast calls for rain, I recommend you save this trip for another time. If you do plan to visit Wine Country during summer or autumn, make lodging reservations early.

You meet with a lot more traffic and tourists on the weekends than on the weekdays. Also, Golden Gate Bridge traffic going north on Friday afternoons and south on Sunday afternoons is amazing. So don't go when all the commuters are taking their weekend trips up to San Rafael. Go while everyone else is at work.

Drinking and driving woes

Although you may be tasting wines all along the 35-mile route through Napa and on the scenic roads through Sonoma, the rules of drinking and driving (and good common sense) are still intact — you can't drink to excess and then drive. Yes, this may affect your wine-tasting tour. Use your judgement. If you need to take a break after a couple of glasses, stop off somewhere and let it wear off. Remember that wine tasting isn't an endurance contest. Wine tasting is about tasting, not drinking it down. Some winery tasting rooms have containers you can spit the wine into so you can taste the wine without actually having it go to your head. Remember that your trip to Wine Country is an opportunity to increase your knowledge of wines. It isn't an opportunity to just drink.

California Highway 29 is very dangerous anyway, even if you're not drinking! This two-lane thoroughfare through the Napa Valley is where many accidents occur, especially at night.

Not going it alone: Taking an organized Wine Country tour

A good option for people who don't feel comfortable driving, or who are on a very tight schedule, are local companies that offer one-day Wine Country tours to the Napa and Sonoma valleys. On these six- to nine-hour tours you can usually visit two to three wineries and have lunch in one of the picturesque villages along the way. The downside of a tour like this is that you won't see some of the great wineries that aren't part of the tour package, you won't have time to relax in places that catch your eye, and you won't be able to choose where you want to eat.

But if you're interested in the package tours, here are a few of the good ones to look into:

- ✔ **Great Pacific Tour Company** (☎ 415-626-4499) picks you up at your San Francisco hotel and delivers you back after tastings at two Sonoma wineries, a picnic lunch, and a tour of Domaine Chandon, a sparkling wine producer in Napa. The cost, including lunch, is $66 for adults, $64 for seniors, and $56 for children 5 to 11.

- ✔ **Grayline** (☎ 800-826-0202) offers several Wine Country outings, as well as a few overnight packages. Its nine-hour tour includes two wineries and a stop in Calistoga for lunch and shopping. The price is $43 for adults and $21.50 for children.

- ✔ **Tower Tours** (☎ 415-434-8687) takes you to Napa and Sonoma Valleys for the day, with stops at three wineries and lunch in Yountville or the town of Sonoma. The charge is $42 for adults and $25 for children.

- ✔ **Wine Country Jeep Tours** (☎ 800-539-5337) will plan a custom three- to four-hour winery tour that can include some off-road trailblazing and a picnic lunch. The cost is $17/hour per person.

- ✔ You can also ride the **Napa Valley Wine Train** (☎ 800-427-4124 or 707-253-9264). The train is basically a gourmet restaurant on wheels that goes along 36 miles through the valley, from the town of Napa to the village of St. Helena. You can get a lunch, brunch, or dinner tour ranging in price from $25 to $85. The tour primarily involves dining and watching the gorgeous scenery go by. The only train that makes a stop is the Grgich Hills Private Winery Tour and Tasting, a luncheon ride that costs $69 per person and stops at one winery. On board the train there is a wine-tasting car with an attractive bar and knowledgeable host. You can buy and taste as much wine as you wish and not worry about getting back to the station safely. The three-hour tours depart from the train station in downtown Napa, at 1275 McKinstry St. You must make reservations for a spot on the train. If you don't want to drive to Napa, **Grayline** (☎ 800-826-0202) arranges, for $99 per person, passage via a Blue and Gold Ferry from Pier 39 to Vallejo, where a bus takes everyone to the wine train station in Napa for the three-hour lunch excursion.

Mapping Out Your Winery Journey

A single day in Wine Country can't do the area justice and will leave you wanting more. But if that's all the time you have, plan to visit no more than three to four wineries, one before lunch and two or three after followed by a late afternoon snack or an early dinner.

If you spend two days and an overnight you can have the chance to check out other enjoyable activities such as a bike ride down a sleepy road or a spa treatment. If you want to do these other activities, cut down on your winery visits the first day, and instead take advantage of whatever your inn has to offer, such as a swimming pool, a garden walk, or just some peace and quiet. Or, you could visit one winery before you check in to your lodgings and visit another one in the early afternoon, followed by a mud bath and a massage, a nap, and dinner. Then, have a substantial breakfast the next morning and consider one of the 11am reservation-only winery tours, such as Niebaum Coppola or Benziger. To occupy any extra time you may have left in your schedule, check out the shopping in the towns and villages along Highway 29.

Touring the Wineries

You will find more than 220 wineries in the Napa Valley and 40 in the Sonoma Valley. Some of these wineries are owned by conglomerates, such as Seagrams. Others are owned by individuals so seduced by the grape that they abandoned other careers to devote themselves to viticulture. There is no direct correlation on wine quality of the larger wineries over the smaller ones. The quality has more to do with the talents of the vintners and variables such as weather and soil conditions. But the bigger wineries offer more to visitors in terms of education and entertainment.

Napa Valley

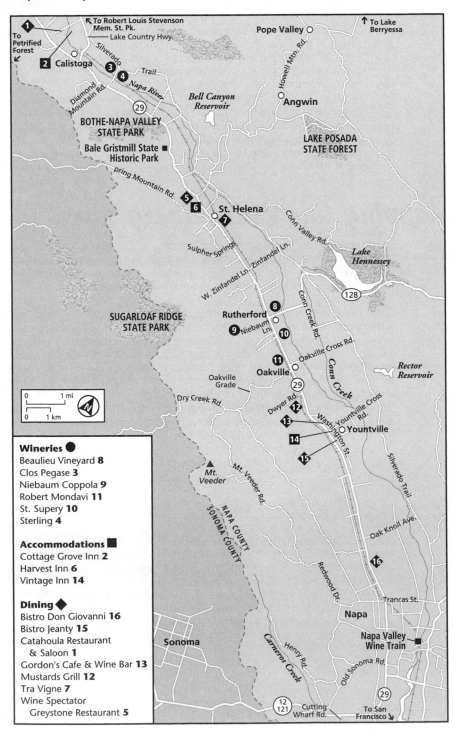

To Petrified Forest

To Robert Louis Stevenson Mem. St. Pk.

Lake Country Hwy.

↑ To Lake Berryessa

1 Calistoga

Pope Valley

Silverado

2

3

4

Trail

Napa River

Diamond Mountain Rd.

Howell Mtn. Rd.

Angwin

Bell Canyon Reservoir

(29)

BOTHE-NAPA VALLEY STATE PARK

Bale Gristmill State Historic Park ■

LAKE POSADA STATE FOREST

pring Mountain Rd.

5

6

St. Helena

7

Conn Valley Rd.

Lake Hennessey

Sulpher Springs

W. Zinfandel Ln. Zinfandel Ln.

(128)

SUGARLOAF RIDGE STATE PARK

Rutherford

8

9 Niebaum Ln.

10

Conn Creek Rd.

Rector Reservoir

11

Oakville Cross Rd.

Oakville

Conn Creek

Oakville Grade

(29)

Dry Creek Rd.

Dwyer Rd.

Yountville Cross Rd.

0   1 mi
0   1 km

12

13

Washington St.

Yountville

14

15

Silverado Trail

▲ Mt. Veeder

Mt. Veeder Rd.

NAPA COUNTY
SONOMA COUNTY

Oak Knoll Ave.

16

Redwood Dr.

Trancas St.

Napa

Sonoma

Henry Rd.

Carneros Creek

Napa Valley Wine Train ■

Old Sonoma Rd.

(12) (121)

Cutting Wharf Rd.

(29)

To San Francisco ↓

Wineries ●
Beaulieu Vineyard **8**
Clos Pegase **3**
Niebaum Coppola **9**
Robert Mondavi **11**
St. Supery **10**
Sterling **4**

Accommodations ■
Cottage Grove Inn **2**
Harvest Inn **6**
Vintage Inn **14**

Dining ◆
Bistro Don Giovanni **16**
Bistro Jeanty **15**
Catahoula Restaurant
   & Saloon **1**
Gordon's Cafe & Wine Bar **13**
Mustards Grill **12**
Tra Vigne **7**
Wine Spectator
   Greystone Restaurant **5**

If you don't know anything about wine (but you know what you like), learn the basics by asking questions of the people hired by the wineries to help you. You can greatly enhance your knowledge of wine by talking to and asking questions of the staff hired by the wineries. Take advantage of them to learn the basics of tasting wine correctly and about the wines they offer. What better classroom to learn about wines than a French-style chateau smack in the middle of a vineyard?

For wine-tasting newbies, the first winery you visit should be one that offers an in-depth tour, so you can familiarize yourself with the wine-making process. If you're traveling from south to north, Sterling Vineyards in Calistoga is a good bet, or Robert Mondavi in Oakville. In Sonoma, the tram operators at Benziger are both knowledgeable and accessible. If you have already developed a fondness for fermented grape juice, ask your local wine merchant for suggestions on smaller wineries that you also might want to visit.

You won't be able to get a deal on wine that you purchase directly from the producers at the wineries. They sell their wines at the full retail price so they don't undercut their primary market, the wine merchants. If you can't get a particular vintage at home, most wineries will mail order it for you.

Becoming a wine connoisseur: Learning about wines

Cabernet Sauvignon, Pinot Noir, and Zinfandel grapes (grown for red wines), and Chardonnay and Sauvignon or Fume Blanc grapes (grown for white wines) are the most prominent grape varieties produced in the area. Identifying one grape variety from another takes a great deal of knowledge. Each one of these varieties contains identifiable flavors and aromas you can only begin to recognize through careful sipping.

Reading the label on the bottle is really the best way to recognize Cabernet from Pinot. The label identifies the type of grape used if the wine contains at least 75 percent of that particular variety, among other bits of information. The appellation of origin indicates where the grapes were grown. The label may state the grapes were grown in either a viticulture area, such as the Carneros region of the Napa Valley, in a certain county, or just in the state itself. Check the vintage date, as well, which explains when at least 95 percent of the grapes were crushed. You also should make a note of the vintage date because many wines taste better aged, and some years produce better grapes than others.

Begin appreciating your wine by analyzing its color, aroma, and taste. First use your eyes, then your nose, then your mouth. Feel free always to ask questions of the person pouring. The more questions you ask, the more you know about the product, the more you are inclined to purchase this product on a regular basis, which benefits everyone involved.

Great Stops for First-Time Tasters

It isn't easy to choose which roads to follow through the vineyards because there are so many vineyards to choose from. The wineries suggested are great for first-time tasters because they make a special effort to accommodate visitors. These vineyards offer tours, exhibits, and/or an extra friendly staff. But there are plenty more, so get a map of the area and, time permitting, explore those back roads.

Start in Calistoga and work your way down the valley along Highway 29 to make your return to San Francisco a bit shorter. Don't take this drive on a summer weekend. The bumper-to-bumper traffic on Highway 29 will ruin your day.

Wineries in Napa Valley

Robert Mondavi

Mondavi was the first winery to conduct public tastings, and it continues to take pride in educating people about wine. It's well-worth it to try the free one-hour tour that is offered daily. And for fees ranging from $15 to $55, you can benefit from the once- or twice-weekly-held seminars on winegrowing, essence tasting, and wine and food. Reservations are required for the seminars. During July, you can enjoy a Saturday evening concert series sponsored by the winery. The concerts sell out quickly, so call or visit Mondavi's Web site for a schedule and tickets.

Wine tasting do's & don'ts

- Before the pour, sniff your glass. It should have a clean aroma.

- Do not pour the wine yourself.

- Taste wines in the appropriate order: whites first, reds second, and dessert wines last.

- Swirl the wine to coat the inside of the glass. This introduces more oxygen and helps open up the wine flavors and aromas.

- Smell the wine. Notice the different aromas — spice, fruit, flowers.

- Take a sip and cover the back of your tongue with the wine.

- Wine tasting is one of the few sports where spitting is not only allowed, it's encouraged. (Just make sure you hit your target, a bucket or some other container available for this purpose.) Tasting, then spitting, is also a nifty way to sample many wines without becoming cloudy-headed.

- Do not bring a bottle of wine from one winery into another.

- Do not bring your friendly neighborhood bar behavior into a tasting room. Leave the chewing gum outside.

7801 St. Helena Hwy. (Hwy. 29), PO Box 106, Oakville, CA 94562. ☎ 800-MONDAVI or 707-226-1395. Internet: www.robertmondavi.com. *Open: daily May–Oct 9:30am– 5:30pm; until 4:30pm Nov–Apr.*

St. Supery

Learn about aromas common to certain varietals with this self-guided interactive tour and about growing techniques at the winery's demonstration vineyard. You will actually experience the aromas of the wines through "SmellaVision." You'll need at least 1 hour and 15 minutes for the tour and wine tasting alone. Have $3 on hand for the tasting fee. Eight dollars will get you a half glass of the really good stuff in the "Divine Wine" room (the new reserve tasting room).

PO Box 38, Rutherford, CA 94573. ☎ 800-942-0809. Open: daily May–Oct 9:30am– 6pm; until 5pm Nov–Apr.

Niebaum Coppola

Yep, Coppola, as in the movie director, Francis Ford Coppola. His wines are fairly sophisticated, but even novice wine lovers can enjoy visiting his impressive estate. There's a museum on the property tracing the history of the winery and the two families connected by its ownership. You'll see movie memorabilia on the second floor of the museum, including the surfboard used in *Apocalypse Now,* Oscar statuettes, and costumes. Make reservations two weeks in advance for an 11am or 2pm in-depth historical tour, which costs $20 a person. Enjoy a formal sit-down tasting in one of the wine cellars after the 1½-hour tour. You'll pay $7.50 for regular tastings — you can even keep the glass. You won't find any picnic facilities at the winery.

1991 St. Helena Hwy. (Hwy. 29), Rutherford, CA 94573. ☎ 707-968-1100. Open: daily 10am–5pm.

Beaulieu Vineyard

At this well-regarded establishment, the vintners pass out glasses of Chardonnay as you walk in to set you in the right mood. After you've enjoyed a glass or two, you can take a free one-half hour tour of the production facility, which is available daily from 11am to 4pm. The winery charges $12.50 for up to five wines for a tasting fee only for Beaulieu's delicious reserve vintages.

1960 St. Helena Hwy. (Hwy. 29), Rutherford, CA 94573. ☎ 707-967-5230. Open: daily 10am–5pm.

Sterling

Visit this hilltop winery by aerial tram and view the spectacular vista. Tasting the wine is also included in the ticket price of $6. After you get to the hilltop, take the self-guided tour that leads you through the entire operation and into the tasting room, where the friendly staff serve you wine at tables rather than at a bar. Plan on spending at least one hour here.

1111 Dunaweal Lane (½ mile east of Hwy. 29), PO Box 365, Calistoga, CA 94515.
☎ *707-942-3344. Open: daily 10:30am–4:30pm.*

Clos Pegase

The official tour takes only about 30 minutes and is offered at 11am and 2pm. The rest of your time at this winery can be spent at happy hour or studying the art collection, walking around the sculpture garden, or picnicking on the vast lawn (you need to reserve your picnic table). You don't need to make reservations for the complimentary tour. Wine tasting is $2.50 for current releases and $2 each for reserve wines.

1060 Dunaweal Lane (between Hwy. 29 and the Silverado Trail), Calistoga, CA 94515.
☎ *707-942-4981. Open: daily 11am–5pm.*

A Sonoma Valley Winery Tour

The Sonoma Valley includes the towns of Sonoma, Glen Ellen, and Kenwood and is frequented a bit less than the Napa Valley because of it's smaller size. Day-trippers will enjoy the smaller, more intimate atmosphere of Sonoma Valley, though. You can drive here in just over an hour, tour a few wineries, shop, have a great meal, and be back in the city — traffic willing — in time for dinner. You may choose to spend the night, in which case you can find many B&Bs and hotels, plus a few resorts sprinkled around the country roads.

Enter the Sonoma Valley by way of Highway 121, and then turn north on Highway 12. This path takes you directly into the charming town of Sonoma. (If you want to go directly to Glen Ellen, take Highway 116 instead.)

This tour includes stops at some smaller wineries that are simply too delicious to miss where you'll get a little wine education and tastings. You'll see country roads bedecked by acres of grapes, old oaks, and flowers. And while the destinations are worthy, the drive itself is divine.

Wineries in Sonoma Valley

Benzinger

Tractor-pulled trams take visitors up a flower-lined path of this beautiful 85-acre ranch for a 45-minute tram tour. The winery, owned by the Benzinger family since 1981, is situated near Jack London State Park. It may seem out of the way, but the tour and winery are very informative about vitaculture. The tram operator is trained to discuss how vines work, insect control, and how the sun and soil together affect the taste of the final product. You can choose from two tasting opportunities, one of which is complimentary, and the other costs $5 for the reserve wines.

1883 London Ranch Rd., Glen Ellen, CA 95442. (Take Hwy. 12 to Arnold Dr. and left on London Ranch Rd.). ☎ *707-935-4046. Open: daily 10am–5pm.*

Sonoma Valley

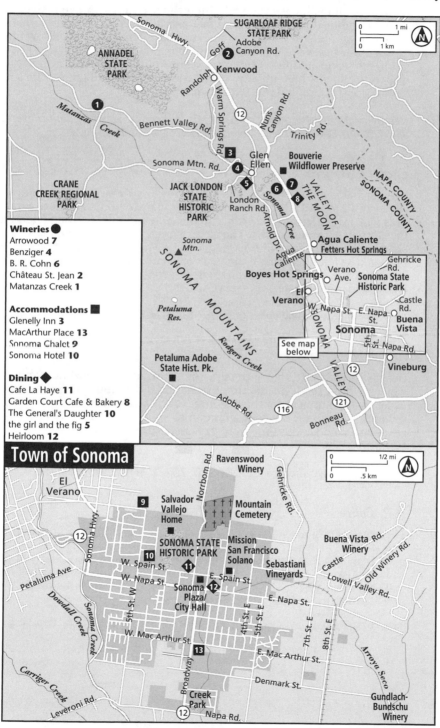

SUGARLOAF RIDGE STATE PARK

Adobe Canyon Rd.

ANNADEL STATE PARK

Kenwood ❷

Goff

Randolph

Warm Springs Rd.

Sonoma Hwy.

Nuns Canyon Rd.

Trinity Rd.

Bennett Valley Rd.

❶

Matanzas Creek

Sonoma Mtn. Rd.

❸

Glen Ellen

❹

Bouverie Wildflower Preserve

CRANE CREEK REGIONAL PARK

❺

London Ranch Rd.

❻ ❼

❽

JACK LONDON STATE HISTORIC PARK

VALLEY OF THE MOON

NAPA COUNTY

SONOMA COUNTY

Arnold Dr.

Sonoma Creek

Agua Caliente

Fetters Hot Springs

Gehricke Rd.

Sonoma Mtn.

Agua Caliente

Verano Ave.

Sonoma State Historic Park

Boyes Hot Springs

El Verano

W. Napa St.   E. Napa St.

Castle Rd.

Sonoma   **Buena Vista**

SONOMA MOUNTAINS

Petaluma Res.

Rodgers Creek

5th St.

Napa Rd.

See map below

Petaluma Adobe State Hist. Pk.

Adobe Rd.

Bonneau Rd.

❶❷   Vineburg

116   121

Wineries ●
Arrowood **7**
Benziger **4**
B. R. Cohn **6**
Château St. Jean **2**
Matanzas Creek **1**

Accommodations ■
Glenelly Inn **3**
MacArthur Place **13**
Sonoma Chalet **9**
Sonoma Hotel **10**

Dining ◆
Cafe La Haye **11**
Garden Court Cafe & Bakery **8**
The General's Daughter **10**
the girl and the fig **5**
Heirloom **12**

0   1 mi
0   1 km

Town of Sonoma

El Verano

Norrbom Rd.

Ravenswood Winery

Gehricke Rd.

❾

Salvador Vallejo Home

Mountain Cemetery

Sonoma Hwy.

❶❷

SONOMA STATE HISTORIC PARK

❿

Mission San Francisco Solano

Buena Vista Rd.

Buena Vista Winery

W. Spain St.

⓫

E. Spain St.

Sebastiani Vineyards

Castle

Lowell Valley Rd.

Old Winery Rd.

Petaluma Ave.

W. Napa St.

Sonoma Plaza/ City Hall

⓬

E. Napa St.

5th St. W.

Dowdall Creek

Sonoma Creek

4th St. E

5th St. E

7th St. E

8th St. E

W. Mac Arthur St.

⓭

E. Mac Arthur St.

Arroyo Seco

Carriger Creek

Broadway

Denmark St.

Creek Park

Leveroni Rd.

❶❷   Napa Rd.

Gundlach-Bundschu Winery

0   1/2 mi
0   .5 km

Matanzas Creek Winery

Enjoy spending an easy time admiring the fragrant and expansive gardens cascading down the hill from the tasting room at this scenic winery. A 30-minute tour shows you the basics of barrel-making, vitaculture, and corks. (Tour times are 10:30am, 1, and 3pm.) Matanzas produces a line of gift items featuring the lavender they grow and dry on the property, as well as producing high-quality, award-winning wine. A flight of wines for tasting costs $3, refundable with a wine purchase.

6097 Bennett Valley Rd. (Hwy 12 to Arnold Dr. to Warm Springs Rd.), Santa Rosa, CA 95404. ☎ 707-528-6464. Open: Mon–Sat 10am–5pm, Sun 11am–5pm.

Chateau St. Jean

Driving back on Warm Springs Drive toward Kenwood, turn left on Highway 12 to find a Mediterranean-style mansion on a 250-acre estate. This winery is a great place for a picnic. You can pick up picnic food at Cafe Citti, 9049 Sonoma Hwy. The winery has an expansive front lawn and shady groves. The magnificent magnolia tree here was planted by Luther Burbank. Self-guided tours only; you can climb the observation tower for a view of the valley. Downstairs, wine tasting is complimentary; $5 is charged for three tastes of reserve wines.

8555 Sonoma Hwy., Kenwood, CA. ☎ 707-833-4134. Open: daily 10am–4:30pm.

Arrowood

Nearby Arrowood is an intimate, high-end, and somewhat exclusive winery with a small production but national distribution. You need to make an appointment for the one-hour tour. Call a day or two in advance. If you do not go on the tour, you can sit on the verandah overlooking grapevines and mountains and try some great wines. There is a $3 tasting fee.

14347 Sonoma Hwy., Glen Ellen, CA 95442. ☎ 707-938-5170. Open: daily 10am–4:30pm.

B.R. Cohn

This tiny tasting room flanked by olive trees is just down the road from Arrowood. The wines are worth trying, although the winery is not the most lush and beautiful one around. Some vintages are sold only at the winery. Also, the olive oil produced here is of the highest quality and makes a great gift. Friendly staff who are happy to talk wine and olives preside over the tasting room. Tastings are free.

15140 Sonoma Hwy., Glen Ellen, CA 95442. ☎ 707-938-4064. Open: daily 10am–5pm.

Taking Advantage of Other Fun Stuff the Valleys Have to Offer

Wine Country offers many fun things to do other than wine tasting. If you're staying overnight, be sure to check out the following sites, sports, and downright sumptuous pleasures in Napa and Sonoma.

Napa excursions

Art turns up in the most unexpected places, but none more so than the di Rosa Preserve. This is a 53-acre indoor/outdoor gallery located 6 ½ miles west of Napa on Highway 121 that displays over 1,700 works in meadows, from trees, and throughout the former winery. Rene di Rosa, a former journalist and vitaculturalist, owns the winery. Guides conduct two-hour tours Tuesday through Saturday. You must make a reservation for the tour; admission is $10 (call % 707-226-5991).

You can enjoy horseback riding in the beautiful countryside here with the help of the **Sonoma Cattle Company and Napa Valley Trail Rides** (☎ **707-996-8566**). You can go on 1½- or 2-hour rides through Bothe-Napa Valley State Park (between St. Helena and Calistoga off Highway 29), available for adults and kids 8 years old and up. Rides start at $46.

Try a pricier diversion, such as a hot-air balloon ride with **Yountville's Adventures Aloft** (☎ **800-944-4408** or 707-944-4408). A preflight snack is included in the early morning lift-off and a post-flight brunch follows with Napa Valley bubbly. The cost is $185 per person.

Do you like bicycling? Contact **St. Helena Cyclery,** 1156 Main St., St. Helena (☎ **707-963-7736**). They'll guide you toward the Silverado Trail for $7 per hour or $25 per day. **Getaway Adventures BHK** (Biking, Hiking, and Kayaking), 1117 Lincoln Ave., **Calistoga** (☎ **800-499-BIKE** or 707-942-0332), runs full-day bike excursions with lunch and winery tours.

Wind down after a busy day of wine-sipping by taking a mud bath. People have been taking mud baths in Calistoga for more than 150 years. If you haven't tried it, this is the place. You can reserve a tub and a follow-up massage at **Dr. Wilkinson's Hot Springs,** 1507 Lincoln Ave. (☎ **707-942-4102**); **Indian Springs Resort and Spa,** 1712 Lincoln Ave. (☎ **707-942-4913**); or **Calistoga Spa Hot Springs,** 1006 Washington St. (☎ **707-942-6269**). A mud bath and one-hour massage is $92 at Calistoga Spa Hot Springs, which is a very good buy.

Sonoma activities

Many olive trees are planted at wineries and in groves around the valley. Olives have become an important crop, and olive oil tastings are a popular activity now. You can debate the merits of various extra

virgin olive oils in Glen Ellen at **The Olive Press,** 14301 Arnold Dr.,
(☎ **707-939-8900**). The press works 24-hours a day between October
and March. Watch the process from the tasting room, while sampling
the olive oil and checking out the olive-themed merchandise.

Jack London State Historic Park, 2400 London Ranch Rd. (☎ **707-
938-5216**), is where the prolific author of *The Call of the Wild* lived
before his death in 1916 at 40. You can walk on trails to the ruins of
Wolf House, London Lake, and Bath House. A museum/library with
first editions of London's works and personal memorabilia are on the
grounds, as well. Open daily from 9:30 to dusk. Take a two-hour group
trail ride through the park through **Sonoma Cattle Company and Napa
Valley Trail Rides** (☎ **707-996-8566**), which has stables on the property. The two-hour ride costs around $45. You can also rent horses for
private rides at $45 per hour.

Even if you have a spa in your hotel, you can enjoy this day spa, **Bella
Luna Ranch,** 21001 Broadway, Sonoma (☎ **707-935-8820**). Facials, massages, or a Sea Gommage Slimming Treatment can help you trim away
all those vacation meals.

The Good Time Bicycle Shop, 18503 Hwy. 12, Boyes Hot Springs,
(☎ **707-938-0453**), delivers bikes to your lodgings and also offers
4½-hour picnic/winery rides for $55, which includes lunch. Rental
is a reasonable $5/hr. or $25/day.

If you have an intense interest in food, sign up for a 3- to 4-hour class at
Ramekins, 450 West Spain St., Sonoma (☎ **707-933-0450**), a small B&B
and culinary school next to the excellent General's Daughter restaurant. During the day, take in the demonstration classes; then in the
evening, glean culinary tips from some major Bay Area chefs. Students
have lots of opportunity to sample the goods with a few glasses of
wine. Call for a catalog. You can register over the phone, in person, or
on the Web at www.ramekins.com.

Fabulous Places to Stay in Wine Country

You'll probably get the impression that it isn't difficult to find a nice
place to sleep because country inns and bed-and-breakfasts inter-
spersed with spas and motels are sprinkled throughout both valleys.
However, supply and demand keep the room rates and the occupancy
on the high side. Even if you're taking your chances on finding a hotel
in San Francisco at the last minute, you need to make reservations in
Wine Country as far in advance as possible for stays between May and
October. Most lodgings have a two-night minimum on the weekends
during the high season.

Here is a breakdown of what the dollar signs represent in the hotel listings:

- ✔ $: Under $100
- ✔ $$: $100 – $150
- ✔ $$$: $150 – $200
- ✔ $$$$: Over $200

It won't be quite as hard to find a substantial and well-prepared meal, although you still need to make reservations. Some great chefs have settled their lives and businesses in charming Wine Country, perhaps realizing that well-to-do tourists and urbanites with second homes love to eat out. Eating out is also one of the few evening activities in Wine Country — not much else to do past 10pm in the country.

Contact **The Napa Valley Conference & Visitors Bureau,** 1310 Napa Town Center, Napa, CA 94559 (☎ **707-226-7459**, Internet: www. napavalley.com), for information on accommodations.

The **Sonoma Valley Visitors Bureau** is located on the Sonoma Plaza at 453 First St. E., (☎ **707-996-1090,** Internet: www.sonomavalley.com). They keep an availability sheet of hotel/B&B/motel rooms in case you didn't make reservations.

Lovely lodgings in Napa

Cottage Grove Inn

$$$$ **Calistoga**

White cottages with porches and wicker chairs are set in two rows among flowers and trees. You'll find beautiful furniture, Jacuzzi tubs, a complimentary bottle of wine, fireplaces, easy chairs, and comfy beds in each cottage. Strictly for couples, this place has a very romantic atmosphere. It's also an easy walk to some terrific restaurants and spas.

1711 Lincoln Ave., Calistoga, CA 94515. ☎ *800-799-2284 or 707-942-8400. Fax 707/942-2653. Parking: free. Rack rates: $195–$245 double including continental breakfast. DC, MC, V.*

Harvest Inn

$$$ **St. Helena**

The spacious rooms in this brick Tudor-style inn are big enough for a family. Two pools and two spas are appealing for just about anyone. For a quiet stroll, you can choose between beautiful gardens or walkways bordering a 14-acre vineyard with a dramatic mountain backdrop. The rooms now feature CD players, VCRs, and feather beds, among other amenities, because of a $2 million renovation that the inn underwent in 1999. Some wineries are within walking distance.

1 Main St., St. Helena, CA 94574. ☎ ***800-950-8466*** *or 707-963-9463. Parking: free. Rack rates: $149–$699 double. AE, CB, DC, DISC, MC, V.*

Indian Springs

$$$ Calistoga

Each of these comfortable, old-fashioned bungalows has a kitchen with a refrigerator and microwave, and there are picnic tables and barbecue grills nearby. The resortlike atmosphere is complete with surreys (bikes with bench seats and awnings) and Ping-Pong tables for guests to use. Lounge and sky chairs surround a warm, Olympic-size mineral pool. The spa, which is located in a bath house from 1913, offers a full range of services. Booking a bungalow in the summer isn't easy, but try edging out the families that come here year after year by calling 48-hours ahead to find out whether you can get in on a cancellation.

1712 Lincoln Ave., Calistoga, CA 94515. ☎ ***707-942-4913***. *Fax 707-942-4919. Parking: free. Rack rates: $175–$260 double. MC, V.*

Vintage Inn

$$$ Yountville

Jacuzzi tubs, fireplaces, and robes complete the rooms in this attractive French-country inn. A heated pool and tennis courts make this a comfortable mini-resort, great for couples who want to get out and explore the area. Pets are also welcome. Check out the terrific restaurants nearby.

6541 Washington St., Yountville, CA 94599. ☎ ***800-351-1133*** *or 707-944-1112. Fax: 707-944-1617. Parking: free. Rack rates: $150–$300 double includes continental breakfast. AE, CB, DC, DISC, MC, V. From Hwy. 29 exit at Yountville and turn left onto Washington St.*

Retreats down Sonoma way

Glenelly Inn

$$ Glen Ellen

A secluded and peaceful, family-run B&B, the modest rooms here are small but decorated quaintly. They each have a private entry, terry robes, down comforters, and most have clawfoot tubs with shower heads. A spa in the garden adds to the quiet magic, and you can sit and gaze at the mountains on the verandahs on both levels in comfortable chairs.

5131 Warm Springs Rd., Glen Ellen, CA 95442. ☎ ***707-996-6720***. *Fax: 707-996-5227. Internet:* www.glenelly.com. *Parking: free. Rack rates: $135–$160 double includes breakfast and afternoon snacks. MC, V. From Hwy. 12 take Madrone Rd. to Arnold Dr.*

MacArthur Place

$$$ **Sonoma**

This divine inn is a renovated Victorian building masterfully connected to newer buildings. The rooms are cushy and spacious, with wonderful four-poster beds. Contented guests can relax at the small, well-staffed spa where the practiced hands of a masseuse can work out their tensions. Afterwards, stroll around the manicured gardens that surround the swimming pool. A restaurant opened recently in the 100-year-old barn, which supplies room service or lunch around the pool.

29 East MacArthur St., Sonoma, CA 95476. ☎ 800-722-1866 or 707-938-2929. Fax: 707-933-9833. Internet: www.macarthurplace.com. *Parking: Free. Rack rates: $150–$375 double with continental breakfast. AE, MC, V.*

Sonoma Chalet

$ **Sonoma**

This farmhouse inn is Swiss-inspired. Although all you see from here are mountains and the ranch next door, it is located less than a mile from the Sonoma town square. Antiques and collectibles decorate the three delightful, spacious cottages. Inside the farmhouse, the upstairs rooms have private facilities while the two downstairs rooms share a bathroom. You get a simple and delicious breakfast, including fresh pastries.

18935 Fifth St. West, Sonoma, CA 95476. ☎ 800-938-3129 or 707-938-3129. Internet: www.virtualcities.com. *Parking: free. Rack rates: $85–$170 double with continental breakfast. AE, MC, V.*

Sonoma Hotel

$$ **Sonoma**

This historic building is located on Sonoma's town square, which makes shopping and dining convenient. There's a new restaurant and remodeled rooms at the hotel, too. Bright bathrooms and stylish furniture make the lodgings attractive and cozy. The small suites work well for nuclear families, and the kids will have a great time in the park across the street.

110 West Spain St., Sonoma, CA 95476. ☎ 800-468-6016 or 707-996-2996. Fax: 707-996-7014. Parking: free. Rack rates: $95–$235 double with continental breakfast.

Feast Your Eyes on These Dining Delights

Wine tasting certainly isn't the only reason to make the trek from San Francisco to Wine Country. The food here is sublime. Take a look at my recommendations and savor the possiblities.

Napa delicacies

Bistro Don Giovanni

$$ Napa ITALIAN

Share a pizza, some antipasti, and a bottle of Chardonnay for a delightful, light Italian meal; or you can go all out with the aged Porterhouse for two. This inviting place attracts a crowd that, when it's warm, gathers at tables on the porch, which is heavenly.

4110 St. Helena Hwy. (Hwy. 29), Napa. ☎ 707-224-3300. Reservations recommended. Main courses: $11.50–$16. AE, DISC, MC, V. Open: lunch and dinner daily.

Bistro Jeanty

$$ Yountville FRENCH

Much applauded around the Bay Area for its great menu, authenticity, and vivacious dining room, this French bistro satisfies both the appetite and the spirit. Rustic dishes like lamb tongue and potato salad or rabbit and sweetbread ragout make up the seasonal menu. Timid and adventuresome eaters will be equally pleased with typical bistro items such as steak frites and coq au vin.

6510 Washington St., Yountville. ☎ 707-944-0103. Reservations recommended. Main courses: $12.50–$22.50. MC, V. Open: lunch and dinner daily.

Catahoula Restaurant and Saloon

$$$ Calistoga AMERICAN/SOUTHERN

The atmosphere and food in this exciting restaurant contain a strong hint of New Orleans. A meal here should end a superb day in Calistoga. Did you forget to make reservations? Don't despair! You can dine in front of the wood-fired ovens at the bar, where plate after plate of seasonal American dishes are cranked out by busy chefs.

1457 Lincoln Ave., Calistoga. ☎ 707-942-2275. Reservations recommended. Main courses: $11–$20. MC, V. Open: lunch daily except Tues; dinner nightly.

Gordon's Cafe and Wine Bar

$–$$ Yountville AMERICAN

Besides breakfast and lunch, Gordon's, a prime destination for food lovers, serves a three-course prix fixe dinner on Friday nights. Known for its meticulous selection of fine wines and gourmet condiments, the store includes a vast array of olive oils. This cafe/store serves delicious food presented in a warm atmosphere that reminds you of a general store.

6770 Washington St., Yountville. ☎ 707-944-8246. Dinner reservations necessary. Main courses: $32 prix-fixe dinner. MC, V. Open: breakfast and lunch daily; dinner Fri only.

Mustards Grill

$$$ Yountville   AMERICAN

The lengthy menu and specials board are filled with scumptious American dishes. The restaurant, the bar, and even the menu are always overflowing, as is the parking lot. If you don't have room for dessert, loosen your belt and give it a go anyway.

7399 St. Helena Hwy. (Hwy. 29), Yountville. ☎ **707-944-2424.** *Reservations recommended. Main courses: $11–$17. CB, DC, DISC, MC, V. Open: lunch and dinner daily.*

Tra Vigne

$$$ St. Helena   ITALIAN

You can enjoy a casual, or more formal, Italian meal in this elegant (but not stuffy) place. Come for lunch on the courtyard patio and feel a bit of Italy in the Napa Valley, especially if the kids are with you. The Cantinetta, a delicatessen, is where you can buy reasonably priced pizza, wine, and prepared foods to eat here or down the road at a winery.

1050 Charter Oak Ave., St. Helena. ☎ **707-963-4444.** *Reservations recommended. Main courses: $12.50–$18.95. CB, DC, DISC, MC, V. Open: lunch and dinner daily.*

Wine Spectator Greystone Restaurant

$$ St. Helena   MEDITERRANEAN

This restaurant, inside a massive former winery, is full of whimsy and color; the food, from tapas to larger plates of seafood and meats, is delicious or disappointing, which is because working chefs come here to hone their skills — so politely send it back! The latest in kitchen necessities and luxuries are available in a store at one end of the building.

2555 Main St. (Hwy. 29), St. Helena. ☎ **707-967-1010.** *Reservations recommended. Main courses: $16–$18.50. AE, CB, DC, MC, V. Open: lunch and dinner daily (closed Tues–Wed Jan–Mar).*

Fantastic food in Sonoma

Cafe La Haye

$$ Sonoma   CALIFORNIA

They serve very good food at this friendly little cafe. It's unlike many other Wine Country restaurants in that there's no attempt to pretend you're in Italy or France. Plain tables and chairs are carefully set about, as if to not disturb the art that fills the walls, making La Haye's single room resemble a gallery. The menu selection, spare but complete, features whatever's seasonal, and offers organic produce.

140 East Napa St., Sonoma. ☎ **707-935-5994.** *Reservations accepted. Main courses: $11.95–$17.95. MC, V. Open: dinner Tues–Sun; weekend brunch.*

Garden Court Cafe and Bakery

$ Glen Ellen AMERICAN

Get a modest breakfast and lunch-to-go, or a tasty, filling breakfast that keeps you going most of the day. Wine glasses and a tablecloth for added panache can be included in picnic lunches. If you are in town on the second Wednesday of the month, the four-course prix-fixe at $23.95 is the bargain of the valley.

13875 Sonoma Hwy. 12, Glen Ellen. ☎ *707-935-1565. No reservations. Main courses: $4.95–$10.95. MC, V. Open: breakfast and lunch daily. Dinner served 2nd Wed of the month.*

The General's Daughter

$$ Sonoma CALIFORNIA

This grand valley landmark is housed by a sunny yellow historic Victorian. Everyone loves the place. The food always merits rave reviews from diners. Here you might have linguine with wild mushrooms, blue cheese, grilled apples and baby spinach, or a mixed grill of Tiger prawns and swordfish with udon noodles.

400 West Spain St., Sonoma. ☎ *707-938-4004. Reservations accepted. Main courses: $8.75–$23.95. MC, V. Open: lunch Mon–Sat; dinner nightly; Sun brunch.*

the girl and the fig

$$$ Glen Ellen COUNTRY FRENCH

This upscale little country bistro can seem to have a measure of provincialism to it due to mix 'n' match chairs and utensils and an assortment of green ceramic collectibles decorating a high ledge. The seasonal menu meets the needs of seafoodies, vegetarians, or carnivores with one or two dishes in each category. The grilled fig salad with arugula is a must-order when fresh figs are available.

13690 Arnold Dr., Glen Ellen. ☎ *707-938-3634. Reservations advised. Main courses: $9–$20. AE, MC, V. Open: dinner nightly.*

Heirloom

$$ Sonoma CALIFORNIA

Located in the Sonoma Hotel, Heirloom was renovated at the same time as the inn with the same charm and rustic warmth. The menu changes according to the availability of local produce, meat, and seafood because that's what the kitchen uses as much as possible. But you can't go wrong with whatever catches the eye of the chef. Lunch or dinner on the secluded patio is a most pleasant and filling experience.

110 West Spain St., Sonoma, CA. ☎ *707-939-6955. Reservations accepted. Main courses: $11.75–$19.75. MC, V. Open: lunch and dinner daily.*

Part VIII
The Part of Tens

"I want a lens that's heavy enough to counterbalance the weight on my back."

In this part . . .

Whipping up this top-ten list was a challenge. I'm just glad I don't have to come up with my ten favorite restaurants (too challenging) or my ten favorite parking places (the first ten available spots, wherever they are). But here I give you my humble opinions on the greatest views, the best pastimes in foul weather, and best ways to look less obviously like a tourist. Not that I have *anything* against tourists, mind you.

Chapter 26

The Top Ten Views

$\mathcal{P}$eople like views. That much is clear from the wrangling that goes on to get a table with a view in restaurants, or the extra tariff imposed on a room with a view, not to mention a home with a view. San Francisco is one major view, owing to all those hills. I admit to a permanent sentimental attachment to the views of San Francisco.

From Twin Peaks

The mother of all views — if the weather cooperates — is surely from **Twin Peaks,** which sits in the center of San Francisco in a residential neighborhood at the top of Market Street. The sightline encompasses the entrance to the bay and reaches all the way 'round to Candlestick Point. If you're driving, head southwest on Market Street, which becomes Portola Drive past 17th Street. The first light past Corbett Street is a right turn only; this is Twin Peaks Boulevard, the road that takes you up the hill.

The 37-Corbett bus, which you can easily catch on Market and Church Streets, takes passengers near, but not all the way to, Twin Peaks. And the rest of the trip is quite a hike up hill. If you'd prefer something slightly less strenuous and want to see one of San Francisco's beautiful "hidden" staircases, here's a tip: Exit the bus at Corbett and Clayton Streets, and look for an old concrete wall on the west side of Clayton marked by a street sign that says "Pemberton." This leads to the Pemberton Stairs. You won't get to the top of Twin Peaks by climbing them, but you'll be treated to bay views in quiet, green surroundings.

From Bernal Heights Park

Look southeast from downtown and you'll spot a prominent hill with a few trees decorating the top. That's **Bernal Heights Park,** the favored dog-walking and fireworks-viewing area for the Bernal Heights neighborhood. The weather in this part of town is far superior to the weather around Twin Peaks, which can get really foggy, much to the dismay of the camera-toting folk on the tour buses. The views here are equally wonderful to my mind, partly because Bernal Hill is closer to downtown and the bay. The 67-Folsom bus drives to the end of Folsom at Esmeralda. Exit and walk up the hill on any of a number of paths.

From Lincoln Park

Lincoln Park is one of the prettiest golf courses in creation, situated as it is around the Palace of the Legion of Honor and above the entrance to the San Francisco bay at Land's End. Standing in front of the museum, you can see in the distance a snippet of downtown framed within the green branches of fir trees. Then walk west down the street. You'll be stunned by a postcard-perfect view of the Golden Gate Bridge from a unique perspective — facing north as if you're entering the bay. Benches have been thoughtfully placed along the street, so you can survey the vista in comfort. The 18-46th Avenue bus stops in the museum parking lot.

From the Beach Chalet Restaurant

The waves along Ocean Beach, at the end of Golden Gate Park on the Great Highway, are at times soothing, and at times violent enough to discourage beachcombing. In either case, you'll be as comfy as a babe in his crib upstairs in the **Beach Chalet restaurant** (☎ 415-386-8439) gazing at the Pacific (ideally, as the sun sets). The building was designed by Willis Polk, and the first floor visitor's center is adorned by murals painted in the 1930s by the same artist who painted the frescoes at Coit Tower. The restaurant is particularly popular for its menu of house-brewed beers, and it serves throughout the day and evening starting at breakfast. If you don't want to wait for a table in the dining room, you can take a seat in the bar and turn toward the view, dramatic in any season. The 5-Fulton, which you can pick up on Market and Powell Streets, takes you to Ocean Beach, a block or so from the Beach Chalet.

Above Dolores Park

From any Muni Metro station (the Powell Street Station being the closest to Union Square) take the J-Church toward Daly City. Exit on 18th and Church Streets, above **Dolores Park.** The city and bay views over this stretch of green on a clear day has been responsible for more than one decision to relocate to the Bay Area. After soaking in the scenery and taking a stroll through the park, walk two blocks north on Dolores Street until you reach **Mission Dolores** at 16th and Dolores Streets, the oldest building in San Francisco.

From Top of the Mark

If you feel like having a cocktail as you drink in a view, head to the **Top of the Mark** in the Mark Hopkins Intercontinental Hotel, 1 Nob Hill at California and Mason Streets (☎ 415-392-3434). Sometimes it's so busy you have to wait in line at the elevator, but the city views are mesmerizing once you get a table.

Sights from the Cheesecake Factory

Union Square is a compact, urban hub, immensely appealing in my mind, especially when it's crowded and bustling. Up until recently, there wasn't a handy place to be among, but not in, the madding crowd; but now Macy's (see Chapter 19) has alleviated that problem by installing a branch of the **Cheesecake Factory** (☎ **415-397-3333**) on the eighth floor of the department store. Management shrewdly included a heated patio for diners who favor a city view in all its sky-scrapered glory. The restaurant is open from 7am until 11pm.

Views from Fisherman's Wharf

If for some unfathomable reason you've skipped to this section without reading what's come before, you won't know that I, like all upstanding San Franciscans, generally avoid **Fisherman's Wharf** (see Chapter 16) like I avoid the Oakland A's baseball team. However, I recently discovered a way to escape the folks crowding the sidewalks, yet still take advantage of the views and freshly cracked crab.

The crab stands are plopped in front of their namesake restaurants along one block off Jefferson Street. Just to the left of Fisherman's Grotto #9 are glass doors marked "Passageway to the Boats," the boats being what remains of the fishing fleet. Take your cracked crab, your beer, and plenty of napkins and push through. You'll be on a pier that leads to the tiny Fisherman's and Seaman's Memorial Chapel on your right, and views of the bay and Telegraph Hill in front and to your left. The pier is parallel to Jefferson Street, but may be gloriously close to empty even on a weekend. You can eat your crab in peace sitting on the dock of the bay, watching . . . well you know. Close by, sea lions jump, swim, and beg in the waters below.

From Fort Point

The remains of **Fort Point,** a 1861 brick artillery fortress, occupy the land at the edge of the bay nearest the Golden Gate Bridge. I remember the first time I visited this area because heavy fog obscured everything around me except the uppermost portion of the bridge. It was a most dramatic vision. On a clear day, you'll be treated to the bridge, of course, but also to bright views of the downtown skyline and Alcatraz. The 29 bus stops as close as the parking lot next to the Bridge visitors' center, a downhill walk to a particularly pretty viewpoint in the midst of eucalyptus trees. If you're up for a hike, follow the joggers past the Marina Green and through the Presidio (see Chapter 17).

From UC Berkeley Botanical Gardens

Drive to the **UC Berkeley Botanical Gardens** located high in the hills behind the campus (see Chapter 23). Find the rose garden. Beyond the plants you can see the bay and San Francisco, small and glowing in the distance. See Chapter 23 for other ideas on what to do in Berkeley after you finish admiring the view.

Chapter 27

Ten Things to Do If It's Raining (Or Just Too Foggy)

• •

San Francisco isn't Seattle by any means, but our rainy days can get in the way of enjoying our city. Actually, a foggy morning is what bothers people most, I think — fog is always cold and damp and gray. But you don't have time to grouse about the weather. You have things to do, places to see, people to meet . . . oh, you don't like getting wet? Okay. Here are a few rainy-day options.

Taking High Tea

High Tea at one of the many hotels that offers it is probably the only civilized way to keep dry. Try the dowdy (in an Englishy way) **King George Hotel,** 334 Mason St. (☎ 415-781-5050); the **Westin St. Francis,** 335 Powell St. (☎ 415-397-7000); the **Sheraton Palace,** Market and New Montgomery Streets (☎ 415546-5010); or **The Clift,** 495 Geary St. (☎ 415-775-4700). **Neiman Marcus** also has a lovely, reasonably priced tea service in the Rotunda restaurant, 150 Stockton St. (☎ 415-362- 4777), from 2:30 to 5pm daily.

Checking Out Japantown

Head to **Japantown** and take cover inside the **Kinokuniya Building** at 1581 Webster St. between Post Street and Geary Boulevard. Although this and the other buildings in the area aren't much to look at from the outside, inside you can get a delicious bowl of comforting noodles at **Mifune** (see Chapter 13), the most authentic noodle house in town, and then entertain yourself in any of a number of interesting stores, such as **Mashiko Folkcraft** (open from 11am to 6pm daily except Tuesday) and the **Kinokuniya Bookstore** (open daily from 10:30am to 7pm). If the sky still hasn't cleared up, take in a movie at the **Kabuki Theater** next door. This multiplex gets all the latest films. There's an underground parking lot off Webster Street. Muni buses 2-Clement, 3-Jackson, 4-Sutter, 22-Fillmore, and 38-Geary will all drop you in Japantown.

Luxuriate at Kabuki Hot Springs

Staying indoors can turn into a modest luxury at **Kabuki Hot Springs,** 1750 Geary Blvd. at Webster Street (☎ **415-922-6000**), a most respectable communal bath house. You can soak your feet, have a massage, and take a steam bath. Women may use the facilities on Sundays, Wednesdays, and Fridays; men get the rest of the week. Shy people may not feel comfortable at first walking around the premises *au natural,* but no one will bother you. Massages are by appointment. To get here, take the 38-Geary bus. Open daily from 10am to 10pm.

Rock Climb (Or Work Out) at the Mission Cliffs Rock Climbing Center

Rather than let the kids climb the walls in your hotel room, take everyone rock climbing (indoors of course) at **Mission Cliffs Rock Climbing Center,** located in the Mission District at 2295 Harrison St. at 19th Street (☎ **415-550-0515**) and open everyday. This world-class facility caters to beginners and experts of all ages and even folks who never dreamed of making like flies. Belay (rope handling) classes are taught regularly, so you can act as assistant to your compadres and vice versa. You don't even need any special equipment, as you can rent whatever is necessary (including shoes) — and there goes your final excuse. There's also a gym on-site with locker rooms and a sauna, perfect for those who prefer to keep their feet on the ground.

Watch the Weather from the Cliff House

Admire the storm from the confines of the **Cliff House,** 1090 Point Lobos Ave. on the Great Highway (☎ **415-386-3330**). I can't recommend the food, but the view of Seal Rocks is impressive, especially if the waves are crashing about. When you tire of staring, dash outside and downstairs into the **Musèe Méchanique** for good, old-fashioned entertainment (see Chapter 17). The closest museum to this spot is the **Palace of the Legion of Honor** (see Chapter 17), another wonderful place to wait out the weather (there's a good cafe). The 18 bus will bring you to both locations.

Find Activities for Everyone at the Metreon and Yerba Buena Gardens

The **Metreon** and **Yerba Buena Gardens** (see Chapter 16) make up a one-stop rainy day haven, particularly if you are traveling with your family. Depending on everyone's ages, you don't have to stick together for the entire day. Teens can flex their independence at **Zeum** or in the **Airtight Garage,** while kids needing direct supervision will enjoy the **Metreon play areas.** The elders, if they aren't needed, can shop, play pool at **Jillian's** (the large restaurant on the first floor), or even dash across the street to the **Museum of Modern Art.** Bowling and ice-skating work for everyone, and when it's time to regroup, you can see what's playing at the movies.

Defy the Weather at the California Academy of Sciences

Try out the **California Academy of Sciences** (see Chapter 16), and stick around to watch one of the planetarium shows. You can find enough to see here to keep you busy until the sun comes back out. If the rain turns to drizzle, put on your baseball cap and take a walk in the **Strybing Arboretum,** across the street. Outside of a few gardeners and squirrels, you'll likely be undisturbed on the paths through this very beautiful garden.

Sightsee and Stay Dry on the F-Market Streetcar

The **F-Market streetcar** (see Chapter 11) is my current public transport ride of choice. Grab an umbrella, then grab a seat for a ride to **The Cannery** (see Chapter 16). Yes, it's really just an enclosed shopping mall, if you want to be blunt and unromantic; but still, it's an attractive enclosed shopping mall with some fun things to do with the kids (see Chapter 17). Then take the streetcar all the way toward **upper Market Street** and reward yourself with a late lunch at **Zuni** (see Chapter 14).

Baby Yourself at Nordstrom

See if you can get an appointment for a manicure, pedicure, and/or a facial at **Nordstrom** in the **San Francisco Centre shopping mall** at 5th and Market Streets (☎ **415-977-5102**). If you have co-visitors to deal with, send them to the fourth floor grill for lunch or a snack. You can find lots of shopping opportunities here as well, although most of the stores are of your typical mall flavors.

Doing Business on a Rainy Day

A great thing to do is sit around your hotel lobby and complain like the locals. Grab a copy of the *Chronicle* and maybe the *Wall Street Journal* for good measure. Whisper into a cell phone while gripping a cup of coffee in your free hand. Then hail a cab and dash to the nearest Internet cafe to check your e-mail: **Club-I,** 850 Folsom St. (☎ **415-777-1448**), and **Cafe.com,** 970 Market St., between 5th and 6th Streets (☎ **415-922-5322**), are closest to Union Square. And if you think the rain is bad, be thankful you haven't been inundated with foggy mornings for 40 days straight. Now you know why anyone who can afford a summer home in Napa puts up with the traffic on Friday afternoons.

Chapter 28

Top Ten Ways to Avoid Looking like a Tourist

*1*don't understand why being a tourist is considered so beneath some people. Even my own dear husband scoffs at tourists — or people he presumes are tourists — and when we travel he does his well-meaning best to look like a local. This generally leads to amusing misunderstandings on behalf of actual citizens, who either ask him something in a language he doesn't understand, or presume he knows where he's going when he hasn't a clue. So, why live a lie, I say. If you're visiting for pleasure and have a keen interest in looking around, you're a tourist. Be proud. Wear that camera around your neck (but maybe leave the fanny pack at home). Rattle a map in frustration. Ask a stranger for directions.

Otherwise, memorize the following tips.

Dress for the Weather

This is not the 90210 zip code; you cannot tan here. In summer, it's foggy and cold in the morning, turning to sunshine in the afternoon, with temperatures in the upper 60s or low 70s. I know this, because the weathermen say the same thing every day in July and August. Dress in long pants, not shorts. Wear a sweater over your tee shirt and a jacket over that. You can always tie extraneous clothing around your waist when you enter one of our famous microclimates. In San Francisco, the temperature changes from neighborhood to neighborhood, so if you're shivering in Golden Gate Park, head to the Mission to warm up.

September and October are the warmest months here. If you look good in shorts, wear them then.

Don't Trust Your Map

Those darn hills have a way of interrupting the streets in ways that may not be apparent to the untrained eye. Telegraph Hill is the worst offender. If you can't go through, you'll have to go around.

Don't Gawk at Tall Buildings

A recent article in the *San Francisco Chronicle* noted that San Franciscans do not gawk at tall buildings, although I don't know if that includes skyscrapers in other towns. Probably. But, the author also noted that San Franciscans are breaking their own rule and gawking like mad at the new downtown ballpark. So, if you don't want to look like a tourist, don't stare at the Transamerica Pyramid — a quick glance should do — but feel free to drool while admiring Pac Bell Park. You'll then resemble a local who didn't buy season tickets.

Don't Eat and Shop like a Tourist

Be picky about where you spend your time and money. Places most residents wouldn't be caught dead in include the Hard Rock Cafe, any restaurant on Fisherman's Wharf, Ripley's Believe It or Not, and the camera/luggage stores on Powell Street.

Wait 'til You Get Back to the Airport to Buy That Delicious San Francisco Sourdough

Don't walk around with loaves of bread wrapped in plastic for the trip home. Around here we buy our baguettes for same-day consumption. Anyway, you can buy that particular brand of bread at the airport, where no one will see you.

Cross the Bridge Before or After — but Not During — Rush Hour

Don't cross the Bay Bridge between 3 and 7pm unless you want to be mistaken for a suburban commuter. Anyway, no one, not even the commuters, are actually crossing the Bay Bridge at this time; rather, they're sitting and fuming and occasionally inching their way forward. This is important to remember if you have friends on the East Bay who ask you to come over for dinner.

Don't Stare at the Locals

Don't point/gasp/shriek at the man/woman/other in the attention-getting tattoo/leather chaps/chartreuse wig no matter how unusual he/she/it appears. That would be unseemly.

Don't Shout at People You Suspect Don't Speak English

Don't raise your voice or speak extra slowly to your waiter if you suspect he doesn't speak English. In fact, he does speak English. He's merely trying to turn your table as quickly as possible.

Do the Farmer's Market Thing

Hang around the Ferry Plaza Farmer's Market on a Saturday morning. Have breakfast, circle the stalls, eat all the samples, buy something non-perishable to take home.

Remove Any Incriminating Evidence

Remove the plastic name tag you attached to your lapel upon leaving the Moscone Convention Center.

Appendix

Quick Concierge

American Automobile Association (AAA)
The office at 150 Van Ness Ave. in the Civic Center provides maps and other information for members traveling by car. Call ☎ 800-222-4357 for emergency service or ☎ 415-565-2012 for general information.

American Express
Several locations, including 295 California St., at Battery Street (☎ 415-536-2686), and 455 Market St., at First Street (☎ 415-536-2600), open Monday through Friday from 8:30am to 5:30pm, Saturday from 9am to 2pm.

ATMs
Easy to find especially downtown, but also on any main business corridor. (See Chapter 12.)

Babysitters
Your hotel concierge can arrange for a babysitter. Otherwise, try A Bay Area Child Care Agency (☎ 415-991-7474).

Camera Repair
Adolph Gasser Inc. is a reputable camera dealer, 81 2nd St. (☎ 415-495-3852). Or try Advance Camera, 118 Columbus, near Jackson Street (☎ 415-772-9025).

Convention Center
The Moscone Convention Center, 747 Howard St. between 3rd and 4th Streets (☎ 415-974-4000), is within easy walking distance of the Montgomery Street Muni and BART stations.

Dentists
Call the San Francisco Dental Society for 24-hour referrals (☎ 415-421-1435).

Doctors
Saint Francis Memorial Hospital (☎ 415-353-6000), 900 Hyde St., between Bush and Pine Streets, offers 24-hour emergency-care service. The hospital's physician-referral service number is ☎ 415-353-6566. Before receiving any treatment, check with your health insurance company to find out how emergency treatment is handled when you are out of your provider area.

Earthquakes
California will always have earthquakes, most of which you'll never notice. However, in case of a significant shaker, you should know a few basic precautionary measures. When you are inside a building, seek cover; do not run outside. Stand under a doorway or against a wall and stay away from windows. If you exit a building after a substantial quake, use stairwells, not elevators. If you are in a car, pull over to the side of the road and stop — but not until you are away from bridges, overpasses, telephone poles, and power lines. Stay in your car. If you're out walking, stay outside and away from trees, power lines, and the sides of buildings. If you're in an area with tall buildings, find a doorway in which to stand.

Emergencies
Dial ☎ 911 from any phone for police, an ambulance, and the fire department.

Hospitals
San Francisco General Hospital, 1001 Potrero Ave. (☎ 415-206-8111), accepts uninsured emergency patients, but the wait can be brutally long and uncomfortable. The patient referral and assistance number is ☎ 415-206-5166.

Hotlines
Poison Control Center (☎ 800-523-2222); Rape Crisis Center (☎ 415-647-7273); Family Service Agency (☎ 415-441-5437).

Information
The San Francisco Convention and Visitors Bureau is in the lower level of Hallidie Plaza, 900 Market St., at Powell Street (☎ 800-220-5747 or 415-391-2000).

Internet Cafes
You can check your e-mail while on the road at Cafe.com, 970 Market St. (near 5th Street), open Monday through Saturday, and at Club-i, 850 Folsom Street (☎ 415-777-1448), open daily.

Liquor Laws
You can't drink or purchase alcohol legally if you are under 21. All the clubs, bars, supermarkets, and liquor stores ID anyone who looks under the age of 30 (try not to be offended if you don't get carded). Bars do not serve liquor from 2am to 6am.

Maps
The visitors bureau (see "Information" in this Appendix) has maps of the city, or stop by the California State Automobile Association (see "AAA" in this Appendix) if you are a member of AAA.

Newspapers/Magazines
The major papers are the morning *San Francisco Chronicle* and the afternoon *San Francisco Examiner,* although the future of the *Examiner* is currently unknown. They are distributed from sidewalk kiosks and boxes. The free weekly *San Francisco Bay Guardian* includes excellent events listings. Find it in cafes and in sidewalk boxes around the city. *San Francisco* magazine is the monthly city magazine (it was formerly *Focus* magazine). You can find it at fine newsstands everywhere.

Pharmacies
Walgreens has taken over the city, and you should be able to find one almost anywhere.

Call ☎ 800-WALGREEN for the address and phone number of the nearest store. You can find a store at 135 Powell St. (☎ 415-391-4433) open Monday through Saturday from 8am to midnight and on Sunday from 9am to 9pm, but the pharmacy has more limited hours. A branch on Divisadero Street at Lombard has a 24-hour pharmacy.

Police
Call ☎ 911 from any phone. No coins are needed. The nonemergency number is ☎ 415-553-0123.

Radio Stations
Find KQED, our National Public Radio affiliate, at 88.5 FM. News and sports may be found at KCBS 710 AM.

Reservation Service
For hotel reservations, call SF Reservations (☎ 800-667-1500 or 415-227-1500).

Rest Rooms
Dark green public bathrooms are located on the waterfront at Pier 39, on Market Street near the cable car turnaround on Powell Street, and by the Civic Center. The rest rooms cost 25¢ and are clean and safe. Also try hotels, museums, and service stations. Restaurants usually let only patrons use their bathrooms.

Safety
Walking around alone late at night is never a good idea. San Francisco is relatively safe, but it still has its share of muggings and more heinous crimes. Areas to be particularly careful in include the Tenderloin (see Chapter 6); the lower Haight; the Mission District anywhere between 16th and 24th Streets east of Mission Street; lower Fillmore Street; and south of Market, particularly on 6th and 7th Streets. Keep your wallet in an inside coat pocket and don't carry around wads of cash. Try to avoid using ATMs at night.

Smoking
Since January 1998, smoking has been prohibited in bars. It is also illegal to smoke in restaurants and public buildings, which is why you see so many well-dressed people loitering on the sidewalks during their coffee breaks.

Taxes
The sales tax of 8.5 percent is added to all purchases except snack food. The hotel tax is 14 percent.

Taxis
Outside of Union Square, expect to have trouble hailing a cab on the street; you'll have to call for one instead: Desoto Cab (☎ 415-673-1414); Luxor Cab (☎ 415-282-4141); Pacific Cab (☎ 415-986-7220); Veteran's Cab (☎ 415-552-1300); Yellow Cab (☎ 415-626-2345).

Time Zone
California is on Pacific standard time, three hours behind New York. Call ☎ 415-767-8900 (415-POPCORN) for a recorded message telling the time.

Transit Information
For Muni (cable cars, streetcars, and buses) route information, call ☎ 415-673-6864. For BART (Bay Area Rapid Transit) information, call ☎ 415-992-2278. Calling ☎ 415-817-1717 connects you to all transit organizations.

Weather Updates
While in town, turn to one of the news stations on the radio (try KCBS 710 AM). Otherwise, www.bayarea.citysearch.com lists comprehensive forecasts.

Toll-Free Numbers & Web Sites

Major North American carriers

Air Canada
☎ 888-247-2262
www.aircanada.ca

Alaska Airlines
☎ 800-426-0333
www.alaskaair.com

America West Airlines
☎ 800-235-9292
www.americawest.com

American Airlines
☎ 800-433-7300
www.americanair.com

Canadian Airlines International
☎ 800-426-7000
www.cdnair.ca

Continental Airlines
☎ 800-525-0280
www.continental.com

Delta Air Lines
☎ 800-221-1212
www.delta-air.com

Hawaiian Airlines
☎ 800-367-5320
www.hawaiianair.com

Midwest Express
☎ 800-452-2022
www.midwestexpress.com

Northwest Airlines
☎ 800-225-2525
www.nwa.com

Southwest Airlines
☎ 800-435-9792
www.iflyswa.com

Trans World Airlines (TWA)
☎ 800-221-2000
www.twa.com

United Airlines
☎ 800-241-6522
www.ual.com

US Airways
☎ 800-428-4322
www.usairways.com

Major hotel & motel chains

Best Western International
☎ 800-528-1234
www.bestwestern.com

Clarion Hotels
☎ 800-CLARION
www.hotelchoice.com

Comfort Inns
☎ 800-228-5150
www.hotelchoice.com

Courtyard by Marriott
☎ 800-321-2211
www.courtyard.com

Crowne Plaza Hotels
☎ 800-227-6963
www.crowneplaza.com

Days Inn
☎ 800-325-2525
www.daysinn.com

Doubletree Hotels
☎ 800-222-TREE
www.doubletreehotels.com

Econo Lodges
☎ 800-55-ECONO
www.hotelchoice.com

Fairfield Inn by Marriott
☎ 800-228-2800
www.fairfieldinn.com

Friendship Inns
☎ 800-453-4511
www.hotelchoice.com/cgi-bin/
res/webres?friendship.html

Hampton Inn
☎ 800-HAMPTON
www.hampton-inn.com

Hilton Hotels
☎ 800-HILTONS
www.hilton.com

Holiday Inn
☎ 800-HOLIDAY
www.basshotels.com

Howard Johnson
☎ 800-654-2000
www.hojo.com

Hyatt Hotels & Resorts
☎ 800-228-9000
www.hyatt.com

ITT Sheraton
☎ 800-325-3535
www.sheraton.com

La Quinta Motor Inns
☎ 800-531-5900
www.laquinta.com

Marriott Hotels
☎ 800-228-9290
www.marriott.com

Quality Inns
☎ 800-228-5151
www.hotelchoice.com

Radisson Hotels International
☎ 800-333-3333
www.radisson.com

Ramada Inns
☎ 800-2-RAMADA
www.ramada.com

Red Roof Inns
☎ 800-843-7663
www.redroof.com

Residence Inn by Marriott
☎ 800-331-3131
www.residenceinn.com

Ritz-Carlton
☎ 800-241-3333
www.ritzcarlton.com

Rodeway Inns
☎ 800-228-2000
www.hotelchoice.com

Super 8 Motels
☎ 800-800-8000
www.super8motels.com

Travelodge
☎ 800-255-3050
www.travelodge.com

Westin Hotels and Resorts
☎ 800-228-3000
www.westin.com

Wyndham Hotels and Resorts
☎ 800-822-4200 in Continental U.S. and Canada
www.wyndham.com

Where to Get More Information

San Francisco Convention & Visitors Bureau

P.O. Box 429097; 900 Market St., San Francisco, CA 94142-9097 (☎ 800- 220-5747 or 415-391-2000).
www.sfvisitor.org

Call or write the Convention and Visitors Bureau if you'd like to receive a nifty booklet with lots of useful information, including maps of the city and a seasonal calendar of events. Of course, the slant is toward the advertisers, so take those glossy ads lightly. There is a $3 mailing charge. If you have a fax and a touch-tone phone, use the 800 number for automated 24-hour fax service and "fast facts."

Napa Valley Visitors Bureau

1310 Napa Town Center, Napa, CA 94559 (☎ 707-226-7459).

This is the second busiest visitors center in California, which either says something about our collective fondness for wine or something about the beauty of the area, or possibly both. They'll send you a free brochure and a list of hotels on request; for $10 (plastic accepted) they'll mail you a 120-page magazine, suggested itineraries, and a handsome map of the area.

Information on the Web

www.bayarea.citysearch.com
A comprehensive, regularly updated site devoted to all things San Francisco, including arts, entertainment, dining, and attractions with links to the hotel reservation network.

www.sfbg.com
The San Francisco Bay Guardian site with event listings and the lowdown on nightlife.

www.sfgate.com
The *San Francisco Chronicle* Web site. Read all about it.

www.qsanfrancisco.com
A Web site for gay and lesbian travelers.

www.sanfran.com
The Web site for *San Francisco* magazine includes dining recommendations and timely entertainment suggestions.

Print Resources

Frommer's San Francisco

This popular guide covers all 46 square miles in great detail, including background on the sites, personalities, and neighborhoods that make San Francisco "everybody's favorite city."

Frommer's Memorable Walks in San Francisco, 3rd Edition

This guide covers 12 easy-to-follow walking tours through San Francisco's most charming neighborhoods. Includes detailed maps.

San Francisco magazine

A monthly glossy with an events calendar, restaurant reviews, and features of local interest.

Transit Information

☎ 415-817-1717 for how to get anywhere in the Bay Area.

Fare Game: Choosing an Airline

Travel Agency: _____ Phone: _____

Agent's Name: _____ Quoted Fare: _____

Departure Schedule & Flight Information

Airline: _____ Airport: _____

Flight #: _____ Date: _____ Time: _____ a.m./p.m.

Arrives in: _____ Time: _____ a.m./p.m.

Connecting Flight (if any)

Amount of time between flights: _____ hours/mins

Airline: _____ Airport: _____

Flight #: _____ Date: _____ Time: _____ a.m./p.m.

Arrives in: _____ Time: _____ a.m./p.m.

Return Trip Schedule & Flight Information

Airline: _____ Airport: _____

Flight #: _____ Date: _____ Time: _____ a.m./p.m.

Arrives in: _____ Time: _____ a.m./p.m.

Connecting Flight (if any)

Amount of time between flights: _____ hours/mins

Airline: _____ Airport: _____

Flight #: _____ Date: _____ Time: _____ a.m./p.m.

Arrives in: _____ Time: _____ a.m./p.m.

Notes

Making Dollars and Sense of It

Expense	Amount
Airfare	
Car Rental	
Lodging	
Parking	
Breakfast	
Lunch	
Dinner	
Babysitting	
Attractions	
Transportation	
Souvenirs	
Tips	
Grand Total	

Notes

Sweet Dreams: Choosing Your Hotel

Enter the hotels where you'd prefer to stay based on location and price. Then use the worksheet below to plan your itinerary.

Hotel	Location	Price per night

Places to Go, People to See, Things to Do

Enter the attractions you most would like to see. Then use the worksheet below to plan your itinerary.

Attractions	Amount of time you expect to spend there	Best day and time to go

Going "My" Way

Itinerary #1

☐ _____
☐ _____
☐ _____
☐ _____

Itinerary #2

☐ _____
☐ _____
☐ _____
☐ _____

Itinerary #3

☐ _____
☐ _____
☐ _____
☐ _____

Itinerary #4

☐ _____
☐ _____
☐ _____
☐ _____

Itinerary #5

☐ _____
☐ _____
☐ _____
☐ _____

Itinerary #6

☐ _____
☐ _____
☐ _____
☐ _____

Itinerary #7

☐ _____
☐ _____
☐ _____
☐ _____

Itinerary #8

☐ _____
☐ _____
☐ _____
☐ _____

Itinerary #9

☐ _____
☐ _____
☐ _____
☐ _____

Itinerary #10

☐ _____
☐ _____
☐ _____
☐ _____

Menus & Venues

Enter the restaurants where you'd most like to dine. Then use the worksheet below to plan your itinerary.

Name	*Address/Phone*	*Cuisine/Price*

Notes

Index

• *N* •

• O •

• ¥ •

Discover Dummies Online!

The Dummies Web Site is your fun and friendly online resource for the latest information about *For Dummies®* books and your favorite topics. The Web site is the place to communicate with us, exchange ideas with other *For Dummies* readers, chat with authors, and have fun!

Ten Fun and Useful Things You Can Do at www.dummies.com

1. Win free *For Dummies* books and more!
2. Register your book and be entered in a prize drawing.
3. Meet your favorite authors through the IDG Books Worldwide Author Chat Series.
4. Exchange helpful information with other *For Dummies* readers.
5. Discover other great *For Dummies* books you must have!
6. Purchase Dummieswear® exclusively from our Web site.
7. Buy *For Dummies* books online.
8. Talk to us. Make comments, ask questions, get answers!
9. Download free software.
10. Find additional useful resources from authors.

Link directly to these ten fun and useful things at
http://www.dummies.com/10useful

For other technology titles from IDG Books Worldwide, go to
www.idgbooks.com

Not on the Web yet? It's easy to get started with *Dummies 101®: The Internet For Windows® 98* or *The Internet For Dummies®* at local retailers everywhere.

Find other *For Dummies* books on these topics:
Business • Career • Databases • Food & Beverage • Games • Gardening • Graphics • Hardware
Health & Fitness • Internet and the World Wide Web • Networking • Office Suites
Operating Systems • Personal Finance • Pets • Programming • Recreation • Sports
Spreadsheets • Teacher Resources • Test Prep • Word Processing

IDG BOOKS WORLDWIDE BOOK REGISTRATION

We want to hear from you!

Visit **http://my2cents.dummies.com** to register this book and tell us how you liked it!

- ✔ Get entered in our monthly prize giveaway.

- ✔ Give us feedback about this book — tell us what you like best, what you like least, or maybe what you'd like to ask the author and us to change!

- ✔ Let us know any other *For Dummies®* topics that interest you.

Your feedback helps us determine what books to publish, tells us what coverage to add as we revise our books, and lets us know whether we're meeting your needs as a *For Dummies* reader. You're our most valuable resource, and what you have to say is important to us!

Not on the Web yet? It's easy to get started with *Dummies 101®: The Internet For Windows® 98* or *The Internet For Dummies®3* at local retailers everywhere.

Or let us know what you think by sending us a letter at the following address:

For Dummies Book Registration
Dummies Press
10475 Crosspoint Blvd.
Indianapolis, IN 46256

BESTSELLING
BOOK SERIES